**Welfare
and Working
Fathers**

Welfare and Working Fathers

Low-Income Family Life Styles

Robert C. Stone
San Francisco State College

Fredric T. Schlamp
California Department of
  Social Welfare

With a foreword by
Everett C. Hughes

Heath Lexington Books
D.C. Heath and Company
Lexington, Massachusetts
Toronto   London

Copyright © 1971 by D.C. Heath and Company.

All rights reserved. No part of this publication may be reproduced or transmitted in any form or by any means, electronic or mechanical, including photocopy, recording, or any information storage or retrieval system, without permission in writing from the publisher.

Published simultaneously in Canada.

Printed in the United States of America.

Standard Book Number: 0-669-73858-1

Library of Congress Catalog Card Number: 70-151786

**To the Memory of
W. Lloyd Warner**

Table of Contents

	List of Figures	ix
	List of Tables	xi
	Foreword, by Everett C. Hughes	xxi
	Preface	xxiii
	Acknowledgements	xxv
	Staff	xxvi
Chapter 1	Introduction	1
Section I:	**Problems of Study Design and Field Work**	9
Chapter 2	The Sample Cases and California's Low-Income Population	11
Chapter 3	Classification of the Cases	29
Section II:	**Social Characteristics of the Cases**	47
Chapter 4	Kinship Bonds	49
Chapter 5	Non-Kin Social Relationships	65
Section III:	**Economic Characteristics of the Cases**	81
Chapter 6	Level of Living and Economic Security	83
Chapter 7	The World of Work	105
Section IV:	**The Orientation of the Cases**	131
Chapter 8	Psychological Dependency and Anomie	133

Chapter 9	Husband-Wife Roles within the Family	147
Chapter 10	Life Style Themes by James Hirabayashi, Anita Spring and Gerardo Rosal	159
Chapter 11	Case Histories by James Hirabayashi, Anita Spring and Arthur Rotman	173
Section V:	**Overview**	193
Chapter 12	Summary of Findings	195
Chapter 13	Comparing the Poor and the Affluent	203
Chapter 14	Interpretation of Findings	225
	Bibliography	249
	Appendixes	253
	Index	281

List of Figures

2-1	Income of Sample Families Compared with Social Security Administration Poverty Index	20
2-2	Number of AFDC-U Cases in California for 1964-1965	26
3-1	Frequency Distribution of Dependency Index Scores for the 808 Families with Some Welfare Experience	30
3-2	Frequency Distribution of Number of Months on Welfare Status and Number of Months Away from Welfare Status for 808 Families with Some Welfare Experience	31
3-3	Median Family Income by Family Size for AFDC-U Cases, Matching Cases, and Total Sample Cases	37
3-4	Median Family Income by Family Size for Dependency Groups	38
3-5	Median Family Income by Family Size and Geographic Areas	39
3-6	Median Family Income by Family Size for Ethnic Groups	39
6-1	Median Income per Person by Household Size for Sample Families	86
8-1	Scores of Respondents by Dependency Status for Questionnaire Items 97 and 98	143

List of Tables

2-1	Income Levels for Selected Cases for Matching with AFDC-U Families	12
2-2	Characteristics of Statewide 19% AFDC-U Sample Compared with Survey Sample of 1200 Families	13
2-3	Median Family Income and Median Education for Four Sample Areas of California in 1960 and Percent of Families with Incomes under $4,000	15
2-4	Characteristics of California's White, Spanish Surname, and Nonwhite Population in 1960	15
2-5	Percentage Distribution by Major Occupational Group of Male Employed Persons, in California, Heads of Low-Income Families, and Two Samples of AFDC-U Family Heads	16
2-6	Unemployment Rates in Percent by Occupational Group for Males in the Experienced Civilian Labor Force in Four Sample Areas and for the State, 1960	19
2-7	Number and Percent of the Employed Labor Force by Major Industry Group for Sample Areas and for the State of California in 1960	22
2-8	Percentage Distribution of Males (14 Years and Older) in Each Major Occupational Group for Sample Areas in California in 1960	23
2-9	Characteristics of the White, Spanish Surname, Nonwhite Population of Four Sample Areas in California in 1960	25
3-1	Distribution of Families Cross-Classified as to: Ethnicity by Area, Dependency by Area, and Dependency by Ethnicity	35
3-2	Distribution of Families Cross-Classified by Dependency, Geography, and Ethnicity	36
3-3	Percent of Husbands with a History of Rural Residence, and Median Years of Residence	41

3-4	Percentage Distribution of Families by Number of Residence Changes in Last Two Years and Median Number of Moves	41
3-5	Percent of Families Living in Current Neighborhood More than Five Months, and Median Length of Residence	42
3-6	Length of Time Husband and Wife Have Lived Together in Same Household	42
3-7	Percentage Distribution of Families by Household Size and Median Household Size	43
3-8	Median Education of Husband	44
3-9	Percent of Husbands by Age and Median Age	44
3-10	Indexes of Socioeconomic Status for a Sample of 1200 Low-Income Families Classified by Dependency Experience	46
4-1	Percentage Distribution of Families by Number of Relatives in Local Area and Median Number of Relatives	51
4-2	Number of Relatives in Area by Type and Rank Order	52
4-3	Percentage Distribution of Relatives by Location in Local Area	54
4-4	Percent of Families Visiting Relatives in Local Area and Median Number of Visits per Year	54
4-5	Percent of Husbands and/or Wives Visiting Distant Relatives, Median Number of Visits, Median Distance Travelled, and Median Amount Spent per Year (1960-1964).	56
4-6	Percentage Distribution of Families' Relationships with Relatives in Each of Four Types of Activities	57

4-7	Percentage Distribution of Persons Involved in Family Crisis Mutual Aid Relationships by Type of Participant	57
4-8	Percent of Husbands without Confidants and Percent of Husbands' Confidants Classified as Kin or Non-Kin	58
4-9	Husbands' Use of Relatives as Confidants Compared with Relatives Available in Local Area	58
4-10	Percent of Husbands Paying Money to Relatives in Last Year	60
4-11	Percentage Distribution of Families Receiving Gifts by Source	60
4-12	Percent of Husbands Who Received Help from Relatives in Getting a Job	61
4-13	Percent of Husbands Who Have Worked for Relatives	61
4-14	Subgroups Showing Highest and Lowest Scores on 14 Indexes of Kinship Relations	62
5-1	Percent of Husbands Who Know One or More Neighbors and Median Number of Families Known	67
5-2	Percentage Distribution of Families by Number of Crisis Mutual Aid Relationships in the Last Twelve Months and Median Number of Relationships	67
5-3	Percentage Distribution of Husbands by Number of Friends	69
5-4	Percent of Husbands Who Listed Friends, and Median Number of Visits	70
5-5	Percentage of Husbands by Number of Organizational Memberships	71
5-6	Percent of Husbands' Memberships by Type of Organization	71

5-7	Percent of Husbands Participating in One or More Organizations and Median Attendance per Year	72
5-8	Subgroups Showing Highest and Lowest Scores on 12 Indexes of Non-Kinship Social Relations	73
5-9	Percentage Distribution of Persons Involved in Family Crisis Mutual Aid Relationships by Source	75
5-10	Percentage Distribution of Persons Involved in Men's Routine Mutual Aid Relationships by Type of Participant	75
5-11	Percentage Distribution of Persons Involved in Men's Routine Mutual Aid Relationships by Source	77
5-12	Percentage Distribution of Husbands' Friends by Source	77
5-13	Percentage Distribution of Husbands' Relationships with Friends by Type of Activities	78
6-1	Average Income of Families for Last 12 Months	84
6-2	Percent of Families Having Specified Types of Household Possessions, Including Automobiles	87
6-3	Subgroups Showing Highest and Lowest Scores for Material Possessions	89
6-4	Percent of Husbands and Wives with Social Security Coverage	91
6-5	Percent of Husbands Who Have Ever Drawn Unemployment Compensation during Their Work History	92
6-6	Percent of Families Expecting Pensions or Other Monies on Retirement	92
6-7	Percent of Husbands with Union Jobs and Number of Union Jobs	94

6-8	Percent of Families with Savings and Median Amount of Savings	94
6-9	Percent of Families with Life Insurance by Size of Policy and Median Amount of Insurance	95
6-10	Percentage of Families with Burial Insurance and Median Amount of Insurance	96
6-11	Percent of Husbands with a Checking Account or Membership in a Credit Union	96
6-12	Percent of Families with Debts and Median Amount of Debt	98
6-13	Percent of Families Purchasing from Second-Hand Stores	98
6-14	Family Median Monthly Payments for Housing	99
6-15	Percent of Families Owning Their Own Homes and Median Number of Rooms in House, for Both Renters and Owners	99
6-16	Subgroups Showing Highest and Lowest Scores for Economic Security	101
7-1	Percent of Husbands in Each Major Occupational Group (Usual Occupation)	106
7-2	Percent of Husbands in Each Job History Type	108
7-3	Percent of Husbands in Each Occupational Mobility Pattern	109
7-4	Percentage Distribution of Husbands by Current Employment Status	109
7-5	Percentage Distribution of Wives by Current Employment Status	110
7-6	Unemployment of Husbands for Entire Job History by Percent Unemployed, Longest Period, Number of Periods, and Total Months	110

7-7	Percentage Distribution of Husbands by Number of Jobs in the Last Three Years	112
7-8	Percentage Distribution of Husbands by Number of Seasonal Jobs in the Last Three Years	112
7-9	Husband's Minimum and Maximum Median Wage during Last Three Years, and Median Wage for Job of Longest Duration	114
7-10	Subgroups Showing Highest and Lowest Scores on 13 Indexes of Socioeconomic Status	114
7-11	Subgroups Showing Highest and Lowest Scores on 6 Indexes Related to Income Production and Expenditures	119
7-12	Percentage of Family Members Whose Work or Schooling is Limited by Illness or Injury	119
7-13	Percent of Husbands Listing Difficulties in Getting a Job	120
7-14	Percent of Husbands Using Various Sources of Aid in Finding Jobs	124
7-15	Percentage Distribution of Husbands' Statements Concerning the Most Important Ways of Getting a Job	126
7-16	Positive Characteristics of Work, Rank Ordered by Percent of Husbands Listing Each Characteristic	126
7-17	Negative Characteristics of Work, Rank Ordered by Percent of Husbands Listing Each Characteristic	127
8-1	Mean Score of Repondents on 14 Attitude Scales	136
8-2	Subgroups Showing High and Low Scores on Psychological Dependency Scales	137
8-3	Subgroups Showing High and Low Scores on Scales of Intergenerational Dependency and Child Autonomy	141

8-4	Subgroups Showing High and Low Scores on Scales of Child and Parent Responsibility	141
8-5	Subgroups Showing High and Low Scores on the Anomie Scale	141
9-1	Percentage Distribution of Husband-Wife Roles within the Family—Household Chores	151
9-2	Percentage Distribution of Husband-Wife Roles within the Family—Dealing with Children	153
9-3	Percentage Distribution of Husband-Wife Roles within the Family—Control over Spending Money	154
9-4	Woman's Attitude toward Her Role as Housewife and Mother	155
9-5	Percent of Husbands and Wives with Favorable Attitude toward Wife Working	156
10-1	Number of Respondents	161
10-2	Number of Respondents' Statements Classified by Theme and Dimension	162
10-3	Respondents' Average Scores on Five Themes Classified by Ethnicity and Dependency	163
13-1	Background Characteristics of High- and Low-Income Families	205
13-2	Indexes of Interaction with Kin for High- and Low-Income Families	207
13-3	Indexes of Interaction with Non-Kin for High- and Low-Income Families	208
13-4	Three Indexes of Interaction of High- and Low-Income Families, Classified by Source of Participants	209
13-5	Indexes of Health and Economic Security for High- and Low-Income Groups	211

13-6	Occupational History and Employment Continuity for Husbands of High- and Low-Income Groups	212
13-7	Material Possessions, Including Indexes of Reading, for High- and Low-Income Families	213
13-8	Most Important Sources of Aid in Job-Finding as Specified by High- and Low-Income Husbands	214
13-9	Positive Characteristics of Work Mentioned by High- and Low-Income Husbands	214
13-10	Husband-Wife Roles: Sharing of Household Tasks and Child Care by High- and Low-Income Couples	215
13-11	Attitudes of Anomie and Dependency for High- and Low-Income Husbands	217
13-12	Indexes That Do Clearly Differentiate High- and Low-Income Families	219
13-13	Indexes That Do Not Clearly Differentiate High- and Low-Income Families	221
A-1	Distribution of AFDC-U Sample Families in Stanislaus and Merced Counties by Distance, in Months, from Public Assistance Status	257
A-2	Distribution of Cases by Ethnic Status in the Group Designated "Other"	257
B-1	Items Comprising Each Attitude Scale, Identified by Source and Question Number	259
B-2	Weighted Mean Scores for Items Used in the Attitude Scales	260
B-3	Groups Showing Highest and Lowest Scores on the Lamphere Dependency Scale's Factored Scores	262
B-4	The Differences in Mean Values of Attitude Scales Required for a 5% Level of Significance (2 sigma) for a Tight Dispersion Made up of ,"N" Items	265

B-5	The Differences in Mean Values of Attitude Scales Required for a 5% Level of Significance (2 sigma) for a Broad Dispersion Made up of "N" Items	265
B-6	Attitude Items	267

Foreword

W. Lloyd Warner, to whom the authors most appropriately dedicate this volume, was the pioneer student of the life-styles of families in a series of American communities—in New England, the Deep South and the Midwest. Warner included the rich and well-born along with the poor, the old-stock American and the "ethnics" of more recent immigration, the black and the white. While he was not looking for the "poverty line," the studies which he and his numerous associates undertook always did distinguish the "lower-lower" class from the somewhat better off "upper-lower."

The distinction between those dependent on "the town" and those who—though poor—remained independent, has long been of interest to economists, public officials and moral philosophers.

Toward the end of the 19th century, the English shipowner Charles Booth, in his seventeen-volume *Life and Labour of the People of London*, presented a series of maps of London, showing in colors, block by block, how he rated the population in relation to a poverty line which he defined. He used economic and moral indices. A decade later Seebohm Rountree did a similar study of York entitled *Poverty: A Study of Town Life*.

This new book about the poor in California half a century and more after the classic English surveys, and decades after the earlier Warner studies, makes one consider in what sense it is true that the poor are always with us. The poor of Booth's London pawned their Sunday suit on Monday and got it out on Saturday. If one missed a Saturday, he might lose the suit. The pawnshop has been replaced by the man who comes to repossess the refrigerator or the sofa. Rountree's poor lived close to their kin; the young lived at home and paid board and room to the parents after they started to work and until they married and started their own households. The California poor visit their kin but seem to have few money dealings with them; they have no money to help each other. The English poor were cramped into small space, and had no cars or refrigerators. California is big. It is warm the year 'round. The car and the refrigerators are necessities even for the very poor.

But life is still precarious for the poor. And the difference between the life-style of the upper middle-class and the poor may be greater than ever. Clearly the tale has to be retold in every generation and in every region in this epoch of great change. Each retelling will require new kinds of data, new definitions, and new statistical devices. The authors of this volume have done the job well for their time and region, combining good statistical analysis with lively social anthropology of kinship and personality in true Warner fashion.

It is still no fun to be poor, and it looks as if dependence is as much a result as a cause.

Everett C. Hughes
Cambridge, Massachusetts
August 1971

Preface

This report provides statistics on a sample of 1200 California families whose incomes fall below the "poverty line." Six hundred of them were current welfare cases, and six hundred were not. Each of these families included a mother, father, and one or more minor children.

It needs to be emphasized, at the outset, that these 1200 able-bodied, early-middle-aged men, and their families, represent a small and specialized segment of a much wider poverty population. Considering the vastly larger group of welfare and nonwelfare families who have even fewer resources for coping with poverty, such as the aged, and female heads of households (not to mention specialized groups such as reservation Indians and newly arrived Chinese and Puerto Rican immigrants), it becomes clear that our cases constitute a blue-ribbon sample of the poverty population. What use, then, can be made of the statistics describing these 1200 cases?

First, our data constitute a baseline for fine-grained comparisons with other groups, both above and below the poverty line. It is the *details* of poverty, in addition to the grand moral conceptions of it, that allow all of us to define more clearly what we wish to change and in what degree. While it seems obvious that anything we have to say in this book about the plight of these 1200 families would hold true more strongly for other more disadvantaged groups within the poverty population, only detailed comparisons can show exactly how much more disadvantaged they are.

Second, looking *within* the sample of cases, important differences in life changes and life style among the families were found to be linked with variation in the length of a family's welfare experience. Additional comparison of these cases to a small sample of affluent, upper-middle-class families buttressed the conclusion that the long-time welfare and the nonwelfare families represent significantly different *types* of poverty.

Our comparison of welfare and nonwelfare cases leads us to conclude that, taken separately, neither the motivations of the welfare father, nor his environmental circumstances, offer a sufficient explanation of his dependent condition. It is the interplay—the complex feedback—of these factors that is the "true" cause of welfare dependency.

Acknowledgements

The study which this book describes was sponsored jointly by the California State Department of Social Welfare and the U.S. Department of Health, Education and Welfare (Welfare Administration Project 207), and appeared originally under the title, *Family Life Styles below the Poverty Line* (1966).

The authors wish to acknowledge their indebtedness first to all those families who afforded us the opportunity to interview them. Their consideration and cooperation could not be met by any direct reciprocation on our part, but it is hoped that this book will materially help to clarify issues involving their welfare.

It is with special pleasure that the authors acknowledge the substantive and methodological contributions made by Charles McConnel and Sheridan Clinchard, graduate students in economics; and Robert Meyer and Velma Parness, graduate students in sociology, at San Francisco State College.

Thanks are due to Mr. Wilbur Parker, Chief of the Research and Statistics Division of the State Department of Social Welfare, whose cooperation eased in major degree the task of coordinating a research project involving a state college and a line agency of the State of California. Our thanks also go to Mr. Jerome Sampson, Executive Secretary of the State Social Welfare Board, for his valuable aid in getting the project under way.

Special thanks are due to Mr. Walter Kaplan, Research Analyst, California State Department of Social Welfare; Mr. Ray Lower, Field Supervisor, San Francisco Regional Unemployment and Insurance Claims Office, California State Employment Service; and Mr. Quentin Emery, Administrative Assistant, Santa Clara County Welfare Department, for their aid with critical problems in the field work.

The listed cooperating agencies whose aid made possible the successful completion of the field work receive our heartfelt thanks: *St. Vincent de Paul Society of San Jose*, Paz Varella, Office Secretary; *Salvation Army*, San Jose, Captain Mervyn Morelock, San Jose Corps Officer; *Goodwill Industries of San Jose*, Al Diludovico, Director of Personnel and Rehabilitation Services; *San Jose Juvenile Probation Department*, Kenneth Fare, Assistant Chief Probation Officer; *San Jose City Health Department*, John M. Hayakawa, Chief Health Educator, and Margaret F. Nelson, Chief Public Health Nurse; *Santa Clara County Hospital*, Edris Coon, Director of Social Services; *Our Lady of Guadalupe Church*, San Jose, Father Anthony Soto, Manuel Vierra and Sister Maria Bravo; *St. Mary's Church*, Gilroy, Father Thomas Burke; *Hunters Point Boys' Club*, San Francisco, Jay LaFoe, Program Director; *Red Shield Youth Association of the Salvation Army*, San Francisco, Jack J. Wolf, Director; *Potrero Hill Neighborhood House*, San Francisco, John H. Heiden, Executive Director, and Ed Weaver, Social Worker; *St. Peter's Church*, San Francisco, Father James Casey; *St. Anthony's Church*, San Francisco, Father Ernesto Sanchez; *University of California Medical Center*, San Francisco, Kenneth C. Abernethy, Assistant Director Outpatient Clinic; *San Francisco General Hospi-*

tal, Lena Leong, Medical Social Work Supervisor; *St. Luke's Hospital*, San Francisco, Gerald Cole, Assistant Hospital Administrator; *Mt. Zion Hospital*, San Francisco, Shirley Chase, Supervisor of Outpatient Clinic; *Presbyterian Medical Center*, San Francisco, J. Milo Anderson, Executive Vice President, and Richard Fitz, Administrative Assistant; *Children's Hospital*, San Francisco, Juliet Goldman, Director Outpatient Clinic; *San Francisco Hospital Conference*, Rolland E. Wick, President; *California State Employment Service*, San Jose, Dayton Stoddard, Unemployment and Insurance Claims, Office Manager; *San Francisco Public Health Department*, Mission Health Center, Dr. Hope Corey, Health Officer; San Francisco Public Health Department, Westside Health Center, Dr. Marian Mykytew, District Medical Officer; *Youth Guidance Center of San Francisco*, Jane Cassedy, Assistant Chief Probation Officer, and Ben Okada, Liaison Officer of the Juvenile Court; *San Francisco City and County Public Welfare Department*, Paul J. Yuke, Assistant Director-Administrative; *San Francisco Housing Authority*, Fred S. Threefoot, Manager of Tenant Selection; *Canon Kip Community Center*, San Francisco, Sterling Osborne, Director; *Mission Neighborhood Centers*, San Francisco, Irving Kriegsfeld, Executive Director; *San Francisco Boys' Club*, Mission Branch, Ernest Ingold Branch; *Columbia Park Boys' Club*, San Francisco; *The George Washington Carver Community Center*, South Dos Palos, Merced County, Mr. Harry Owen; *Stanislaus County Welfare Department; Merced County Welfare Department; Office of the Stanislaus County Superintendent of Schools; Office of the Merced County Superintendent of Schools*, Dr. William Stockard; *Stanislaus County Housing Authority; Los Angeles County Department of Charities; Los Angeles County General Hospital; Avalon Community Center, Los Angeles; Welfare Information Service, Los Angeles; Los Angeles City Housing Authority*.

It is possible that the names of one or more cooperating agencies have been inadvertently omitted from the preceding list, and we trust that this oversight will be forgiven.

Staff

Study Director	Robert Stone, Director, Institute for Social Science Research, Professor of Social Welfare and Sociology, San Francisco State College
Associate Director	Fredric Schlamp, Research and Statistics, California State Department of Social Welfare, and Director, Institute for Study of Family Life and Mental Health, 655 "P" St., Sacramento.
Research Associates	Ramona First, Associate Professor of Economics, San Francisco State College
	James Hirabayashi, Assistant Professor of Anthropology, San Francisco State College

Consultants	Earl Raab, Consultant to California State Social Welfare Board
	Seaton Manning, Professor of Social Welfare, San Francisco State College
	Bernice Madison, Professor of Social Welfare, San Francisco State College

Secretarial Staff
- Executive Secretary: Marilyn Blechman
- Secretaries:
  - Caroline Jackson
  - Joan Masunaga
  - Sharron McCuistion
  - Marilyn Miller
  - Ellen Stone
  - Alice Westbrook

Field Work Coordinator Morgan Yamanaka, Assistant Professor of Social Welfare, San Francisco State College

Field Work Supervisors

Los Angeles — Lloyd Street, Research Director, Welfare Planning Council
Assistant Supervisors — Stephen Weiner, Ward Belding, and Ida Powell

San Jose — Donald Johnston
Assistant Supervisor — Sumner Stone

Stanislaus & Merced — Reginald Corder — Stanislaus County Department of Education
Assistant Supervisor — Stella Thill

Graduate Assistants
- Sheridan Clinchard
- Sam Johnston
- Louis Kemnitzer
- Charles McConnel
- Sharron McCuistion
- Robert Meyer
- Richard Morton
- Velma Parness
- Ray Rivers
- Arthur Rizzo
- William Weaver
- Henry Zaretsky

Undergraduate Assistants
- David Cossock
- Carl Dahlke

　　　　　　　　　　　Beth de la Fuente
　　　　　　　　　　　Patricia Roberts
　　　　　　　　　　　Edward Roquette
　　　　　　　　　　　Gerardo Rosal
　　　　　　　　　　　Sumner Stone
　　　　　　　　　　　Miriam Weinberg

Programmers　　　　Larry Selmer
　　　　　　　　　　　Mary McMaster

Interviewers
　San Francisco　　　Fernando Arroyo
　　　　　　　　　　　Norman Carlin
　　　　　　　　　　　Gary Carrington
　　　　　　　　　　　Velia Cockrum
　　　　　　　　　　　Marilyn Cook
　　　　　　　　　　　Maxine Cooper
　　　　　　　　　　　Adolph Cordova
　　　　　　　　　　　Margaret Cottle
　　　　　　　　　　　Diane Dixon
　　　　　　　　　　　Michael Duggleby
　　　　　　　　　　　Norman Gehlke
　　　　　　　　　　　Alke Gleeson
　　　　　　　　　　　Judith Golubchick
　　　　　　　　　　　John Hassett
　　　　　　　　　　　Esther Kahn
　　　　　　　　　　　Nicholas King
　　　　　　　　　　　John Lamont
　　　　　　　　　　　Mary Landels
　　　　　　　　　　　Roger Levin
　　　　　　　　　　　Celestino Luque
　　　　　　　　　　　Harold Lyster
　　　　　　　　　　　Irwin Matus
　　　　　　　　　　　Lawrence Newmark
　　　　　　　　　　　Richard Reeve
　　　　　　　　　　　Gerardo Rosal
　　　　　　　　　　　Sandra Sjoberg
　　　　　　　　　　　Dorothy Tappin
　　　　　　　　　　　Joanne Tornatore
　　　　　　　　　　　Claude Ury
　　　　　　　　　　　Beverly Watkins
　　　　　　　　　　　Miriam Weinberg
　　　　　　　　　　　Hermund Wong

San Jose	Teresa Bello
	George Berg
	Kathryn Chamberlin
	Manual Fojo
	Martha Foshi
	Judith Hirshfeld
	Lionel Maldanado
	Nancy Mason
	Robert McAlear
	David Pantoja
	Frank Peralta
	Jack Pockman
	Henry Quintero
	Ramon Reyes
	Thomas Richards
	Mardi Rubalcava
	Gale Thompson
	Jesse Torres
	Peter Wakeland
	Lois Yennie
Los Angeles	Richard Belding
	Ward Belding
	James Berland
	Warren De Ley
	Lorenzo Foster
	Monasch Helfman
	Tony Luna
	David Pantoja
	Ida Mae Powell
	Lisa Ramsuer
	Frank Rivera
	Ron Sirota
	Andrew Wright
Stanislaus and Merced Counties	Basilio Castaneda
	Alicia Cochran
	Mae Hensley
	Nicholas Ochava
	Harry Owens
	LaRue Patterson
	Elmon Peterson
	Doris Powell
	Robert Saenz
	Stella Thill
	Donald Trammell

**Welfare
and Working
Fathers**

1 Introduction

In February 1964, in response to federal enabling legislation, California instituted a new welfare program designed to aid needy children of families having a male head of household. The older program of Aid to Dependent Children (AFDC) was intended to provide financial support to children deprived of a father's support due to his death, absence, or incapacity to work. The new 1964 program (AFDC-U) was designed to provide a family with public assistance for its needy children if the father was capable of work but was underemployed or unemployed. This same program now operates in 26 of the 50 states.

The controversy over paying welfare to able-bodied fathers is merely an extension of the on-going conflict about the older AFDC program of aid to the dependent children of broken homes. The critics of the original AFDC program base their arguments on the premise that welfare clients have much the same environment to contend with as nonwelfare, low-income persons. Welfare clients, it is argued, respond to their environment by laziness and chiseling, and show a general lack of initiative. These same critics always emphasize that they do not wish to punish those persons or families who represent *genuine* cases of hardship and distress. Nevertheless, it is insisted that welfare programs *increase* dependency by reducing individual initiative.

Advocates of the older AFDC program argue in exactly the opposite way. Arguments in defense of public assistance start with the premise that the individual motives of all low-income people are much the same, but that their environmental circumstances are different at various points in time; therefore, the difference between welfare and nonwelfare clients is more a matter of circumstance than it is of individual initiative. Viewed from this framework, lack of individual initiative is held to be of minor importance compared to the unemployment, illness, or other family crises that engulf a low-income family. Defenders of welfare programs always point out that they do not wish to reward laziness and lack of initiative, but they insist that such problems are *minor* compared to the *genuine* need of the bulk of welfare families.

It is easy to see that the same arguments over the program which aids the broken family become even more sharply focused in the case of the new AFDC-U program. The reason for giving financial assistance to families with unemployed fathers is not due to problems of blindness, old age, or physical inability to work—or because the family lacks a male breadwinner. It is because the male head of the household is unemployed and/or unable to earn an income that reaches certain minimum standards. The AFDC-U family's central problem is the husband's lack of employment and/or level of income.

The moral debate over public assistance payments to the unemployed husband with a wife and children centers simultaneously on the issues of destitution versus decency, and dependency versus self-reliance. In the public conscience, receipt of income without work is unacceptable unless mediated through the institution of private property. Neither the coupon clipper nor the welfare recipient work for their money, but the former's status is highly respectable while the latter's is not. At the same time, public morality is equally offended by conditions of destitution that erode away the indigent person's decency. If welfare payments are not forthcoming, destitution occurs; if they are made available at minimum health and decency standards, the moral demand for economic self-reliance is violated. The result is a moral dilemma.

It can be seen that one's moral position about welfare tends to affect—indeed, may well determine—one's convictions as to the facts in the case. Moral judgments aside, the facts about welfare, employment and worker motivation in the low-income population are by no means self-evident. Consequently, this book centers on those factors that affect the linkage between the low-income worker and the world of jobs—both for the welfare and the nonwelfare low-income father. The range of factors that was investigated includes length of public assistance, the character of rural and urban labor markets, the ethnic status of workers and their families, family organization, level of living, the occupational history of workers, and their psychological characteristics.[1]

From the study of these factors, a conception was developed of the linkage between the lower-class worker and the world of work, ranging from the worker who has never received welfare to the long-time public assistance case. In contrast to the single-factor conceptions underlying the two moral positions that have been outlined, this conception emphasizes the significance of a range of social, economic and psychological factors that operate as feedback cycles in determining a worker's relationship to the labor market and the welfare system.

Study Design

Given the importance attached to the differences between welfare and nonwelfare families, it is all the more surprising to find that there are few, if any, studies which focus on a range of factors to be found in the two groups. A comprehensive survey by Dr. Henry Miller (1965) reveals that the only reliable comparisons of welfare and nonwelfare families focus on questions of family size and other related census characteristics that cast little light on the causes of presumed differences in the family life styles of the two groups. Because of the paucity of current reliable knowledge, our study involved matching welfare and nonwelfare families in terms of socioeconomic status in order to determine those

---

[1] These public policy issues are reflected in two resolutions passed by the California Senate in 1963. Senate Resolutions 220 and 232 ask about the causes of unemployment that have created a need for the new AFDC-U program, and request the State Department of Social Welfare to make appropriate studies.

factors that might explain the welfare status of the one group and the nonwelfare status of the other.[2]

The study design called for control of key factors whose effects might otherwise obscure possible differences between welfare and nonwelfare clients. The first consideration was to control for income by matching the welfare and nonwelfare families on this factor. The second control was to sample equal numbers of persons from the three ethnic groups who constitute the bulk of California's low-income population. The third control was to sample from both rural and urban areas of the state in order to measure this factor as it might affect a family's economic fortunes. By this method, it was expected that differences between welfare and nonwelfare families that were not due to differences in family income, ethnic status, or rural-urban location could be identified. At the same time, the inclusion in the sample of rural and urban families, and families from California's major ethnic groups, assured representation of persons from a range of poverty-producing circumstances and from the major cultural and racial groups which comprise the state's low-income population.

A sample size of 1200 cases was chosen, and it was decided that 600 welfare and 600 nonwelfare families would be selected in equal numbers from four areas in California, including one rural area in the San Joaquin Valley. In each area, an equal number of cases would be drawn from the white, Spanish-speaking, and black population. The result would be a stratified sample with an equal number of cases in each of the six subgroups of the overall sample.

Using this sampling method, the proportion of subgroups in the sample, e.g., the ratio of black to white families, does not correspond to the proportion of these same groups in the state's low-income population. The advantage of choosing equal numbers in each subgroup in constructing the sample resides in the increased ability to determine the relationship of one variable to another. The disadvantage of this method is the lowered ability to draw inferences from the distribution of characteristics in the sample to the distribution of characteristics in the universe population.

It is also important to note the consequences of selecting 600 public assistance families[3] from AFDC-U caseloads rather than from the full range of

---

[2] Because the idea for the study came first from the California Senate and was initiated by the State Department of Social Welfare, the original study design was developed by Mr. Earl Raab, consultant to the State Social Welfare Board, who has also served as consultant for the project.

[3] The term "welfare" in popular parlance means money payments or the giving of commodites by private or public agencies to indigent persons. The correct term to designate such payments from a public agency is "public assistance," and is used by such agencies to differentiate this particular service from other nonmonetary services rendered to clients. "Welfare," then, correctly refers to services in general, and "public assistance" refers to the specific service of money payments. We have, however, followed popular usage in this book. Thus, the terms "aid," "welfare," "welfare case" and "welfare history" all refer to persons on public assistance or to public assistance payments. While recognizing the sensitivity of welfare agencies to usage that is technically incorrect, we have employed popular usage for reasons of readability and flexibility.

public assistance programs. As these households were all *intact* families, i.e., they included a father, mother, and one or more children, the 600 matching families also had to be intact family units. Thus, the sample did not include broken families with a female head of household, childless couples, or single persons. In this sense, the sample was a highly specialized one and not representative of the total low-income population. The study focuses on intact families and on the problems of the male head of the household.

In selecting the cases, the first requisite was that the 600 nonrecipient families have the same income level as the 600 families on welfare. A systematic effort was made to select nonwelfare families whose income matched the public assistance cases. While the average income of the nonrecipient families was some 17.2 percent higher than that of the sample families currently on welfare, other measures of socioeconomic status indicated that the two groups were surprisingly closely matched in this respect. A similar effort was made to see that ethnic groups were equally represented in the two halves of the sample. A number of factors made it impossible to achieve this goal fully in each of the sample areas, but each of the ethnic groups (white, Spanish-speaking and black)[4] comprised approximately one-third of the cases in the over-all sample of 1200 families.

Four geographic areas in California were chosen for sampling and were represented equally in the sample. The first area consisted of two rural counties at the northern end of the San Joaquin Valley (Stanislaus and Merced counties). The second area was Santa Clara County, one of the outer ring of counties surrounding the Bay Area. The rapid growth in the last twenty years of San Jose, Santa Clara's primary city, has changed the county's economic base from a heavy reliance on agriculture to a primary emphasis on industry and trade. The last two areas chosen were California's two major urban centers—Los Angeles and San Francisco.

Because over 200 of the nonrecipient families had received assistance from public or voluntary social agencies at some time in the past, it became evident that the families should be classified in terms of their welfare history, rather than simply in terms of their current welfare status. Using a dependency index, the families were divided into three groups: (1) those who had never received assistance—392 families; (2) a short-time assistance group (median duration: four months)—571 families; and (3) a long-time assistance group (median: twenty-six months)—237 families. These groups are referred to in the text as the "NOA" or Never on Aid, the "STA" or Short-Time Aid, and the "LTA" or Long-Time Aid groups.

In addition to the 1200 interviews with husbands, 300 wives were also interviewed. These interviews were conducted only in San Jose and San Francisco. In the women's interviews, the subjects of family dynamics and child-rearing attitudes replaced the focus on work experience that characterized the men's questionnaire. Some data from the women's interviews have been

---

[4]The term "white" will be used throughout the report even though the term "Anglo" would be more appropriate in comparing this group to the "Spanish-speaking" families of Latin-American descent.

included in a section on husband-wife roles. The larger part of the women's interviews were much less structured than the men's interviews were and made a content analysis of the *values* expressed in the interview material possible. This analysis of values, based on the women's interviews, served as a separate and independent check on many of the conclusions drawn from data in the men's questionnaires. This project was carried out independent of the larger study and was under the direction of Dr. James Hirabayashi. It constitutes Chapters 10 and 11 of this book. The results of Dr. Hirabayashi's project confirm in broad outline the conclusions drawn from the major part of the project.

In addition to the 1500 questionnaires obtained in the summer of 1964, a small sample of upper-middle-class families were studied in the fall of 1965, utilizing the same questionnaire. Some 43 families were surveyed. This work was conducted without sponsorship or funding from the California State Department of Social Welfare. The total number of questionnaires utilized in this book equals 1586, covering 1200 low-income husbands and 300 wives, and 43 high-income husbands and their wives.

Theoretical Framework

A brief description of the central guiding ideas and major conclusion provides a framework for the detailed analysis to be given in the ensuing chapters.[5] The relationship between the lower-class person and the world of work follows a different mode than is true in the case of the middle-class worker. In the middle class, the *character* of the work done and the self-definition of the worker are intertwined. Achievement, status, contribution, and service are the symbols that have significance. *Work* and *income* in and of themselves are taken for granted. They are the most important elements in the work situation, but they are nevertheless taken as given. The investment of self in work tends to be maximized (Gans, 1962). Work is seen as an extension of self. When extended to its maximum degree, this orientation produces a pathology that has been labeled "The Work Addict" (Bradley, 1961). Such cases represent the Protestant ethic writ supreme over all other considerations or values.

For lower-class persons, the character of the work done is secondary to the fact of working. Working and income are most important, but in contrast to the middle-class assumption of these elements as given, lower-class workers consider work and income as goals to be *achieved*. Working and income arise from the same source, and hence income—and particularly the prospect of steady income—is foremost as the goal to be achieved (Freidmann and Havighurst, 1962). The first identification of the lower-class person is then with the working process that produces the income.

---

[5] Various theoretical models of worker motivation and attitudes have been advanced in the past. While the conception to be outlined here is consistent with some of these studies and conflicts with others, only a few relevant sources will be cited in this introductory statement. A fuller critique of relevant research will be given in the body of the book.

The second factor involved in work is that of the microculture and informal social system associated with the work setting. Characteristic of this system are the horseplay, jokes, resentment against bosses and authority, and the sharing of gripes and complaints. The microculture involved in work also relates to the use of tools, machinery, materials being worked on, work rhythms and routines, etc. The cultural elements and informal social relations emerging from work settings constitute a system of male sociability. Studies of human relations in industry have documented the ubiquitous character of such relationships in work settings and have demonstrated the importance of such relationships for workers *during* the time they are at work (Gardner, 1945). For lower-class men, these relationships constitute a system of male sociability.

It can be seen that working, income, and male sociability are interconnected aspects of a particular work setting. The worker can shift from one job to another, and one job can be more taxing or unpleasant than another, but the three elements we have described are relatively constant. Working, income, and sociability are all continuing aspects of the work setting itself.

These three elements are tied up in the worker's conception of himself as a *breadwinner*. In turn, his self-definition as a breadwinner is tied up with his self-definition as a man. Thus, his male ego—his conception of himself as a man—is expressed and reinforced by working, by income, and by participation in the microculture and informal social relationships on the job.

Given the fact of such linkages between the lower-class person and the work world, the strength of such linkages is difficult to assess unless something more is known about the other aspects of a worker's life that may have to do with his self-definition. If his basic life interests are focused on areas other than work, then these linkages to the work world may be offset by other more powerful motives or social forces (Dubin, 1956). The conception emerging from studies on lower-class life is that the "local social world" of kin, friends, acquaintances, and neighbors is a dominant interest. This world of buddies, chums, kinsmen, and pals is a major matrix for the expression and reinforcement of the lower-class male ego. Family and church may also be focal points of identification, but they are usually thought to be less significant than the informal peer groups.

If the local social world is a dominant focus for male identification, the crucial question to be answered is whether or not this world interconnects at any point with the world of work. Are these two spheres of life totally separate for lower-class persons? Closely connected? Or somewhat connected? (Dyer, 1962.) The interconnection between the work and nonwork worlds of lower-class people is primarily through friendships and informal social relationships. Some of the friends met at work are subsequently involved at various points in the lower-class man's local social world. The sources of friendship are a sensitive index to the relative psychological importance of the various sectors in a man's life. Furthermore, the interconnections between circles of friendship are one clue at the social level to the social-psychological process of identification. In the case of lower-class male workers, we found the first source of friends to be from the neighborhood, the second source from work, and the third source from family and kin. Investigation of mutual-aid activities and recreation indicated that the friends made at work were included in these activities.

From the data to be presented, it is clear that there are systemic linkages between work and nonwork worlds, even though the nonwork world may be the dominant life interest of lower-class workers. Consequently, the lower-class worker's definition of himself as breadwinner is not separate from his participation in his local social world. From this we would conclude that, by comparison with the upper-middle-class man, work is *secondary* but *not lacking in importance* in the lower-class male's maintenance of his self-image.

The proof of this psychological and social interconnection between work and nonwork worlds is found when *work* is absent, i.e., when long-time unemployment takes place. If work and nonwork worlds are quite separate—if lower-class workers have no identification with work but only with money—then the nonworking, long-time welfare case should show the same pattern of social relationships as does the working person (Morse and Weiss, 1962). The only disturbance that should be manifested is that resulting from the lowering of income level. In fact, there may be little or no disturbance in continuity of income, if the continuity of the welfare check is superior to the continuity of income created by intermittent employment.

This study and earlier studies of unemployment point to significant changes in a worker's self-definition and to a developmental pattern of social withdrawal that accompanies long-time unemployment (Bakke, 1940; Bakke, 1940a; Cavan, 1938; and Angell, 1936). The social withdrawal that takes place includes both kinship and non-kinship relations. The inclusion of friends first met at work in the local social world of the unemployed man shows a decline as unemployment lengthens and welfare dependency increases.

This brief sketch of how various factors combine to destroy the linkage between the worker and the world of work is only a generalized picture. The several factors which may combine to produce variations in the feedback cycle that results in long-time welfare dependency are taken up in the body of this book.

Returning to the point that the "work addict" is a pathological form of the middle-class orientation to work, we can see that the pathology of the lower-class worker's orientation is in the opposite direction. Whereas the upper-middle-class professional and executive is plagued by his tendency to let his work world swallow up all other aspects of his life, the lower-class worker is plagued by his tendency to dissociate money and working. His pathology is that of the drone.

These two pathologies have quite different consequences in the public conscience. The middle-class worker's pathology is looked upon as a private problem to be solved by his own efforts, even though the consequences of his condition may have severe effects on family life and possibly on the adequacy of the family's child-rearing practices. The lower-class worker's pathology is defined as a public problem because the public conscience cannot stand the thought of starvation or destitution on the one hand nor, on the other hand, can it tolerate a belief in income without work.

Outline of Sections

In Section I, we include, first, a discussion of how representative of the low-income population of California the study sample may be. In the second chapter, we describe the index of dependency that was utilized to classify the cases into three dependency groups, and include a detailed description of the matching process which was used to ensure that in comparisons of welfare and nonwelfare families, key factors were held constant in order to assess the effects of the dependency experience.

In Section II, we are concerned with the social characteristics of the families and describe kinship and nonkinship relations. Frequency of interaction with kin, neighbors, and friends is reported with an analysis of the functions such social relations perform.

We devote Section III to an analysis of the relationships between current income, level of living, economic security, and wage and occupational history of the subgroups within the sample.

In Section IV, we deal with the subjective outlook or orientation of the families to the world around them, including the influence of early childhood experience, the effects of the welfare dependency experience itself, and influences arising from membership in an ethnic or racial group.

In Section V, we summarize the empirical results, offer a comparison of the affluent and the poor, and present a theory of male welfare dependency which shows how social, economic and psychological factors affect the relationship of the worker to the labor market.

**Section I:
Problems of Study Design
and Field Work**

2

The Sample Cases and California's Low-Income Population

The sampling procedure required by the study design involved a combination of stratification and matching. The 600 cases to be drawn from lists of current AFDC-U families were to be chosen in equal numbers from four geographic areas, and in equal numbers from each of three ethnic groups. Initially, it was planned to draw welfare cases at random from these segments or strata of the total population of welfare families. Random sampling was abandoned when preliminary field experience proved that the number of welfare cases in each ethnic group in each county that could actually be contacted at their dwelling places was barely sufficient to fill the sample quota. In effect, the sample of welfare cases in the four counties came to equal the *available* universe. The major bias in the welfare sample that may have been created by these field work procedures was the tendency to select those persons who showed less geographic mobility than would be true of the total AFDC-U welfare population.

A similar, though not identical, experience took place in finding the matching cases to fill the various quotas dictated by the sample design. As a preliminary step, a sample of San Francisco city blocks with lowest rental levels was selected by utilizing U.S. Census city block data. A survey of households from these blocks made it clear that use of any probability procedure would require screening several thousand cases by direct contact in order to find 600 families who would fit the criteria of the sample.

In place of this procedure, it was decided to use institutions and agencies of any or all types (hospitals, Boys' Clubs, social service agencies, etc.) which function as catch basins of information on low-income families. Lists of families were secured from these agencies, and interviewers made contact with these families at their places of residence.[1] Screening procedures then led to

---

[1] Clearly, the sampling of cases from the population in contact with institutions that serve the low-income population leaves out those families who have not been in touch with such agencies. Furthermore, just as with the AFDC-U families, we found in using lists of clients, that if the list was four or five months old, as many as 50% of the families had moved and had left no forwarding address. Consequently, the sample of matching families was weighted toward those who had been in contact with an agency within the last three or four months. In an effort to offset biases created by this procedure, we asked families who were interviewed to furnish us with the names of friends or acquaintances who might fit the criteria of the sample. This effort met with little success as the number of cases in the sample derived from this procedure is a small proportion of the total. During the last two weeks of field work, lists of persons receiving unemployment compensation were also utilized in the search for matching cases. This particular procedure may have introduced additional bias into the matching sample in that the sample cases may show a higher unemployment rate than would be true for the appropriate universe that they are presumed to represent.

interviewing of those families who fitted the sampling requirements. The first requirement was that the family not be receiving public assistance or monetary support from a voluntary agency, with a second requirement that the family consist of a father, mother and at least one minor child. The income requirements for inclusion within the sample as a "matching" family are given in Table 2-1.

The net result of the preliminary field work procedures led to the decision that the advantages derived from the use of stratification and matching procedures in the sampling design should not be abandoned, even though probability methods of selecting the cases could not be used. Thus, the sample was designed to maximize needed controls in comparing welfare and nonwelfare cases, and was not intended to be a probability sample of a designated segment of California's population.

Having described the procedures by which the sample cases were chosen, we can now address ourselves to the question of how representative the sample may be of California's low-income population. In this case, the method for assessing the "representativeness" of the sample is to compare it to known characteristics of the appropriate population universe. If the sample accurately reflects known characteristics of a designated parent population, then it is plausible to assume that other characteristics of the sample would also be representative of the universe population.

The population to which the sample should be compared consists of all current AFDC-U families in California, and all intact families with male heads of

Table 2-1
Income Levels for Selecting Cases for Matching with AFDC-U Families[1]

No. in Family	Matching Case, Annual Income	Matching Case, Monthly Income
3	$2,172	$181
4	2,492	208
5	3,120	260
6	3,591	299
7	3,936	328
8	4,485	373
9	4,766	397
10	5,265	438
11	5,342	445
12	5,533	461

[1] Income levels are approximately 4% above average family annual incomes of a sample of AFDC-U families surveyed by the California State Department of Social Welfare. The 4% differential corresponds to costs related to employment and therefore is not present in a welfare family's budget.

household in the experienced civilian labor force whose annual income is equivalent to AFDC-U families of comparable size. No published statistics are available to refer to *this* particular segment of California's population. Therefore, limited comparisons were made with another sample of AFDC-U cases, with rural-urban differences in California's population that should be reflected in the sample, with differences in the characteristics of California's ethnic populations that should appear in the sample, and with the characteristics of California families having incomes under $4000 per year. These comparisons can tell us first if the sample accurately reflects certain differences between various population groups that appear in the sample. Additional comparisons can tell us if the sample group is representative of California's low-income population or is representative of only a segment of low-income households.

A first comparison can be made between the characteristics of the 1200 sample families and a 19% statewide probability sample of AFDC-U families made by the State Department of Social Welfare in 1964. Table 2-2 gives the comparative figures for the two groups. The characteristics of the two samples look much alike, though the sample of 1200 families shows a 5% higher income, larger average family size, and slightly older age for heads of households.

Assuming that the statewide AFDC-U sample is representative of all AFDC-U cases, then the sample of 1200 families reflects these known characteristics rather closely. Furthermore, it reflects not only those characteristics that define the universe population (i.e., a given income level related to family composition), but it also reflects with some accuracy characteristics such as family size, education, and previous welfare experience, which are attributes not related *per se* to those defining criteria that place families within this population group.

The reader will note that the comparison just made involves dissimilar groups

Table 2-2
Characteristics of Statewide 19% AFDC-U Sample Compared with Survey Sample of 1200 Families

Characteristics	19% Statewide AFDC-U Sample[1]	Survey Sample of 1200 Families
Percent of Applicants on General Relief at Intake	33.4	33.3[2]
Median Family Size	6.0	6.8
Unemployed Parent's Median Education (in years)	9.5	9.4
Median Age of Unemployed Parent	34.9	36.9
Average Family Income (annual)	3,204	3,367
Median Family Income	3,109	3,306

[1] Source: *Aid to Families with Dependent Children: Characteristics of Unemployed Parent Families at Intake*. Sample of Recipients – February through July 1964, State of California, Department of Social Welfare, Research and Statistics Division, Sacramento, 1964.

[2] The 33.3% represents that proportion of the 1200 families on *some type* of welfare program at the time the new AFDC-U program came into being.

since the State Department of Social Welfare samples are all AFDC-U cases, whereas the sample used in this study is composed of both AFDC-U and nonwelfare families. The dissimilarity in the composition of the two samples does not, however, vitiate the comparison if it is recalled that the nonwelfare half of the sample used in this study was to be *matched* with the welfare cases. The comparison to the State Department of Social Welfare sample is useful, for it tests whether or not the matching process in our sampling procedure produced a set of 1200 cases that are similar to the universe of AFDC-U cases in California.

Known Population Characteristics Reflected in the Sample

A second procedure is to ask if the sample cases reflect known differences between rural and urban groups and between ethnic segments of California's population. Table 2-3 shows that the median education of males in the two valley counties to be 9.5 and 9.8 years, respectively, whereas the three urban areas show median educational levels from 11.8 years to 12.2 years. This differential is reflected in the Valley *sample* cases which record an educational level of 8.3 years for the male head of household; in comparison, the cases drawn from urban areas show an educational level from 9.3 to 10.8 years (Table 3-8). Rural urban differences in family income shown in Table 2-3 are also reflected in the sample families. The Valley median family income for the sample cases drawn from that area is $3009, whereas median income for sample families in the three urban areas varies from $3330 to $3586 (Table 6-1).

Known differences in the characteristics of California's ethnic groups are also accurately reflected in the sample of 1200 families. Table 2-4 shows the larger family size and lower median education for Spanish-speaking families and males. For the sample cases, median family size of the Spanish-speaking cases was 7.4 compared with 6.9 for the black cases and 6.2 for whites. Median education for the Spanish-speaking male head of household was 7.6, whereas the median for blacks was 11.1 and 9.9 for whites (Tables 3-7 and 3-8).

Differences between the Study Sample and California's Low-Income Population

The comparisons made so far indicate that the sample of 1200 families is probably quite similar to the AFDC-U population in California and accurately reflects the rural-urban and ethnic differences found in the larger population. Our final comparisons are between the sample cases and California's low-income intact family population.

The first comparison centers on occupational status. In Table 2-5, the first column delineates the occupational distribution of California's employed labor force in 1960.

Table 2-3
Median Family Income and Median Education for Four Sample Areas of California in 1960 and Percent of Families with Incomes under $4,000[1]

Sample Areas	Family Median Annual Income (Dollars)	Median Education (Highest Grade) Completed for Males 25 Years and Over	Percent of Families Under $4,000
San Francisco			
City and County	6717	11.8	21.0
Santa Clara			
City of San Jose	6949	12.1	17.5
County	7417	12.2	15.5
Valley			
Stanislaus			
City of Modesto	6357	12.0	24.7
County	5260	9.5	35.2
Merced			
City of Merced	5638	11.3	33.5
County	4806	9.8	40.1
Los Angeles			
City	6896	12.2	21.8
County	7046	12.1	19.1

[1] Source: U.S. Bureau of the Census. *U.S. Census of Population: 1960*. Volume I, *Characteristics of the Population*. Part 6, California. U.S. Government Printing Office, Washington, D.C., 1963.

Table 2-4
Characteristics of California's White, Spanish Surname, and Nonwhite Population in 1960[1]

Population Groups	Percent of Total Population	Median Age	Percent Urban	Median Family Size	Median Education
All groups	100.0	–	–	–	12.1
White	82.9	25.0	86.0	3.6	12.1
Spanish Surname	9.1	22.7	85.4	4.5	8.4
Nonwhite	8.0	26.1	91.4	4.0	10.5

[1] Source: U.S. Bureau of the Census, *U.S. Census of Population: 1960*. Volume I, *Characteristics of the Population*. Part 6, California. U.S. Government Printing Office, Washington, D.C., 1963; and Subject Reports, *Persons of Spanish Surname* Final Report. PC (2) – 1B.

Table 2-5
Percentage Distribution by Major Occupational Group of Male Employed Persons, in California, Heads of Low-Income Families, and Two Samples of AFDC-U Family Heads

Major Occupational Group	Male Employed Persons in California 1960	Family Heads in Experienced Civilian Labor Force with Incomes under $4,000 1960[1]	Statewide 19% AFDC-U Sample 1960[2]	Survey Sample of 1200 Families 1964[3]
All Groups	100[1]	100[1]	100[2]	100[3]
Professional & Managerial	25.4	13.7	1.8	1.6
Clerical and Sales	14.7	14.8	2.5	5.8
Service	6.5	14.0	6.7	11.7
Agriculture	5.3	12.6	22.2	21.8
Craftsmen	20.2	12.6	7.2	10.0
Semiskilled (Operatives)	16.5	17.8	27.3[4]	20.9
Unskilled (Laborers)	6.2	8.7	30.9	28.2
Other	5.2	5.8	1.4	0

[1] Source: U.S. Bureau of the Census. *U.S. Census of Population: 1960*. Volume 1, *Characteristics of the Population*. Part 6, California. U.S. Government Printing Office, Washington, D.C., 1963. Heads of low-income families are represented by the census category–Family Heads in the Experienced Civilian Labor Force with Incomes under $4,000.

[2] Source: *Aid to Families with Dependent Children: Characteristics of Unemployed Parent Families at Intake*. Sample of Recipients–February through July 1964, State of California, Department of Social Welfare, Research and Statistics Div., Sacramento, 1964.

[3] N = 1198 husbands; NR = 2 (0.2% persons were never employed).

[4] Defined in the State Social Welfare Report as follows: Operatives, kindred skilled, semiskilled workers.

These data can be used as a base line against which to compare the occupational composition of various segments of the population. Column two describes the occupational composition of family heads in the experienced civilian labor force with incomes under $4000 (1960). Whereas 25% of all *employed* workers are in the professional and managerial category, only 13.7% of the *low-income family population* fall in this occupational group. It can also be noted that the low-income family population has the same proportion of workers in the clerical and sales category as is true for the total employed labor force.

The last two columns show the occupational distribution of the State Department of Social Welfare sample and our sample of 1200 families. As expected, the occupations of the husbands in these two groups are concentrated in low-status occupations. Perhaps the most startling difference between the AFDC-U samples and the state's low-income population is with reference to white-collar occupations. Whereas 13.7% of the low-income population fall in this occupational group, only 2.5% and 5.8% of the State Department of Social Welfare sample and the sample for this study were classified as white-collar workers. These comparisons make it quite clear that in terms of the vital dimension of occupational status, our sample is drawn from the lowest occupational levels of California's low-income population.

A second comparison can be made between the study sample and low-status occupational groups in terms of unemployment rates. While data on unemployment rates are not available for the low-income population (under $4000), such facts are given by occupational groups. Table 2-6 presents data on unemployment rates for 1960 by occupational groups for the four areas from which the sample cases were drawn as well as for the state at large. From the data in Table 2-5, it can be seen that the bulk of the sample cases are concentrated in agricultural, semiskilled (operatives), and unskilled (laborers) occupations.

By comparing the unemployment rate of our study sample to the unemployment rates of the occupational groups just listed, we can determine whether these sample cases are better or worse off than the average worker in these occupations.

Considering the two occupational categories of operatives and laborers, we find a variation in county unemployment rates from a low of 6.1 to a high of 11.2 for the former and a low of 10.6 to a high of 16.8 for the latter. While 44.1% of the husbands in our sample of 1200 families were unemployed, this figure is not meaningful for comparison because it includes all the AFDC-U families who had an unemployment rate of 88.1% (at the time of interviewing). A more accurate comparison can be made by utilizing only those families within the sample who have never received public assistance.[2] These 392 husbands

---

[2] It is possible that the inclusion of some families within the sample who were unemployment compensation cases may have created an upward bias in the unemployment rate for the entire sample. However, it does not seem probable that this bias would be larger than the 2.2% that differentiates the unemployment rate of the 392 NOA families from the unemployment rate for laborers in Merced and Stanislaus counties. The employment data

showed an unemployment rate of 19%. This figure is higher than the highest unemployment rate given in Table 2-6 and indicates that our sample families are worse off in terms of employment continuity than the average worker. This finding holds true for all four counties as well as for the state at large.

One other comparison can be made between the socioeconomic status of our sample and California's low-income population. While the published census volumes do not include a cross-tabulation of income by education for heads of families in the experienced civilian labor force, this type of cross-tabulation is reported for males over twenty-five, and serves for purposes of rough comparison with our sample cases. The median school years completed for men in the $2000 to $2999 class is 9.6, and for men in the $3000 to $3999 class is 10.5. The median number of school years completed by the husbands of the 1200 sample families is 9.4. Again, this comparison documents the conclusion that the sample cases have been drawn from the bottom level of California's low-income population.

The various comparisons that have been made between the characteristics of the study sample and the population groups in California lead to the following conclusions. The study sample appears to be representative of California's AFDC-U population. Differences between rural and urban subgroups and ethnic subgroups of the sample accurately reflect the differences between these groups in California's entire population. Again, the sample is representative in this respect.

The sample is not representative of California's low-income intact family population, but rather appears to be more nearly representative of the bottom stratum of this segment of California's population. Because there are no published statistics describing the universe to which the sample refers, the sample statistics necessarily have to be used as the best estimate for describing the universe population.

Figure 2-1 indicates graphically the fact that the sample families are living not at the margin of poverty but well below the statistical yardstick described by a poverty line. As has been shown by comparisons with California's low-income population, the sample families manifest the lowest occupational and educational levels. The population that these sample families represent can be described, then, as having the interlocking characteristics of low income, large family size, low occupational level, low educational level, and a high unemployment rate. The population to which the sample refers consists of current AFDC-U families and all other families (not currently on welfare) having the same socioeconomic characteristics.

for counties were collected by the U.S. Census during the spring of 1959, a period of high unemployment in agricultural counties. The data on the 1200 sample families were collected during the summer of 1964, a period of low unemployment for agricultural workers.

This bias would operate to diminish the difference in unemployment rate between the 392 sample families and the occupational groups reported on by the U.S. Census. Thus, the bias created by using unemployment compensation rolls as a source for sample cases is probably more than offset by the bias in the data created by seasonality in employment. This leaves the original conclusion unchanged.

Table 2-6
Unemployment Rates in Percent by Occupational Group for Males in the Experienced Civilian Labor Force in Four Sample Areas and for the State, 1960[1]

Unemployment Rates for Occupational Groups	San Francisco County	Santa Clara County	Stanislaus & Merced Counties	Los Angeles County	State
Total Labor Force	6.5	4.3	7.4	5.6	5.7
Professional and Managerial	2.7	1.1	1.9	2.9	2.2
Clerical and Sales Workers	4.8	2.8	3.0	4.2	3.8
Service Workers, Including Private Household	8.5	5.8	6.2	6.9	6.7
Craftsmen, Foremen, and Kindred Workers	7.0	5.0	7.7	5.7	6.1
Operatives and Kindred Workers	7.8	6.1	11.2	7.3	7.6
Laborers, Except Farm and Mine	10.6	12.6	16.8	10.6	12.6
Farmers, Farm Managers, Farm Laborers, & Farm	14.2	5.8	7.4	5.2	6.3
N.R.	10.6	7.2	9.3	8.6	8.6

[1] Source: U.S. Bureau of the Census. *U.S. Census of Population: 1960.* Volume I, *Characteristics of the Population.* Part 6, California. U.S. Government Printing Office, Washington, D.C., 1963.

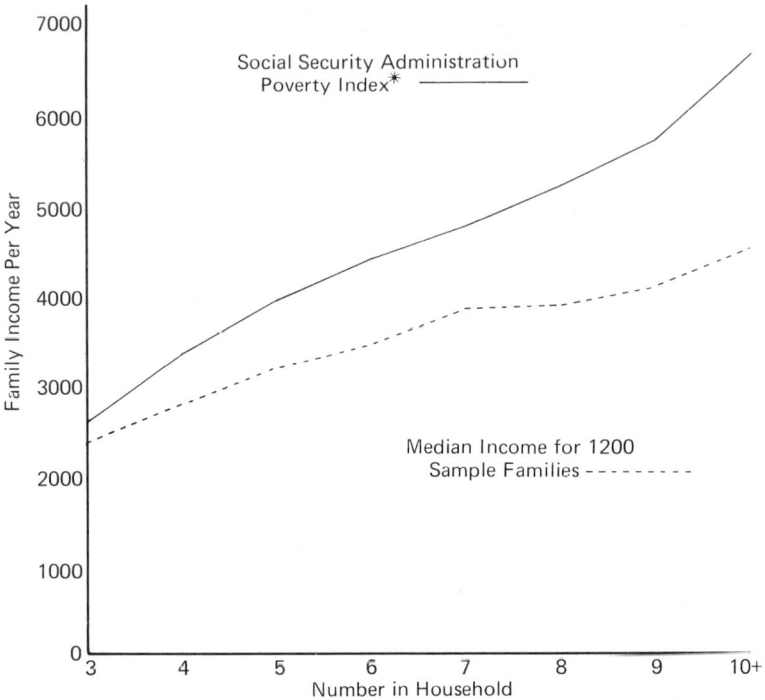

*For comparability with the 1200 sample families, the Social Security Administration Poverty Index was extrapolated (at the rate of $450 per extra person/per year) to cover family size larger than six persons.

Figure 2-1. Income of Sample Families Compared with Social Security Administration on Poverty Index. Source: Orshansky, Mollie, "Counting the Poor: Another Look at the Poverty Profile," *Social Security Bulletin*, Vol. 1, No. 28 (January, 1965), 3-29.

Representativeness of the Four Sample Areas

The remaining sampling issue concerns whether or not the four sample areas selected for the survey cover the range of conditions to be found in California's major labor markets. The four areas were picked to represent first, the agricultural labor market conditions of California's Central Valley, second to represent an urban fringe area, and third to represent the state's two major metropolitan areas.[3]

---

[3]Only two major geographic areas of California are not represented by the four sample areas. These are the Imperial Valley area in Southern California and the large block of

Santa Clara County with its central city of San Jose was chosen as characteristic of a type, the fringe urban area, that has until the last two decades been heavily agricultural in its economic base, and since that time has undergone rapid industrialization and urbanization. Table 2-7 indicates that the composition of its labor force closely approximates the labor force composition for the entire state. Santa Clara County is 95.5% urban, and its central city of San Jose contains one-half the county's population. The agricultural component of the county labor force is statistically engulfed by the characteristics of the urban and industrial population. In actuality, the county today contains two types of economies, with the agricultural sector constituting a submerged secondary level that does not show up in countywide statistics on average income, education, etc.

The third sample area—San Francisco (a combined city and county)—is a port and administrative city, whose characteristics are reflected in the high proportion of workers in the transportation industry (Table 2-7) and in the high proportion of workers classified as clerical (Table 2-8). Los Angeles County, the fourth sample area, shows a diversified economy, and since it contained some 41% of the employed labor force in California in 1960, it is hardly surprising that it approximates closely the characteristics of the entire state economy.

The geographic concentration of low-income families and ethnic groups in these four areas show certain important differences and similarities. In Los Angeles and San Francisco, low-income families reside in zones or belts that are determined by a combination of rent levels and by ethnic and racial ties and barriers. Families of Mexican descent suffer from somewhat less rigid segregation barriers than does the black population, but they still live within clearly defined areas of these inner cities. It is important to point out that these racial and ethnic slums from which our cases were drawn are not homogeneous in income, in family composition, or in the social types who live there. Based on the barriers created by segregation, a wide variety of types of persons are contained within such subcommunities. While the areas are characterized by poverty, the population can be characterized as socially heterogeneous.

Merced and Stanislaus counties—the two rural areas in the San Joaquin

---

agricultural counties in Northern California. We are assuming that the Sacramento Valley is basically the same type of labor market as the San Joaquin Valley and is therefore represented by Stanislaus and Merced counties. The major issue involved is whether or not the agricultural sector of California's labor force has been adequately represented by the two counties from the San Joaquin Valley. Census data show that Imperial County is 63.5% urban, whereas Merced County in the San Joaquin Valley is only 36.1% urban. Consequently, we have not excluded a large labor market area that is significantly more agricultural than the two counties chosen from the San Joaquin Valley. A computation was made for fourteen northern counties in California as to the rural-urban distribution of the population. Six of these fourteen counties showed a higher proportion of rural residents than the sample county of Merced. Despite this fact, and despite the fact that these counties constitute some one-fourth of the state's land area, they constitute only 2.8% of the state's population. There is, then, little reason to believe that lack of inclusion of one of these counties within the sample alters the representativeness of the four areas that were selected.

Table 2-7
Number and Percent of the Employed Labor Force by Major Industry Group for Sample Areas and for the State of California in 1960[1]

Industry	San Francisco		Santa Clara (San Jose)		Stanislaus & Merced (Valley)		Los Angeles		California	
	Number	Percent	Number	Percent	Number	Percent	Number	Percent	Number	Percent
Agriculture	1,498	0.5	7,896	3.5	16,125	21.0	29,052	1.2	267,836	4.6
Mining	260	0.1	243	0.1	198	0.3	6,826	0.3	25,973	0.5
Construction	14,049	4.2	18,163	8.0	4,323	5.6	124,170	5.2	361,691	6.3
Manufacturing	54,467	16.4	67,469	29.6	11,846	15.4	728,823	30.7	1,391,110	24.1
Transportation	34,211	10.3	12,771	5.6	4,685	6.1	150,411	6.3	393,804	6.8
Sales	67,864	20.5	37,271	16.3	15,103	19.6	440,180	18.5	1,081,730	18.8
Finance, Insurance, & Real Estate	30,276	9.1	10,313	4.5	2,702	3.5	127,350	5.4	291,349	5.1
Services	82,743	25.1	55,125	24.1	15,311	19.8	541,551	22.9	1,324,969	23.0
Public Administration	22,987	6.9	9,274	4.1	3,443	4.5	102,262	4.3	354,008	6.1
Industry Not Reported	22,801	6.9	9,631	4.2	3,202	4.2	123,066	5.2	268,983	4.7
Total	331,156	100.0	228,153	100.0	76,938	100.0	2,373,691	100.0	5,761,433	100.0
Percent of State	5.7		4.0		1.3		41.1		100.0	

[1] Source: U.S. Bureau of the Census. *U.S. Census of Population: 1950*. Volume 1, *Characteristics of the Population*. Part 6, California. U.S. Government Printing Office, Washington, D.C., 1963.

Table 2-8
Percentage Distribution of Males (14 Years and Older) in Each Major Occupational Group for Four Sample Areas in California in 1960[1]

Major Occupational Groups	San Francisco City and County	Santa Clara County	Santa Clara City of San Jose	Valley Merced County	Valley Merced City	Valley Stanislaus County	Valley Stanislaus City of Merced	Los Angeles County	Los Angeles City
All occupations	100.0	100.0	100.0	100.0	100.0	100.0	100.0	100.0	100.0
Professional	11.8	19.2	15.8	6.4	11.6	7.8	14.1	14.7	16.0
Farm Managers	0.2	1.8	0.6	16.9	2.5	10.4	1.4	0.7	0.8
Managers & Proprietors (except farm)	11.1	11.2	10.3	9.2	16.4	10.6	17.2	12.0	12.1
Clerical	11.8	6.8	7.9	3.2	5.6	4.1	5.6	7.8	8.2
Sales	8.3	7.5	8.2	5.5	11.0	7.7	12.9	8.2	8.7
Craftsmen	15.8	21.3	21.4	13.4	15.5	16.4	14.9	20.2	17.3
Operatives	13.3	14.5	17.0	12.0	10.3	16.1	13.8	18.3	16.2
Household Servants	0.4	0.1	0.1	0.0	0.1	0.0	0.0	0.2	0.2
Service (nonhouse)	12.7	5.7	6.4	4.8	6.7	4.7	5.9	6.4	7.6
Farm Laborers	0.2	2.0	1.0	18.5	4.5	10.3	2.1	0.5	0.3
Laborers (except farm & mine)	6.9	5.5	6.2	5.7	8.1	7.1	6.0	5.3	5.4
N.R.	7.5	4.4	5.1	4.4	7.7	4.8	6.1	5.7	7.2

[1] Source: U.S. Bureau of the Census. *U.S. Census of Population: 1960*. Volume I, *Characteristics of the Population*. Part 6, California. U.S. Government Printing Office, Washington, D.C., 1963.

Valley—have about 23% of their populations contained in the two central cities of Merced and Modesto. Thirty-six and 52%, respectively, of the populations of these counties live in communities of 2500 or more persons. A large percentage of this area's population lives in small hamlets. These small hamlets contain few white-collar workers or other persons in the middle class. A high proportion of the population in such places live at poverty standards. Frequently, they are racially or ethnically homogeneous. From these few facts, it can be easily seen that the low-income segment of the population in these rural counties are so distributed that their communities are much more homogeneous and show less variation in social and economic characteristics than the big city slum does.

The distribution of low-income families in Santa Clara County is more complex, because of its large central city, its suburban population, and its agricultural labor force, some of whom live in hamlets and small towns and some of whom live in the central city. While it contains some of the elements of both the major metropolitan areas and the rural central valley, its dominant characteristics appear to be that of the large urban complex, and therefore, the bulk of its low-income population probably tends to show the same social and economic heterogeneity.

In terms of ethnic composition, the San Jaoquin Valley area and Santa Clara County have a very small black population and a high proportion of Spanish surname families in comparison to San Francisco and Los Angeles (Table 2-9). These facts are reflected in the proportion of ethnic families included in the samples drawn from each of the four areas (see Tables 3-1 and 3-2).

In examining how our four sample areas represent socioeconomic conditions in California, we must consider two additional factors: (1) the policies of county welfare departments; and (2) seasonality of employment for the labor force. As might be expected, the rural Central Valley is strongly affected by seasonal employment. During the summer of 1964, the AFDC-U rolls in Stanislaus and Merced counties declined to almost zero. It can be expected that many families who were receiving AFDC-U assistance prior to summer employment will be back on the public assistance rolls in the winter.

At the same time, the first two years of experience with the AFDC-U program show a statewide decline in AFDC-U caseloads during both the summer of 1964 and 1965 (Figure 2-2). It is difficult to determine whether or not this decline is accounted for by increased employment in the agricultural sector of the state's experienced civilian labor force; it may be that the same trend is manifested in AFDC-U caseloads in San Francisco and Los Angeles.

Seasonality may be associated with the policies of county welfare departments in a particular way—namely, to be more strict in enrolling families under the AFDC-U program during the summer months when more jobs are available, and to be less strict during the winter months when low-skilled jobs are in shorter supply. If true, the combined interaction of seasonality in employment and county welfare department policies would be reflected in a higher rate of short-time unemployment for rural families with welfare experience than would be true for urban families who are also receiving or have received public assistance.

Table 2-9
Characteristics of the White, Spanish Surname, Nonwhite Population of Four Sample Areas in California in 1960[1]

Sample Areas	Percent of Population	Median Family Income
San Francisco		
All groups	100.0	
White	74.7	6,717
Spanish Surname	7.0	5,921
Nonwhite	18.4	5,305
Santa Clara		
All groups	100.0	
White	84.7	7,417
Spanish Surname	12.1	5,931
Nonwhite	3.2	6,280
Valley		
Merced		
All groups	100.0	
White	77.7	4,806
Spanish Surname	14.8	3,862
Nonwhite	7.5	2,887
Stanislaus		
All groups	100.0	
White	91.1	5,260
Spanish Surname	7.5	4,458
Nonwhite	1.4	3,820
Los Angeles		
All groups	100.0	
White	80.8	7,046
Spanish Surname	9.5	5,759
Nonwhite	9.7	5,157

[1] Source: U.S. Bureau of the Census, *U.S. Census of the Population: 1960*. Subject Reports. *Persons of Spanish Surname*, Final Report. PC (2) – 1B. U.S. Government Printing Office, Washington, D.C., 1963.

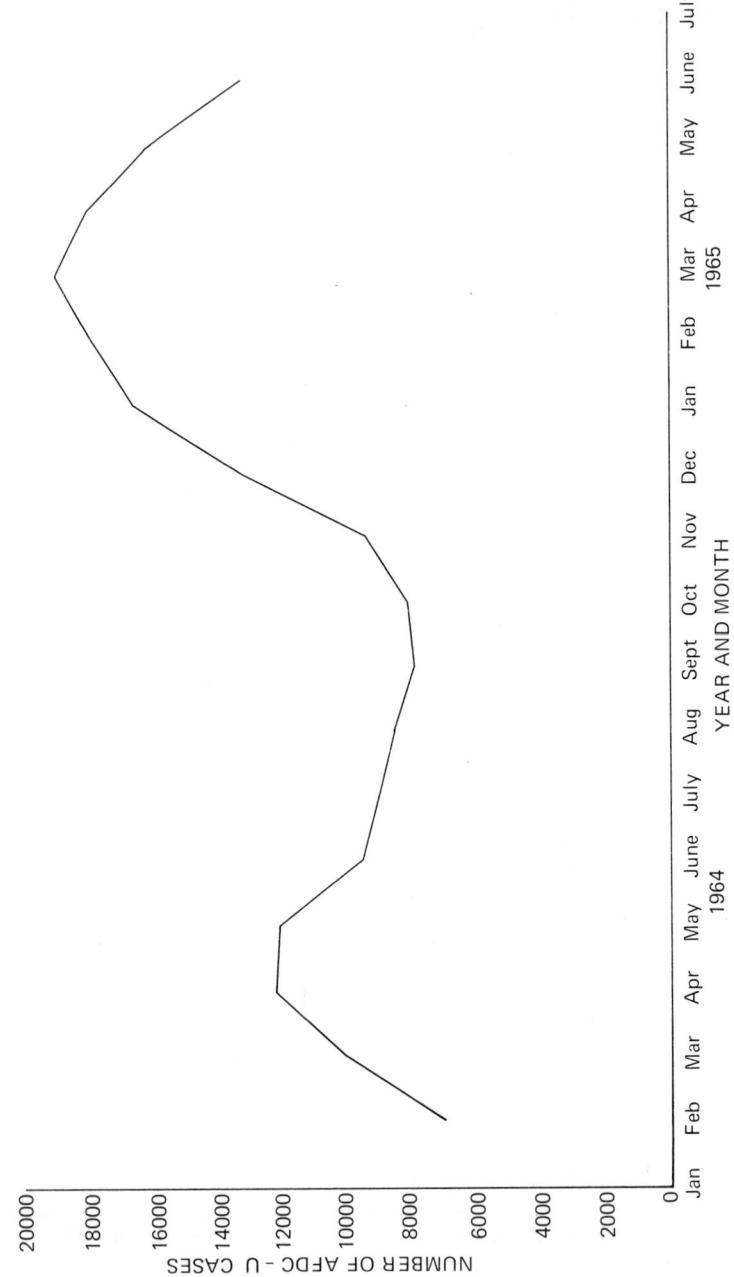

Figure 2-2. Number of AFDC-U Cases in California for 1964-65. Source: Special AFDC-U tabulation by California State Department of Social Welfare, unpublished.

Still another possible effect arising from differences in county welfare policies centers on the strictness or leniency in administering state and federal law. Based on the statements of the families interviewed, it would appear that counties differ. We cannot offer any proof that the range of strict or lenient policies displayed by counties in California is accurately reflected in the four sample areas, but it seems likely that these areas are representative of conditions commonly met by the bulk of California's low-income population.

While no survey of institutional services for low-income families was made, data collected by the State Social Welfare Board and presented in its first annual report indicate that the urban areas contain more organizations and associations which function to serve the low-income population than is true for rural counties. Whether or not these organizations are *effective* in achieving their goals is, however, still another question.

Summary

The sample of 1200 families appears to be quite similar to a statewide sample of AFDC-U cases drawn by the State Department of Social Welfare. The sample also reflects accurately certain characteristic differences in the state's population with reference to rural-urban residence and ethnic status. Comparisons of the sample characteristics to those of the state's low-income population reveal that the sample families are a group whose income, occupational level, educational level, and employment continuity place them at the bottom or close to the bottom of the low-income intact-family population in California.

As this distinct population group is not described in any available published statistics, the sample of 1200 families described in this book constitutes the best available current estimate of this population's characteristics, even though the sample itself was not drawn by probability methods.

Comparison of the four areas where sampling was carried out indicates that these counties cover the range of *major* labor market conditions and institutional and ecological patterns characteristic of poverty areas in California.

3 Classification of the Cases

Though the 1200 cases were selected in terms of each family's current welfare status, it soon became evident that many of the matching families had experienced welfare status at some point in their working lives. Thus, it was decided that the families should be classified in terms of their welfare history rather than simply in terms of their current welfare status. This simple and important decision has the effect of translating the concept of welfare experience from that of a population containing welfare and nonwelfare cases, to that of a population of persons manifesting varying degrees of welfare experience at various times in their life history as workers.

A Dependency Index

Length of welfare experience (aid in the form of money or commodities from a private or public agency) is easily expressed as an index ranging from zero months to some upper limit. Ninety-nine months (eight years and three months) was chosen as the upper limit for the index of aggregate welfare experience. The time during a worker's life history when welfare aid was experienced was expressed in terms of the number of months in the past that the latest welfare experience had occurred. A person currently receiving public or private assistance was specified to be zero months away from an aid status, and a person whose welfare experience occurred eight years and three months from the time when the survey was taken received a score of 99.

By a simple process of inverting[1] the second of these scales, the two scores describing an individual's welfare history were added together and divided by two in order to provide a single index number indicating his dependency status. This index of dependency ranged from zero to 99. The index gives equal weight to the *amount* of aid (expressed in months) received by a person, and the location in time of that aid (in months) relative to the present (defined as the time when the person was interviewed during the summer of 1964).

On this scale, a score of zero means that the individual has never had welfare experience. A score of 99 means that his aggregate months of assistance was 99,

---

[1] The scale representing numbers of months away from aid status was subtracted from 99. Thus, a family currently receiving public assistance was given a score of 99 (99 − 0 = 99). A family whose aid status ended one month prior to the present (time of interview in summer of 1964) would receive a score of 98 (99 − 1 = 98).

and that his current status is that of a welfare recipient—namely, zero months away from aid status, which is inverted to 99. When these two scores are added and divided by two, the resultant index is 99.

A plot of 1200 dependency index scores produced a graph that is a profile of the welfare histories of the 1200 families. If the 392 families with no welfare history are excluded and the remaining 808 scores are plotted, the form of this graph (shown in Figure 3-1) is that of the familiar bell-shaped curve, or normal distribution. Without going into the details of the procedure, we can state that the combined index produces a very different statistical picture than that derived from graphing only the aggregate months of welfare experienced by a family without reference to the time *when* it occurred. Figure 3-2 shows the two elements in the index when each dimension is graphed separately. The plot of aggregate months on welfare takes the form of a "j" curve, with most of the cases showing short-time aid experience. The plot of scores calculated only in

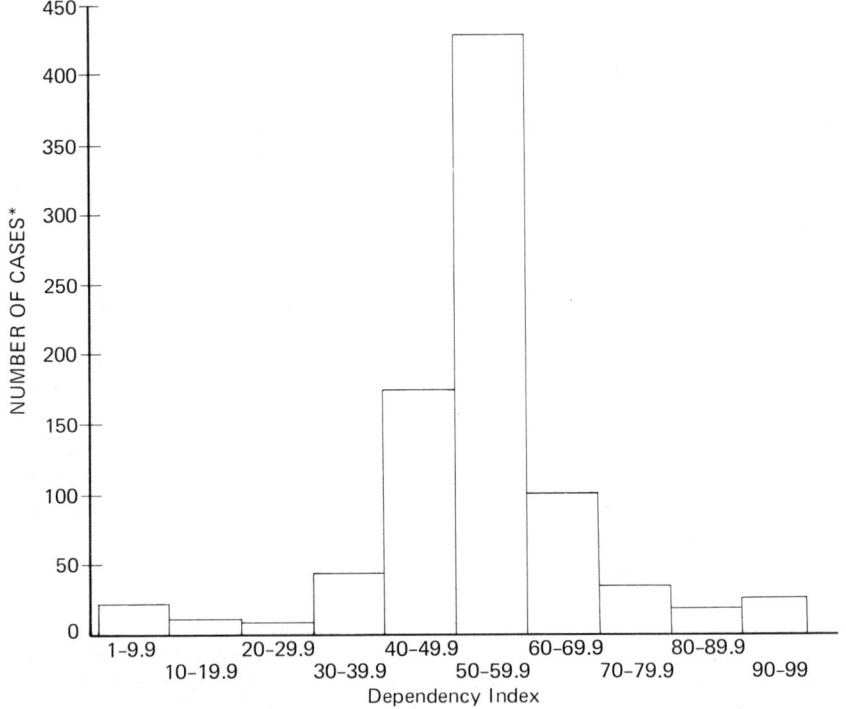

*Total number of cases is 808 (STA+ LTA); the NOA cases equal 392 at a dependency index of zero.

Figure 3-1. Frequency Distribution of Dependency Index Scores for the 808 Families with Some Welfare Experience.

terms of when the aid experience occurred shows the same "j" shape, indicating that the aid experience of most of the 808 families is recent. The bell-shaped curve in Figure 3-1 results from combining these two indexes into one index of welfare dependency.

Comparing this bell-shaped distribution to studies done of current welfare recipients in California (Schlamp, 1962), we find that the computation of aggregate months on welfare for *current* cases when graphed shows the same "j"-shaped curve as that given in Figure 3-2. The vast majority of cases show less than a year's welfare experience, and only a minority would be characterized as long-time welfare cases. When it is recognized that the analysis of current cases excludes all those families in the population not now on welfare but who have been on welfare at some previous time, it becomes obvious that any adequate

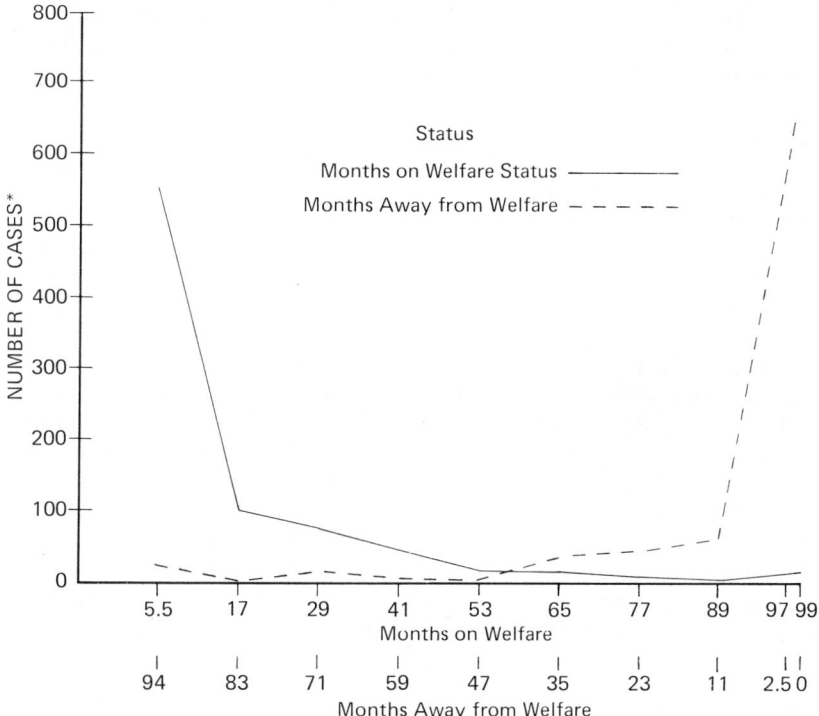

*Total number of cases is 808 (STA+LTA), NOA's equal 392 cases at zero month on aid.

Figure 3-2. Frequency Distribution of Number of Months on Welfare Status and Number of Months away from Welfare Status for 808 Families with Some Welfare Experience.

description of welfare rates requires inclusion of all persons who have had such experiences in the past.

The dependency index that has been described covers those families who have never received public assistance, as well as those who have received assistance both in the present and the past. Thus, it leads directly to the notion that welfare experience may be viewed statistically in the same way that accidents, sickness, or other recurrent human phenomena are considered—namely, from an actuarial viewpoint. While individual accidents or illnesses may be difficult to predict, accident rates or sickness rates for *groups* of persons can be predicted with considerable accuracy. The actuarial approach to such things as sickness or accidents involves the definition of a risk population, and the calculation of the probabilities of the frequency of sickness or accidents for this group based upon the group's experience over time.

If the low-income population is viewed as a risk group with reference to public assistance experience, we can then ask what the incidence of such experience is in this population in any given year or over several years' time.

The first and obvious approach is to talk about a crude rate such as the number of current welfare cases per 1,000 population. However, this does not tell us how long these persons have been on welfare, nor does it relate particular welfare programs to the appropriate segment of the low-income population that constitutes the risk group for that particular program. We would not expect, for example, that insurance companies would calculate rates for deaths of mothers due to childbirth for both males and females. It makes no more sense to relate the number of current AFDC-U welfare cases to the low-income population that includes both single persons, childless families, and families with a female head of household.

The risk population for AFDC-U public assistance consists *only* of intact families (mother, father, and one or more children under 18) whose income at a given level is related to family size. Without some estimate of the number of such families at given points in time, it is difficult if not impossible to estimate what the AFDC-U public assistance rate per thousand families may be for the AFDC-U risk program.

The ideal method for calculating the dependency rates of risk populations with reference to particular welfare programs requires, then, accurate knowledge of a population cross-classified by age, income, health, family composition, and labor force participation potential. That segment of the population constituting the risk population for a given program can then be accurately estimated. Accurate data concerning the amount of welfare experience in any given year for persons or families falling in the risk population would then allow computation of a reasonably accurate dependency rate. If such rates were calculated annually, trends in the dependency rates for a given welfare program could be easily ascertained.

These brief remarks concerning the ideal method for determining the welfare dependency condition of a population are included in order to make clear that there is very little knowledge at present by which data on current welfare cases can be linked to census population data to provide any estimates of dependency rates. Our sample of 1200 cases is not a probability sample, and was not drawn in order to provide estimates of the larger risk population. Nevertheless, the construction of a dependency index for the 1200 cases highlights the point that our interest is in a risk population. Use of the dependency index for the 1200 families provides a ratio of cases who have never experienced welfare to those who have, and indicates for those with some welfare experience the duration and location in time of that experience.

An equally important derivative of using a dependency index is the emphasis it places on the need for the prevention of dependency as well as for rehabilitation. Just as with accident cases or illness, reducing the risk of dependency would result in a lowering of the dependency rate in a given population over a given period of time.

In order to make effective comparisons of families with varying welfare experience, it was decided to classify the sample into three groups. The first group consisted of 392 families who had never been on aid (NOA). The remaining 808 cases were arbitrarily split into two groups, a short-time (STA) and a long-time aid (LTA) group. The dependency scores of the 571 STA cases ranged from 1 to 55, and for the 237 LTA cases from 56 to 99.[2] The reader can see that the score dividing the STA and the LTA groups falls almost exactly at the midpoint of the bell-shaped curve given in Figure 3-1.

Matching the Cases by Income Ethnicity, and Geography

Having provided a method for classifying the cases by their dependency experience, we can now ask about the matching of the cases by income and by ethnicity, and can also describe how well the cases are matched for other variables such as family size, education, years of rural residence, etc. It will be

---

[2] The original definition of the STA group was constructed as follows: All cases with 12 months or less of welfare experience, and all cases whose aid experience was more than 12 months in the past, regardless of amount of welfare experience. These definitions produced 567 cases with scores ranging from 1 through 55. The remaining four cases had scores, respectively, of 68, 74, 77, and 81. These were all cases where the welfare experience had taken place more than 12 months distant from the present, but the aggregate amount of welfare experience was so large that the respective scores were above the cutting point of 55.9.

Originally, the LTA cases were defined as those with more than 12 months of welfare aid whose experience was 11 months or less away from the present. This definition produced 231 cases with scores ranging from 56-59. Six cases were below the cutting point of 56. The scores of these cases were as follows: one case, 53; one case, 54; and 4 cases, 55.

These original definitions of the STA and LTA cases were utilized to classify the cases *before* the dependency index was constructed and resulted in a classification that produced 10 errors (4 STA cases and 6 LTA cases). The number and size of the errors in classification do not materially affect the definition of the STA group as that group having dependency scores from 1-55 and the LTA group as that group having dependency scores from 56-99.

remembered that the original intent of the research design was to sample in such a manner that rural-urban differences would be controlled for, and to draw an equal number of cases from each of the three ethnic groups to be represented in the 1200 cases. At the same time, the dependency groups were to be matched for present income level, i.e., income for the last 12 months. As will be seen in the following discussion, the problems involved in meeting the requirements of the design derive first from reclassifying the cases into three dependency groups, secondly, from the differences in population characteristics in the four areas where the sampling was conducted, and, thirdly, from biases in the sampling procedure arising from difficulties encountered in doing the actual field work.

In reclassifying the cases into three dependency groups, the proportions did not result in one-third of the cases falling into each subgroup. Rather, the proportions were NOA 32.6%, STA 47.6%, and LTA 19.8%. When these cases were cross-classified by ethnicity, the number of cases in each subgroup of the sample were not equal.

A second difficulty arose in sampling by ethnicity. Because the number of black cases in Santa Clara County and the two Valley counties were not sufficient to provide one-third of the total sample families for each of these areas, a disproportionate number of black families in the San Francisco area were included in the sample drawn from that county. In addition, 44 cases were collected that did not readily fall into any one of the three ethnic groups, and these cases are included in the tables under the category of "other." As a result, the proportions of the three ethnic groups and the "other" group are as follows: white, 33.3%; black, 26.3%; Spanish-speaking, 36.7%; and "other," 3.7%.

The results of this procedure produced the subgroup totals shown in Table 3-1. When this two-way classification is turned into a classification of the cases based on geographic location, dependency status, and ethnic status, a 48-cell table results. The distribution of the sample resulting from this cross-classification is shown in Table 3-2.

Because of the disproportions in the distribution of cases in Table 3-2, it was not possible to utilize all the features of a study design based on the logic that each welfare case would be matched with a nonwelfare case with ethnicity held constant. The black cases were disproportionately concentrated in San Francisco, and the Spanish-speaking cases disproportionately concentrated in San Jose and Los Angeles.

Our method for dealing with these difficulties was to analyze the data first in terms of the single variable of dependency. If patterned differences showed up in terms of the dependency dimension for a factor such as education, it could then be asked whether differences in education were also found when the 1200 cases were classified by ethnicity. The third step was to ask if differences were manifested by the geographic location of the cases. If differences in education were found when the cases were classified by the dependency variable, it still remained to be proved that such differences were not due to the confounding effect of disproportionate distribution of the ethnic groups. The only way to control for this bias was to find a difference that was free of the confounding effect created by disproportions in the sampling.

Table 3-1
Distribution of Families Cross-Classified as to: Ethnicity by Area, Dependency by Area, and Dependency by Ethnicity

A. Ethnicity by Area

Ethnicity	S.F.	S.J.	VAL.	L.A.	Total
Black	172	6	43	95	316
Spanish	53	198	87	102	440
White	59	92	154	95	400
Other	16	4	16	8	44
Total	300	300	300	300	1200

B. Dependency by Area

Dependency	S.F.	S.J.	VAL.	L.A.	Total
Never on aid	107	74	94	117	392
Short time on aid	119	170	182	100	571
Long time on aid	74	56	24	83	237
Total	300	300	300	300	1200

C. Dependency by Ethnicity

Dependency	Black	Spanish	White	Other	Total
Never on aid	108	149	111	24	392
Short time on aid	125	207	225	14	571
Long time on aid	83	84	64	6	237
Total	316	440	400	44	1200

For example, the lower educational level of Spanish-speaking families, who constituted a disproportionately large segment of the San Jose sample, did not obscure the difference between urban (San Jose) educational levels and rural educational levels (the Valley cases). The median educational level of the San Jose cases was higher than that of the Valley families, and can be considered a true rural-urban difference.

Matching for Income

In matching for income, we used Table 2-1 to provide an upper income ceiling for nonwelfare families who were to be paired with public assistance cases. As the field work progressed during the summer of 1964, it became more and more clear that finding matching families was not difficult in the Valley counties, but in the three urban areas, finding nonwelfare families who were living at the income level of welfare families proved to be a much more difficult task. In the last weeks of the field work period, the income ceiling used to choose matching families was raised to 10% above welfare levels, then to 20%, and even to 30% in order to complete the sample quota of 600 nonwelfare families.

The results of this field work difficulty produced a set of matching cases that were not identical in income level with the welfare cases. Figure 3-3 shows this differential in income by family size. As stated in Chapter 1, the median annual family income of the nonwelfare group was 17.2% higher than the welfare cases.

When the cases were reclassified into three groups based on the dependency index, a rather different picture was obtained. As shown in Figure 3-4, the income level of the STA and LTA groups looks much the same, whereas the median income of the NOA group is 20% higher than the LTA cases.

The ease in finding low-income families in the two rural counties is clearly reflected when family income is plotted by geographic area. Figure 3-5 shows that for families of three to six persons, income levels are very similar in the four geographic areas. For larger families, the Valley area shows much lower incomes, and the San Francisco cases much higher incomes, than the average for the total sample.

When the cases are classified by ethnic status, income levels look much the same. Figure 3-6 shows that family income is higher for those black families with a large number of members. As the black cases are disproportionately represented in the San Francisco sample, this difference probably reflects geographic rather than ethnic factors.

Table 3-2
Distribution of Families Cross-Classified by Dependency, Geography, and Ethnicity

	S.F.	S.J.	VAL.	L.A.	Total
Black – Never on aid	56	01	16	35	108
Black – Short time on aid	71	02	21	31	125
Black – Long time on aid	45	03	06	29	83
Spanish – Never on aid	21	55	33	40	149
Spanish – Short time on aid	20	102	51	34	207
Spanish – Long time on aid	12	41	03	28	84
White – Never on aid	23	17	34	37	111
White – Short time on aid	23	63	105	34	225
White – Long time on aid	13	12	15	24	64
Other – Never on aid	07	01	11	05	24
Other – Short time on aid	05	03	05	01	14
Other – Long time on aid	04	00	00	02	06
Total	300	300	300	300	1200

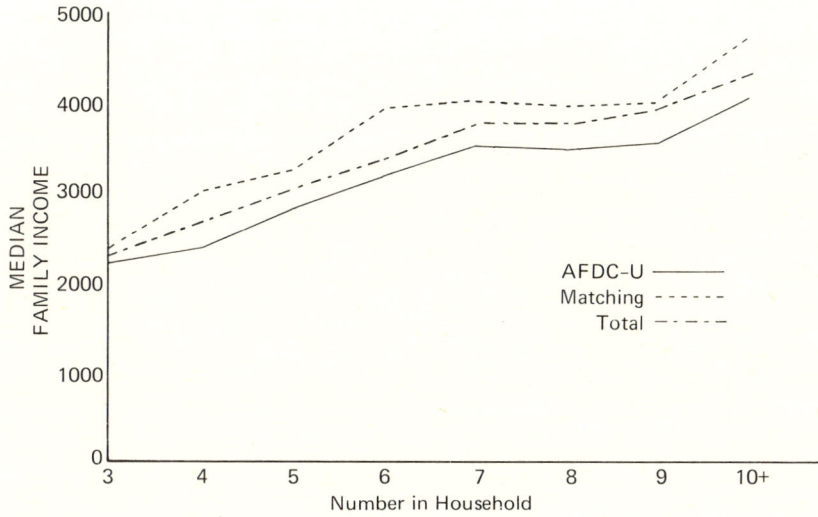

Figure 3-3. Median Family Income by Family Size for AFDC-U Cases, Matching Cases, and Total Sample Cases.

In terms of the original study design, the method used to find matching cases rested on the assumption that families could be matched in income at the same time that they were selected for welfare status, ethnic status, and geographic location. In actuality, it is clear that we were sampling from populations where significant differences existed in average family income between welfare and nonwelfare families and between rural and urban families.

Despite efforts to implement the initial assumption underlying the study design, differences in the income characteristics of the populations being studied were reflected in the sample subgroups that were selected. In effect, the field work procedures produced subsamples that are more representative of the various segments of the universe population than would have been true if each subsample showed the same median income.

Additional Matching Variables

An additional and unexpected complication arose in selecting current public assistance cases in the two Valley counties. During the summer months of 1964, the AFDC-U rolls in these counties were reduced almost to the vanishing point as the demand for agricultural labor increased. As a result, only 44.7% of the AFDC-U sample in the Valley were current cases at the time they were interviewed, and the remaining cases were from one to three months removed

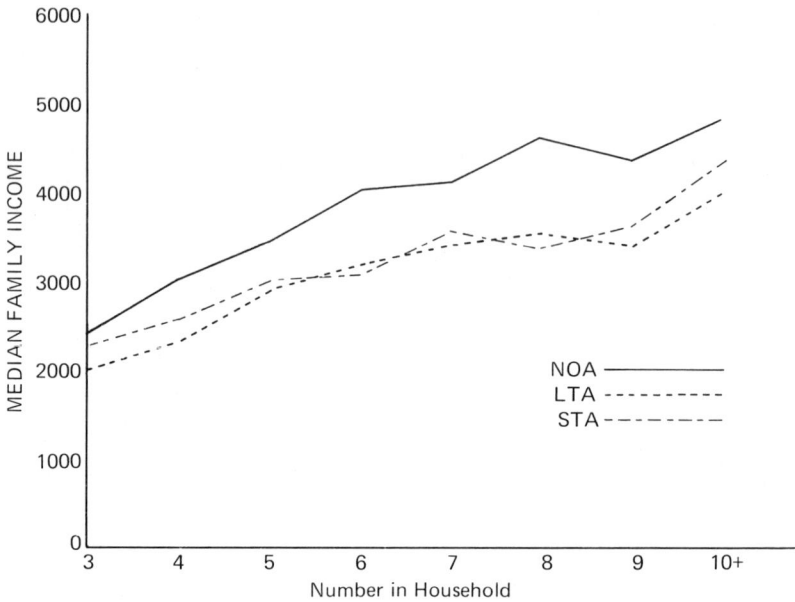

Figure 3-4. Median Family Income by Family Size for Dependency Groups. (Standard deviations for the distributions are: NOA, $1,400; STA, $1,359; and LTA, $1,100. Mean income is, respectively; $3,679, $3,263, and $3,099.)

from a welfare status. The bias created by this deviation from the original study design turned out to be of minor significance when the cases were reclassified in terms of the dependency index. A fuller discussion of this problem can be found in Appendix A.

Another question of classification and matching concerns the definition of a family as rural or urban. The rural status of a family or person consists of some combination of residence and labor force participation both in the past and present. Table 3-3 describes the history of rural residence for the husbands of the 1200 families. Rural residence was defined as residence on a farm or in a small town. Both indexes in the table show that the Valley families have had more rural residence in the past than the families in the three urban areas. The data in Table 2-7 document the obvious fact that the Valley has much larger percentage of its labor force in the agricultural sector than is true of the urban counties. Fifty-seven % of the sample cases drawn from the Valley show a current occupation within the agricultural sector of the economy, whereas the next largest proportion of the sample families involved in agricultural pursuits is San Jose (20%). From these indexes, it is clear that the Valley families are more rural than the sample families from the other three areas.

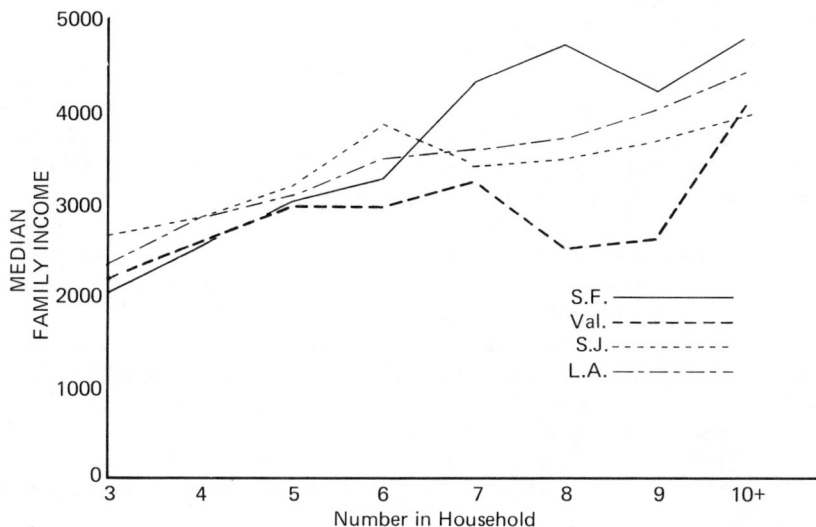

Figure 3-5. Median Family Income by Family Size and Geographic Areas.

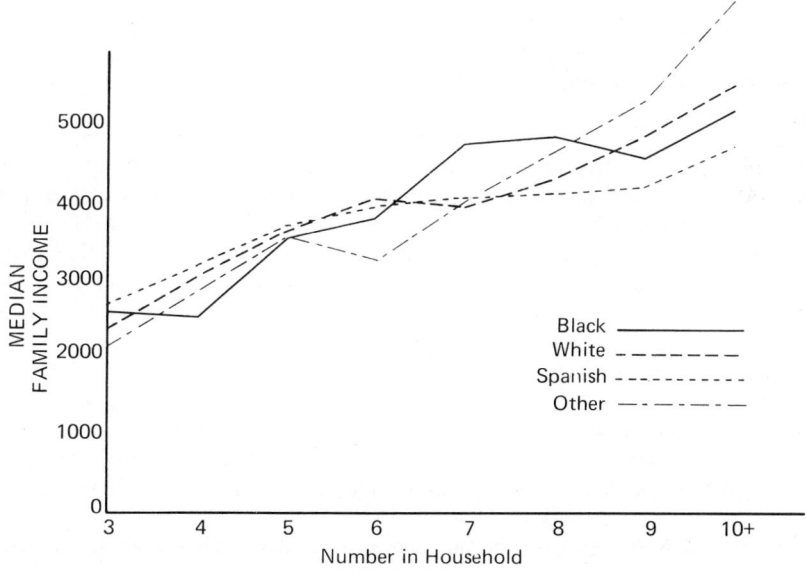

Figure 3-6. Median Family Income by Family Size for Ethnic Groups.

Another variable that should be held constant in comparing the cases is that of geographic or residential mobility. Table 3-4 shows that the median number of residence changes within the last two years has been 2.3 moves. This does not tell us, however, how far the families moved. Table 3-5 shows that the median length of stay in the neighborhood where families were living at the time of the interview was 25.4 months. If the indexes in the two tables are considered jointly, it seems clear that these families change residence frequently, but tend to make these changes within a neighborhood area.

The two tables on stability of residence allow us to disprove the possibility that the NOA cases are all without welfare experience in California because they are newcomers to the state. On the average, the NOA cases have been living in their current neighborhood as long as the LTA cases. As explained in Chapter 2, certain features of the field work procedures make it plausible to conclude that the sample cases may be biased in the direction of greater residential stability than is true in the parent population.

The sample cases may also be biased in the direction of greater stability of marriage. Table 3-6 shows that the median length of time that husband and wife have shared the same household is 11.2 years. Family stability in the universe population may not be this high.

Even though the cases were selected for income level by household size, in comparing subgroups within the sample, it is important to control for household size. Table 3-7 shows that the median number of persons in the household remains almost the same for the subgroups in the sample, with the exception of the Spanish-speaking families who show a median of 7.4 persons in contrast to the overall sample median of 6.8 persons.

The data on education show almost no variation in educational achievement for the cases when classified by dependency. In contrast, when classified by geographic area and by ethnicity, the subgroups show significant variation around the overall median of 9.4 years of education.

Another variable that affects comparison of the subgroups in the sample is that of age. Table 3-9 shows the median age of the husbands to be 36.9 years. The greatest variation from this over-all sample median is found in the LTA cases which show a median age of 40.4 years. Any comparison of the dependency groups must then take account of the fact that age is not held constant.

Summary

The original study design was based on the concept of matching welfare and nonwelfare families for income, with equal representation of ethnic group members in the two halves of the sample. The cases were to be drawn from four geographic areas, one of which was a rural area.

Recognition that a more adequate measure of dependency was needed than the simple classification of a family as a welfare or nonwelfare case led to the construction of a dependency index which combined length of public assistance

Table 3-3
Percent of Husbands with a History of Rural Residence, and Median Years of Residence

Rural Residence	Cases Classified by Dependency				Cases Classified by Area					Cases Classified by Ethnicity				
	NOA	STA	LTA	Total	S.F.	S.J.	VAL.	L.A.	Total	Black	Span.	White	Other	Total
Those with a history of rural residence	71.4	70.8	65.8	70.0[1]	67.0	69.3	79.0	64.7	70.0[1]	69.0	61.8	79.0	77.3	70.0[1]
Median number of years rural residence	18.8	15.4	15.7	16.5[2]	15.1	12.9	20.8	17.6	16.5[2]	16.1	13.7	18.2	26.3	16.5[2]

[1] N = 1200 husbands.
[2] N = 840 husbands, those reporting one or more years of rural residence.

Table 3-4
Percentage Distribution of Families by Number of Residence Changes in Last Two Years and Median Number of Moves

Residence Change	Cases Classified by Dependency				Cases Classified by Area					Cases Classified by Ethnicity				
	NOA	STA	LTA	Total	S.F.	S.J.	VAL.	L.A.	Total	Black	Span.	White	Other	Total
All Moves	100.0	100.0	100.0	100.0[1]	100.0	100.0	100.0	100.0	100.0[1]	100.0	100.0	100.0	100.0	100.0[1]
No moves	47.5	40.3	48.0	44.2	47.1	38.7	43.0	48.0	44.2	49.6	50.2	33.3	43.2	44.2
1 move	23.2	24.1	27.7	24.5	27.3	26.7	20.5	23.7	24.5	29.0	21.0	25.8	15.9	24.5
2 moves	13.5	14.8	11.1	13.6	12.5	14.3	15.4	12.3	13.6	11.8	13.5	14.3	22.7	13.6
3 moves	7.9	9.9	7.2	8.7	8.4	9.0	4.4	8.0	8.7	6.1	8.7	10.8	9.1	8.7
4 moves	7.9	10.9	6.0	9.0	4.7	11.3	11.7	8.0	9.0	3.5	6.6	15.8	9.1	9.0
Median number of moves in last two years	2.2	2.4	1.9	2.3[2]	1.9	2.3	2.5	2.2	2.3[2]	1.9	2.3	2.5	2.6	2.3[2]

[1] N = 1195; NR = 5 (0.5%).
[2] N = 667 families, those who did move one or more times within the last two years.

Table 3-5
Percent of Families Living in Current Neighborhood More than Five Months, and Median Length of Residence

Months	Cases Classified by Dependency				Cases Classified by Area					Cases Classified by Ethnicity				
	NOA	STA	LTA	Total	S.F.	S.J.	VAL.	L.A.	Total	Black	Span.	White	Other	Total
Living in neighborhood 5 months or more	83.2	81.0	85.2	82.5[1]	88.0	77.2	79.3	85.6	82.5[1]	88.9	82.5	76.8	88.6	82.5[1]
Median number of months in neighborhood	26.2	22.8	25.8	25.4[2]	26.5	16.0	29.0	26.3	25.4[2]	29.8	26.1	17.2	27.0	25.4[2]

[1] N = 1196 families; NR = 4 (0.3%).
[2] N = 987 families; those living in current neighborhood more than five months.

Table 3-6
Length of Time Husband and Wife Have Lived Together in Same Household

Years	Cases Classified by Dependency				Cases Classified by Area					Cases Classified by Ethnicity				
	NOA	STA	LTA	Total	S.F.	S.J.	VAL.	L.A.	Total	Black	Span.	White	Other	Total
Median number of years	11.1	11.1	11.6	11.2[1]	9.8	10.9	12.3	12.1	11.2[1]	9.9	12.7	10.8	9.0	11.2

[1] N = 1200 marital pairs.

Table 3-7
Percentage Distribution of Families by Household Size and Median Household Size

Number in Household	Cases Classified by Dependency				Cases Classified by Area					Cases Classified by Ethnicity			
	NOA	STA	LTA	Total[1]	S.F.	S.J.	VAL.	L.A.	Total[1]	Black	Span.	White	Other	Total[1]
All households	100.0	100.0	100.0	100.0	100.0	100.0	100.0	100.0	100.0	100.0	100.0	100.0	100.0	100.0
2	0.3	0.7	0.0	0.4	0.7	0.3	0.7	0.0	0.4	0.6	0.2	0.5	0.0	0.4
3	7.4	8.1	10.1	8.3	11.7	5.7	7.7	8.0	8.3	7.0	5.5	12.5	6.8	8.3
4	12.0	11.6	13.5	12.1	11.7	11.7	13.0	12.3	12.1	12.0	8.6	15.8	13.6	12.1
5	17.9	16.1	13.1	16.1	12.2	16.0	17.7	18.2	16.1	16.9	13.6	17.8	18.2	16.1
6	15.1	15.5	17.3	15.8	13.8	17.6	16.3	15.7	15.8	14.9	15.4	17.4	13.6	15.8
7	13.3	15.7	12.7	14.3	13.6	15.7	13.0	14.7	14.3	13.0	15.7	13.3	18.2	14.3
8	13.5	10.9	6.8	10.9	11.0	9.0	12.3	11.3	10.9	9.8	13.4	9.3	9.1	10.9
9	6.9	8.8	8.9	8.2	10.0	9.0	5.0	8.7	8.2	12.3	8.6	5.0	2.3	8.2
10	6.4	6.0	6.3	6.2	6.3	5.3	7.3	5.7	6.2	6.0	8.2	4.0	6.8	6.2
11	3.1	2.8	5.4	3.4	4.0	4.3	3.3	2.0	3.4	3.5	4.8	1.8	4.5	3.4
12	2.5	2.3	3.0	2.6	3.3	3.7	3.0	0.3	2.6	2.8	3.2	1.8	2.3	2.6
13	0.8	1.1	1.7	1.1	1.0	1.7	0.0	1.7	1.1	0.6	1.8	0.8	0.0	1.1
14	0.5	0.0	0.8	0.3	0.7	0.0	0.0	0.7	0.3	0.3	0.5	0.0	2.3	0.3
15	0.3	0.4	0.4	0.3	0.0	0.0	0.7	0.7	0.3	0.3	0.5	0.0	2.3	0.3
Median number in household	6.8	6.9	6.8	6.8	6.9	6.9	6.7	6.7	6.8	6.9	7.4	6.2	6.8	6.8

[1] N = 1200 families. Families with two in household were cases where the wife was pregnant.

Table 3-8
Median Education of Husband

Highest Grade Completed	Cases Classified by Dependency				Cases Classified by Area						Cases Classified by Ethnicity				
	NOA	STA	LTA	Total[1]	S.F.	S.J.	VAL.	L.A.	Total[1]		Black	Span.	White	Other	Total[1]
Median grade	9.4	9.5	9.1	9.4	10.8	9.3	8.3	9.9	9.4		11.1	7.6	9.9	8.9	9.4

[1] N = 1163 husbands; NR = 37 (3.1%).

Table 3-9
Percent of Husbands by Age and Median Age

Age in Years	Cases Classified by Dependency				Cases Classified by Area					Cases Classified by Ethnicity				
	NOA	STA	LTA	Total	S.F.	S.J.	VAL.	L.A.	Total	Black	Span.	White	Other	Total
All age classes	100.0	100.0	100.0	100.0[1]	100.0	100.0	100.0	100.0	100.0[1]	100.0	100.0	100.0	100.0	100.0[1]
Below 16	0.0	0.0	0.0	0.0	0.0	0.0	0.0	0.0	0.0	0.0	0.0	0.0	0.0	0.0
16 – 20	3.8	4.8	2.9	3.4	3.7	4.0	3.8	1.6	3.4	3.2	2.5	4.5	0.0	3.4
21 – 25	11.4	11.5	6.5	10.4	12.5	10.6	10.9	8.0	10.4	10.7	8.1	11.4	25.6	10.4
26 – 30	17.6	16.2	9.9	15.6	18.9	13.2	15.5	15.0	15.6	20.7	15.2	13.1	9.3	15.6
31 – 35	15.1	18.8	16.4	17.4	17.3	22.2	12.0	17.9	17.4	16.9	19.2	15.6	18.6	17.4
36 – 40	17.0	16.6	17.1	17.0	17.1	15.6	14.8	20.6	17.0	17.4	17.9	16.4	9.3	17.0
41 – 45	12.3	11.8	15.5	12.8	11.5	13.2	13.4	13.1	12.8	12.2	12.9	13.2	11.6	12.8
46 – 50	9.5	9.1	11.2	9.6	10.1	8.4	12.4	7.7	9.6	10.9	8.3	10.1	9.3	9.6
51 – 55	6.4	5.7	11.6	7.1	5.0	7.8	8.9	6.7	7.1	5.5	8.1	7.6	4.7	7.1
56 – 60	3.3	4.1	7.2	4.5	3.3	3.0	5.9	5.7	4.5	1.6	4.8	6.0	7.0	4.5
61 – 65	2.1	1.2	1.3	1.5	0.3	2.0	1.4	2.4	1.5	0.6	2.3	1.3	2.3	1.5
66 and over	1.5	0.2	0.4	0.7	0.3	0.0	1.0	1.3	0.7	0.3	0.7	0.8	2.3	0.7
Median age of husband in years	36.6	35.9	40.4	36.9	35.6	36.1	38.9	37.8	36.9	35.9	37.8	37.9	35.5	36.9

[1] N = 1187 husbands; NR = 13 (1.1%).

experience with the location of that experience in time. The cases were then reclassified into three dependency groups.

This reclassification created a disproportionately large number of cases in the Short-Time Welfare (STA) group. Further disproportions were created by the inability to select equal numbers of ethnic group members from each of the four geographic areas. As a result, the subgroups of the sample do not contain an equal number of cases. In coping with this difficulty, it was decided that, with certain exceptions, the cases would not be cross-classified by dependency, ethnicity, and geographic location.

The tables in the text present the 1200 cases classified first in terms of dependency, then classified separately in terms of geographic location, and thirdly, classified separately in terms of ethnicity. In interpreting the results, problems of bias created by disproportions in the subgroups of the sample have been taken into account.

A second major shift in the study design resulted when the sampling procedure produced subgroups showing variation in median income when the cases were classified by dependency, ethnicity, and geography.

In comparing the three dependency groups for variables such as residential stability and marital stability, it was concluded that the sample may be biased toward stability higher than is true for the universe population. When the three dependency groups were compared in terms of household size, age of husband, and education, the major difference was in the higher age level of the Long-Time Aid (LTA) group.

These various modifications in the original study design did not vitiate the original plan to control various factors in order to compare a welfare and nonwelfare group. When it is recognized that current income is only one measure of a family's socioeconomic status, the true goal of the study design can be made clear. This goal is to match families for socioeconomic status while allowing welfare experiences to vary.

Table 3-10 shows three key measures of socioeconomic status for the cases when they are classified by dependency status. The groups are virtually identical in education, slightly different in occupational status, and somewhat different in terms of current income.

Other relevant variables that need to be held constant in order to compare the dependency groups are listed under the heading of demographic variables. The major difference between the NOA, STA, and LTA groups is in the older age level of the LTA cases. The third section of the table gives two dependency measures for the three groups, and for this variable large differences appear.

Viewed in terms of the overall goals of the study design, Table 3-10 demonstrates that the three dependency groups show only small differences in socioeconomic and demographic characteristics when compared to the very large differences on the dependency index. Hence, several key characteristics of the sample population are held relatively constant, while welfare experience is allowed to vary. This makes it possible to look for characteristics of the sample families that may be associated with varying dependency experience. At the

Table 3-10
Indexes of Socioeconomic Status for a Sample of 1200 Low-Income Families Classified by Dependency Experience

Characteristics	Cases Classified by Dependency			
	NOA	STA	LTA	All Cases
Socioeconomic Indexes				
1. Median Annual Income	3682	3190	3068	3306
2. Median Education	9.4	9.5	9.1	9.4
3. Occupational History (all unskilled & semiskilled jobs) %	81.8	86.4	88.8	85.4
Demographic Indexes				
4. Family Size	6.8	6.9	6.8	6.8
5. Median Age	36.6	35.9	40.6	36.9
6. Median Months Residence in Same Neighborhood	26.2	22.8	25.8	25.4
7. Those with a History of Some Rural Residence %	71.4	70.8	65.8	70.0
Dependency Indexes				
1. Median Months on Welfare	0.0	4.5	26.7	3.6
2. Median Dependency Index Score	0.0	51.4	62.5	50.6

same time, because the cases are also classified by geographic area and ethnic status, we can test to see if differences in life style are associated more strongly with rural-urban and ethnic differences than with the dimension of dependency.

Section II:
Social Characteristics of the Cases

4 Kinship Bonds

Our first topic centers on relationships between kin members. If we include nuclear family ties between husband, wife, and minor children within the meaning of this term, kinship bonds are the most fundamental of man's relationships. Kinship is unique as a social system, for it welds together the impersonal attribute of obligation with the dimension of personal intimacy. Personal relations are usually viewed as resting on voluntary choices, but relations between kin members are both personal and obligatory at the same time. Added to the obligatory and personal quality of kin relations is the unbroken continuity this system gives to human relationships. It anchors the individual to the past, defines his relationships in the present, and predicts those kinship bonds that will connect him with the future. The fourth quality of kinship, making it unique among man's social systems, is the link it provides between the biological facts of descent and the symbolic social definition of relationships between persons who are called kin.

These attributes make kinship so fundamental to man's social nature that interpersonal relations cannot be evaluated against a more fundamental standard. To evoke an ideal standard of human relations at a public level, we specify that all men are brothers. Christianity itself is grounded in the use of kinship terms. Crimes against kin members are the archetype of the unspeakable.

Although the nature of kinship is everywhere the same, the functions that it performs and its structural characteristics show enormous variation. Historically, kinship has been the primary system utilized to take care of dependent children, the aged, the infirm, and others who must be cared for. Even today, for a large part of the world, kinship systems continue to perform this function. The obvious fact that governmental and private agencies in the United States have taken on some of the traditional functions of kinship in providing for the dependent should not obscure the vital functions still performed by means of kin relationships. Despite variations due to social class and ethnic group, the enduring and basic functions of kinship in our society still include socialization of the young, control over property, performance of ritual or ceremonial activities, maintenance of bonds of affection, and participation in mutual aid.

These background remarks indicate that even though welfare families by definition do not receive adequate economic support from relatives, a variety of functions may still be performed through the mechanism of kinship. Our investigation of kin relations among low-income families centers on frequency of contacts, intimacy of relationships, mutual aid, ritual, and a comparison of the kinship system with other social systems. From these subjects, it will be possible to say how specialized or diffuse kinship functions may be for low-income families, and how variations in function may be associated with dependency, ethnicity, and rural-urban status.

Propinquity of Relatives

Table 4-1 shows that on the average only 14.5% of the families were without relatives in the local area, and the median number of kin (either family units or individuals) available was 3.5. There were only small differences in the subgroups of the sample as to the availability of relatives, with Los Angeles showing the lowest median.

Table 4-2 shows that the available kin members are predominantly brothers, sisters, parents, and adult children. Hence, available kin are also characteristically close kin.

An additional measure of availability is provided in the data concerning proximity of relatives to a given family within the local area. The data in Table 4-3 show the following significant differences: LTA families have fewer relatives in their immediate neighborhood; San Jose shows the lowest percentage of relatives in the neighborhood; Spanish-speaking families have fewer relatives who are neighbors, while black families show the reverse condition. If propinquity is the major determinant of social contact, then these same groups should show correspondingly high or low rates of interaction with relatives.

Frequency of Interaction with Relatives

Table 4-4 describes visits with relatives, and indicates first that 98% of the 1,026 families with relatives in the local area are involved in reciprocal visiting patterns. Median visits are roughly once per week with a first relative, showing a steady decline to approximately once per two weeks for families with a fourth relative.[1] This gradient in visiting pattern indicates that social contacts are not exclusively with one relative if more than one relative is available. This same steady gradient in the visiting pattern is also true for all the subgroups in the table.

The first difference between groups to be noted is the decline in the rate of visiting as welfare dependency increases. This gradient holds for visits with first, second, third, and fourth relatives. The San Joaquin Valley area shows a high visitation rate and Los Angeles shows a low rate, while blacks show the highest visitation rate among ethnic groups.

When these differences in interaction rate are paired with the facts about the

---

[1] Komarovsky (1964) reports 66% of blue-collar wives and 52% of husbands involved in weekly visits with local relatives. The comparable calculation for our data gives a figure of 70%.

Table 4-1
Percentage Distribution of Families by Number of Relatives in Local Area and Median Number of Relatives[1]

Number of Relatives	Cases Classified by Dependency				Cases Classified by Area					Cases Classified by Ethnicity				
	NOA	STA	LTA	Total	S.F.	S.J.	VAL.	L.A.	Total	Black	Span.	White	Other	Total
All relatives	100.0	100.0	100.0	100.0	100.0	100.0	100.0	100.0	100.0	100.0	100.0	100.0	100.0	100.0
No relatives	15.8	12.4	17.3	14.5[2]	12.7	12.0	12.4	20.6	14.5[2]	12.4	15.7	15.0	13.6	14.5[2]
One relative	19.7	14.7	13.9	16.3	12.7	18.8	15.0	18.7	16.3	14.6	18.0	14.8	25.0	16.3
Two relatives	16.9	17.9	17.4	17.4	13.0	18.8	20.0	18.0	17.4	16.5	19.8	16.5	9.1	17.4
Three relatives	18.4	16.8	19.8	17.9	19.6	12.0	18.6	21.3	17.9	20.4	14.3	19.2	22.8	17.9
Four relatives	14.6	17.6	13.9	15.8	17.3	18.1	18.0	10.0	15.8	15.2	14.5	18.2	11.4	15.8
Five relatives	8.2	9.6	9.7	9.2	10.0	11.0	8.0	7.7	9.2	9.2	8.6	9.3	13.6	9.2
Six relatives	6.4	11.0	8.0	8.9	14.7	9.3	8.0	3.7	8.9	11.7	9.1	7.0	4.5	8.9
Median number of relatives	3.3	3.7	3.5	3.5[3]	3.9	3.6	3.5	3.1	3.5[3]	3.6	3.3	3.6	3.4	3.5[3]

[1] Relatives include those of both husband and wife. A kin unit composed of more than one relative was counted as one. Thus, an individual relative and a family of relatives were equally weighted. "Compadres" and "comrades" were classified as kin or non-kin by the respondent *himself*. Sons and daughters were counted as relatives, rather than members of the nuclear family if they were living away from their parents' home. There were 114 such cases.
[2] N = 1200 families.
[3] N = 1026 families, those who had relatives in the area.

Table 4-2
Number of Relatives in Area by Type and Rank Order[1]

Rank Order	Husband's Relatives		Wife's Relatives	
1	Brothers	457	Sisters	384
2	Sisters	383	Parents	376
3	Parents	366	Brothers	332
4	Others	222	Aunts or Uncles	128
5	Aunts or Uncles	210	Others	115
6	Cousins	150	Cousins	87
	Total	1788	Total	1422

[1] N = 3210 relatives of 1026 families.

propinquity of relatives, we find that in four out of six comparisons, a high ratio of relatives in the local area corresponds to a high rate of visiting.[2]

The next set of facts concerns visits with distant relatives. Table 4-5 shows that slightly over one-third of the sample families visited distant relatives in the last two years, with a median number of visits of 3.6. The median one-way distance traveled was 252 miles. The median expenditure per year was $35. The number of respondents visiting distant relatives declines as dependency status increases. Because the Long-Time Aid group has a slightly lower median income (and a smaller proportion who own cars), this difference is probably due, in part, to economic factors. But the dependency groups show the same pattern of decrease in visits to relatives in the local area which cannot be accounted for by economic factors.

The measures of frequency of interaction with near and distant relatives indicate a web or network of relationships quite sufficient to fulfill a variety of functions. This network includes several relatives rather than being concentrated solely on one kinsman. As expected, these low-income families do not spend large sums of money to visit distant relatives nor do they travel long distances.

It is evident that propinquity is an important fact in determining interaction rate with relatives. At the same time, the data show a consistent tendency for interaction with relatives to decline as dependency increases.[3] Additional indexes will show this same tendency where propinquity is not involved as a key factor; thus indicating the independent function of dependency as a factor related to participation with kin.

[2] This finding is parallel to that reported by Reiss (1962) and Bernard (1964).

[3] This same relationship is reported by Bakke (1940), Bernard (1964), and MacDonald (1964).

Functions of Kinship

When type of participation with relatives is considered (Table 4-6), we find recreation to be the most important category, accounting for 55% of activities. Mutual aid was second in importance (24%); ritual, third (18%); and joint activity in voluntary associations, last (3%).

A gradient of decreasing use of relatives for purposes of mutual aid as dependency increases can be seen in Table 4-6. The Los Angeles cases, and Spanish-speaking families also, show the lowest usage of relatives for purposes of mutual aid by contrast with other functions.

When relatives and nonrelatives are compared as a source for mutual aid, the data in Table 4-7 show that the former are used 45% of the time, and are by far the most important source when compared with friends (28%) or neighbors (15%).

Tables 4-6 and 5-13 provide data on the respondents' coparticipants in ritual activities. Participation with relatives in ritual activities occurs 18% of the time, whereas such activities take place only 8% of the time with friends. These facts concerning mutual aid and ritual activities of the 1200 families with their relatives reflect the enduring, fundamental attributes of kinship that were briefly touched on in the first part of the chapter.

The next index centers on degree of intimacy with kin. Each of the 1200 husbands was asked if he had anyone in whom he confided, i.e., one whose advice he would most rely on. If the respondent specified such a confidant, it was then ascertained whether or not this individual was a relative. Table 4-8 gives the results obtained from this question.

One-third of the husbands stated that they confided in no one, 43% specified a relative who served as a confidant, and 23% specified nonrelatives. The importance of relatives to our informants at the level of intimate personal relations is made clear by these ratios. The same decline in the use of relatives can be observed as dependency increases. Propinquity of relatives also appears related to the use of relatives as confidants. When dependency groups are compared for those persons who do not have confidants, there is an unexpected reversal, with the LTA group showing the lowest percent without confidants, whereas the NOA group is highest.

A subsidiary question concerns the type of relatives in whom our respondents confide. Is this choice a direct function of availability? When the choices of respondents by type of relative are rank ordered and compared with the rank order of available relatives (Table 4-9), we find that parents are chosen more frequently than would be expected by their availability in the local area.

Thus, two factors seemed to interact in determining the choice of relatives who were used as confidants—the closeness of a relative defined in kinship terms, and closeness defined in terms of geographic proximity.[4]

---

[4] Komarovsky (1964) reports that the respondents in her study characteristically use *close* kin as confidants.

Table 4-3
Percentage Distribution of Relatives by Location in Local Area

Location	Cases Classified by Dependency				Cases Classified by Area						Cases Classified by Ethnicity				
	NOA	STA	LTA	Total	S.F.	S.J.	VAL.	L.A.	Total		Black	Span.	White	Other	Total
All locations	100.0	100.0	100.0	100.0[1]	100.0	100.0	100.0	100.0	100.0[1]		100.0	100.0	100.0	100.0	100.0[1]
Neighborhood	27.3	23.9	19.1	24.0	28.5	14.9	29.0	22.8	24.0		27.1	22.8	23.0	19.0	24.0
City	42.7	41.0	49.8	43.1	50.4	50.8	21.5	50.6	43.1		53.0	48.6	29.8	35.0	43.1
Less than 2-hour drive	23.9	26.1	24.5	25.2	16.4	26.4	34.1	24.7	25.2		14.5	21.3	36.9	42.0	25.2
More than 2-hour drive	6.1	9.0	6.5	7.7	4.7	7.9	15.4	1.9	7.7		5.4	7.3	10.3	4.0	7.7

[1]N = 3135 relatives; NR = 75.

Table 4-4
Percent of Families Visiting Relatives in Local Area and Median Number of Visits per Year

Interaction with Relatives	Cases Classified by Dependency				Cases Classified by Area					Cases Classified by Ethnicity				
	NOA	STA	LTA	Total	S.F.	S.J.	VAL.	L.A.	Total	Black	Span.	White	Other	Total
Visits with first relative Those listing visits with first relative	83.2	86.0	80.6	84.0[1]	86.3	86.7	85.0	78.0	84.0[1]	86.4	82.7	83.2	86.4	84.0[1]
Median number of visits to first relative	55.3	51.2	44.5	51.4[2]	54.0	45.8	70.0	44.7	51.4[2]	53.0	49.2	52.9	48.9	51.4[2]

55

Visits with second relative													
Those listing visits with second relative	60.2	69.4	63.3	65.2[3]	69.3	65.3	69.3	56.7	65.2[3]	69.6	63.0	65.0	56.8	65.2[3]
Median number of visits to second relative	43.7	41.0	38.0	41.2[4]	42.9	39.9	43.9	36.5	41.2[4]	45.4	39.3	39.9	32.9	41.2[4]
Visits with third relative													
Those listing visits with third relative	41.8	49.7	38.8	45.0[5]	54.0	42.0	44.7	39.3	45.0[5]	51.9	39.8	45.5	43.2	45.0[5]
Median number of visits to third relative	41.7	32.4	25.0	33.9[6]	31.9	32.9	37.6	34.3	33.9[6]	40.5	32.7	29.0	38.0	33.9[6]
Visits with fourth relative													
Those listing visits with fourth relative	21.7	27.8	20.3	24.3[7]	30.7	26.3	22.3	18.0	24.3[7]	30.1	23.2	21.5	20.5	24.3[7]
Median number of visits to fourth relative	31.9	25.4	30.0	29.2[8]	32.0	39.2	22.5	18.4	29.2[8]	26.0	32.2	19.9	50.0	29.2[8]

[1] N = 1200 families.
[2] N = 1008 families, those who visited one or more times per year.
[3] N = 1200 families.
[4] N = 782 families, those who visited one or more times per year.
[5] N = 1200 families.
[6] N = 540 families, those who visited one or more times per year.
[7] N = 1200 families.
[8] N = 292 families, those who visited one or more times per year.

Table 4-5
Percent of Husbands and/or Wives Visiting Distant Relatives, Median Number of Visits, Median Distance Traveled, and Median Amount Spent per Year

Visits with Distant Relatives	Cases Classified by Dependency				Cases Classified by Area					Cases Classified by Ethnicity				
	NOA	STA	LTA	Total	S.F.	S.J.	VAL.	L.A.	Total	Black	Span.	White	Other	Total
Those visiting distant relatives in last two years	40.8	36.4	30.8	36.7[1]	34.3	42.0	38.7	32.0	36.7[1]	34.2	37.7	39.5	20.5	36.7[1]
Median number of visits in last two years	3.6	3.6	3.8	3.6[2]	4.0	3.5	3.5	3.7	3.6[2]	3.9	3.5	3.6	3.0	3.6[2]
Median distance traveled to visit distant relative (one way) in last two years	344	236	189	252[3]	257	268	376	158	252[3]	247	243	295	151	252[3]
Median amount in dollars spent for visits in last four years	51.3	33.1	11.8	35.4[4]	50.4	38.1	27.9	34.9	35.4[4]	51.1	50.4	27.2	28.8	35.4[4]

[1] N = 1200 husbands.
[2] N = 440 husbands, those who did visit distant relatives.
[3] N = 440 husbands, those who did visit distant relatives.
[4] N = 574 families, those who spent money to visit distant relatives. The total number of cases reporting visits is larger than in the previous three rows because the time span is four years rather than two years.

Table 4-6
Percentage Distribution of Families' Relationships with Relatives in Each of Four Types of Activities

Types of Activities	Cases Classified by Dependency				Cases Classified by Area					Cases Classified by Ethnicity				
	NOA	STA	LTA	Total	S.F.	S.J.	VAL.	L.A.	Total	Black	Span.	White	Other	Total
All activities	100.0	100.0	100.0	100.0[1]	100.0	100.0	100.0	100.0	100.0[1]	100.0	100.0	100.0	100.0	100.0[1]
Mutual aid	24.5	24.1	22.8	24.0	28.4	23.1	24.6	16.8	24.0	24.0	22.8	25.0	26.8	24.0
Recreational	51.6	55.2	58.3	54.6	45.2	54.8	56.6	67.7	54.6	54.8	56.3	53.7	45.3	54.6
Rituals	20.4	17.7	16.8	18.4	22.6	18.0	17.8	12.7	18.4	18.5	18.2	18.1	21.9	18.4
Organization	3.5	3.0	2.1	3.0	3.8	4.1	1.0	2.8	3.0	2.7	2.7	3.2	6.0	3.0

[1] N = 4482 relationships with relatives; NR = 14,718.
If all 1200 husbands had each listed four relatives, and if all four types of activities had been engaged in with relatives, N would equal 19,200.

Table 4-7
Percentage Distribution of Persons Involved in Family Crisis Mutual Aid Relationships by Type of Participant

Types of Participants	Cases Classified by Dependency				Cases Classified by Area					Cases Classified by Ethnicity				
	NOA	STA	LTA	Total	S.F.	S.J.	VAL.	L.A.	Total	Black	Span.	White	Other	Total
All types of participants	100.0	100.0	100.0	100.0[1]	100.0	100.0	100.0	100.0	100.0[1]	100.0	100.0	100.0	100.0	100.0[1]
Friend	28.5	28.0	31.2	28.8	29.8	30.8	26.8	27.1	28.8	31.8	27.8	27.6	28.1	28.8
Relative	47.1	46.0	40.9	45.2	42.4	45.5	49.3	44.7	45.2	41.8	49.5	43.2	51.5	45.2
Neighbor	14.9	14.1	19.3	15.4	19.0	7.8	11.0	24.3	15.4	19.7	10.5	16.3	18.8	15.4
Minister	0.4	0.5	0.3	0.5	0.4	0.8	0.0	0.6	0.5	0.5	0.4	0.5	0.0	0.5
Other	9.1	11.4	8.3	10.1	8.4	15.1	12.9	3.3	10.1	6.2	11.8	12.4	1.6	10.1

[1] N = 1543 participants involved with the 1200 families; NR = 203.

Table 4-8
Percent of Husbands without Confidants and Percent of Husbands' Confidants Classified as Kin or Non-Kin

Classification of Confidants	Cases Classified by Dependency				Cases Classified by Area					Cases Classified by Ethnicity				
	NOA	STA	LTA	Total	S.F.	S.J.	VAL.	L.A.	Total	Black	Span.	White	Other	Total
All classes of confidants	100.0	100.0	100.0	100.0[1]	100.0	100.0	100.0	100.0	100.0[1]	100.0	100.0	100.0	100.0	100.0[1]
Relatives	44.1	43.5	41.9	43.4	52.3	35.0	42.6	43.5	43.4	52.2	33.6	46.7	47.7	43.4
Nonrelatives	20.0	23.6	27.2	23.1	25.7	25.9	19.5	21.4	23.1	30.4	21.5	18.3	29.6	23.1
Those with no confidants	35.9	32.9	30.9	33.5	22.0	39.1	37.9	35.1	33.5	17.4	44.9	35.0	22.7	33.5

[1] N = 1191 husbands; NR = 9 (0.8%).

Table 4-9
Husbands' Use of Relatives as Confidants, Compared with Relatives Available in Local Area

	Type of Relatives Used as Confidants[1] by Husbands, Arranged in Rank Order by Frequency of Choice			Husbands's Relatives,[2] in Local Area, Arranged in Rank Order	
1.	Wife	235	1.	Wife	1200
2.	Parents	112	2.	Brothers	457
3.	Brothers	70	3.	Sisters	383
4.	Sisters	27	4.	Parents	366
5.	Aunts or Uncles	18	5.	Aunts or Uncles	210

[1] N = 462, those husbands who used the above listed relatives as confidants.
[2] N = 2616.

The kinship functions that have been described so far have little to do with jobs or money, and it is of vital importance to determine if this web of obligations stretches out to include the pecuniary and job realms. A first question concerns support of relatives in the form of money payments. Table 4-10 indicates that 90% of the 1200 families provide no such aid to relatives.

The characteristic gradient of declining linkage with relatives as welfare dependency increases also shows up in this table. Whites and the Los Angeles cases are low on this index.

The reciprocal of "giving to relatives" is found in "support from relatives." Table 4-11 summarizes the answers to a question that deals with one aspect of such support—the receipt of gifts. Slightly more than one-third of the respondent families received gifts, but the proportion of the 1200 families receiving gifts from *relatives* is roughly 10%. Decreased support from relatives among LTA cases is again documented. On this index, Spanish-speaking families and Valley cases are low.

Economic Functions

In the field of employment, we can expect that if any one of the three ethnic groups has established a monopoly over jobs in any small sector or area of the economy, it may be reflected in reciprocal help between relatives in getting jobs. Table 4-12 indicates that 29% of the 1200 families received help from relatives in getting a job, and that 72% of those who were aided by relatives received such help several times. On the basis of the previous indexes, it is predictable that the LTA group will receive less help from relatives, and Table 4-12 verifies this expectation. Among the geographic areas, Los Angeles is low and Spanish-speaking families are low. No one ethnic group is strikingly high on this index, supporting the view that no given ethnic group has been able to create any specialized control over an area of jobs.

Another index of mutual aid in the job world is *employment* by relatives. Given the socioeconomic position of these families, we would expect a very low degree of support from relatives. The overall average for the sample families is 14% (Table 4-13). Exactly the same pattern of differences between groups is shown in Table 4-12.

The various indexes concerning mutual aid between kinsmen in the area of jobs and money make it clear that kinship support is strikingly restricted by comparison with functions performed in other areas of daily life. The results concerning pecuniary matters are hardly unexpected, but they take on added meaning when *contrasted* with the degree of support that kinship provides in other areas.

Interpretation of Findings

The discussion of kinship bonds has covered frequency of interaction, intimacy of relationships, and type and frequency of functions performed. A summary of

Table 4-10
Percent of Husbands Paying Money to Relatives in Last Year

Money Payments	Cases Classified by Dependency				Cases Classified by Area					Cases Classified by Ethnicity				
	NOA	STA	LTA	Total	S.F.	S.J.	VAL.	L.A.	Total	Black	Span.	White	Other	Total
Those paying money to relatives	11.5	10.5	7.6	10.3[1]	10.7	12.3	12.0	6.0	10.3[1]	10.8	13.0	7.3	6.8	10.3[1]

[1]N = 1199 husbands; NR = 1 (0.1%).

Table 4-11
Percentage Distribution of Families Receiving Gifts by Source

Source of Gifts	Cases Classified by Dependency				Cases Classified by Area					Cases Classified by Ethnicity				
	NOA	STA	LTA	Total	S.F.	S.J.	VAL.	L.A.	Total	Black	Span.	White	Other	Total
Those receiving gifts	30.6	40.5	43.9	37.9[1]	39.0	42.7	35.3	34.7	37.9[1]	31.0	35.9	45.5	38.6	37.9[1]
All sources of gifts	100.0	100.0	100.0	100.0[2]	100.0	100.0	100.0	100.0	100.0[2]	100.0	100.0	100.0	100.0	100.0[2]
Relatives	43.2	28.8	22.8	31.4	43.1	33.7	16.3	30.3	31.4	44.0	21.8	32.6	30.4	31.4
Friends	20.9	14.7	15.4	16.5	20.5	16.0	14.1	15.1	16.5	20.0	15.0	14.1	34.8	16.5
Organizations	17.6	27.4	38.2	27.1	11.3	18.4	51.0	31.9	27.1	14.4	39.4	24.7	17.4	27.1
Church	14.4	17.8	12.2	15.7	17.2	19.6	11.9	12.6	15.7	9.6	14.5	19.8	17.4	15.7
Other	3.9	11.3	11.4	9.3	7.9	12.3	6.7	10.1	9.3	12.0	9.3	8.8	0.0	9.3

[1]N = 1199 families, NR = 1 (0.1%).
[2]N = 568 sources of gifts for 455 (37.9%) respondents.

Table 4-12
Percent of Husbands Who Received Help from Relatives in Getting a Job

Help from Relatives	Cases Classified by Dependency				Cases Classified by Area					Cases Classified by Ethnicity				
	NOA	STA	LTA	Total	S.F.	S.J.	VAL.	L.A.	Total	Black	Span.	White	Other	Total
Those receiving help	31.1	32.0	22.4	29.8[1]	33.0	28.7	31.7	26.0	29.8[1]	30.7	26.6	33.5	22.7	29.8[1]
All job categories	100.0	100.0	100.0	100.0[2]	100.0	100.0	100.0	100.0	100.0[2]	100.0	100.0	100.0	100.0	100.0[2]
Present job only	42.5	17.8	12.5	25.7	34.1	27.7	15.7	25.0	25.7	28.6	27.7	21.5	33.3	25.7
Several jobs	57.5	79.9	83.3	72.5	63.8	69.9	82.1	75.0	72.5	69.2	70.5	77.7	55.6	72.5
All jobs	0.0	2.3	4.2	1.8	2.1	2.4	2.2	0.0	1.8	2.2	1.8	0.8	11.1	1.8

[1] N = 1184 husbands; NR = 16 (1.3%).
[2] N = 352 husbands, those who had assistance from relatives in finding a job.

Table 4-13
Percent of Husbands Who Have Worked for Relatives

Employment	Cases Classified by Dependency				Cases Classified by Area					Cases Classified by Ethnicity				
	NOA	STA	LTA	Total	S.F.	S.J.	VAL.	L.A.	Total	Black	Span.	White	Other	Total
Those who have worked for relatives	13.7	16.4	9.7	14.2[1]	13.0	18.0	15.3	10.6	14.2[1]	13.2	10.9	18.5	15.9	14.2[1]

[1] N = 1200 Husbands.

Table 4-14
Subgroups Showing Highest and Lowest Scores on 14 Indexes of Kinship Relations

Indexes	Cases Classified by Dependency		Cases Classified by Area		Cases Classified by Ethnicity	
	High	Low	High	Low	High	Low
Percent of families who did visit available relatives	Tied	Ranks[1]	S.J.	L.A.	Tied	Ranks
Frequency of visits with locally available relatives	NOA	LTA	VAL	L.A.	Tied	Ranks
Percent of families who did visit distant relatives	NOA	LTA	S.J.	L.A.	White	Black
Number of visits with distant relatives	Tied	Ranks	S.F.	S.J. VAL	Black	Spanish
Amount of money spent in visiting relatives	NOA	LTA	S.F.	VAL	Black	White
Distance traveled to visit distant relatives	NOA	LTA	VAL	L.A.	White	Spanish
Relatives in organizations	NOA	LTA	S.J.	VAL	White	Black Spanish
Use of relatives as confidants	Tied	Ranks	S.F.	S.J.	Black	Spanish
Percent receiving gifts from relatives	NOA	LTA	S.F.	VAL	Black	Spanish
Percent paying out money to relatives	NOA	LTA	S.J.	L.A.	Spanish	White
Percent who have worked for relatives	STA	LTA	S.J.	L.A.	White	Spanish
Percent who received help from relatives in getting jobs	STA	LTA	S.F.	L.A.	White	Spanish
Percent using relatives as a source of crisis mutual aid	NOA	LTA	S.F.	VAL	Black	White
Percent of husbands using relatives as a source of routine mutual aid	Tied	Ranks	S.F.	L.A.	Tied	Ranks

[1] If the difference between the scores of the high and low subgroup was 10% or less, the subgroups were defined to have "tied ranks." The 10% criterion was obtained by taking 10% of the score recorded for all the cases. For example, 84% of the cases listed visits with relatives. The difference between the value of the highest and lowest group (classified by dependency) is less than 8.4%; therefore, it is called "tied ranks."

some 14 indexes covering these dimensions provides a quantitative picture of patterned differences between subgroups of the sample. Table 4-14 shows how often a given subgroup was high or low on these indexes.

This summary table makes it quite clear that the *use* of kin declines as dependency increases. This is the strongest and clearest pattern revealed in the data. A minor pattern by geographic location is shown, as the Los Angeles cases were low on eight out of 14 indexes, while the San Francisco cases were high on seven indexes. An additional minor pattern by ethnicity is seen, with the Spanish-speaking families showing a lower level of interaction with kin. It might have been expected that families in the rural Valley area or the Spanish-speaking families would manifest higher scores on the indexes of kinship bonds, but such is not the case.

The relationship between physical proximity of relatives (propinquity) and the number and intimacy of social contacts indicates that *availability* is an important factor in the maintenance of kinship bonds. Additional indexes of kinship function that are not related to close geographic proximity of relatives indicate that an additional independent factor—degree of welfare dependency—is inversely correlated with use of kin. As welfare dependency increases, interaction with kin declines.

When the data on kinship functions are compared with the data on nonkin relations (to be outlined in the next chapter), it is clear that kinship is the single most important social system in the lives of these low-income families.[5] At the same time, it can be concluded that kinship support is very limited with regard to economic aspects of family life for the 1200 cases.

If kinship is central in the life style of low-income families, then any change, even of small degree, in the network of kinship bonds can be expected to produce repercussions in other areas of the family's way of life. It may be that reduced support from kin is one factor that sets the stage for the onset of welfare dependency. Or it may be that continuing welfare dependency results in reduced kinship interaction. Possibly both of these processes interact such that the end result is a lowered use of kin for LTA families.

E. Wight Bakke's classic study of unemployment and relief during the depression of the thirties shows clearly that reduction in interaction with kin and friends occurs as unemployment and dependency increases. He was not able to point to a control group to show that such reduction is uniquely related to unemployment and welfare dependence. In the present study, families were not followed through a sequence of steps from employment through a period of unemployment and welfare dependency. However, a control group of nonwelfare families provides the comparison to a treatment group, i.e., two samples showing varying welfare experience. Hence, the two studies show the same results, one study being based on a before-and-after comparison of the same

---

[5] This conclusion reaffirms the results of virtually all studies of lower-class life styles, including the recent reports of Rainwater (1959), Komarovsky (1964), and Litwak (1960). The latter suggests that the lower-class family be described as a modified extended family system.

cases, the other based on a treatment group and a control group but without any before-and-after sequence.

In the conclusion of his *Citizens Without Work* (1940), Bakke points to the interaction between the effects of unemployment and the characteristics of the persons who became unemployed. Coupling the results of the present study with his work, it seems plausible to conclude that unemployment and welfare dependency do not operate equally on all families in reducing their ties with kin. The effect of welfare experience will vary depending upon the pattern of kinship relations that characterizes that family as it enters a public assistance status. The physical proximity of relatives appears to be a significant factor in determining patterns of kinship relations.

One important point in this argument needs to be checked. The loss of psychological and social support resulting from the weakening of kinship ties may be balanced by an increase in non-kin social relations that constitute a functional alternative to kinship. If such is the case, the presumed cause-and-effect relationship between kinship ties and welfare dependency would be negated. For the families that Bakke studied, it seemed clear that non-kin social relations did not operate as an effective substitute for kinship ties. The next task is then to describe and analyze the non-kin social world of the 1200 low-income families to determine what functions are fulfilled by this system.

5 Non-Kin Social Relationships

The subject matter of non-kin social relations covers friendships, neighbors, and acquaintances involved in activities such as crisis and routine mutual aid, recreation and ritual. While non-kin social relations do not usually include the major kinship functions of child-rearing or control over property, they do function to provide intimacy, affection, mutual aid, and recreation.

If propinquity is a determinant of a family's frequency of interaction with relatives, stability of residence may operate in a similar manner with reference to friends and neighbors. Accordingly, the subgroups of the sample were compared to ascertain if a family's neighborhood stability was correlated with social interaction in the neighborhood.

One important purpose in describing non-kin relationships was to determine how effectively this system functioned as a substitute for those families who showed lowered participation with relatives. In making such an assessment, the first step was to determine the frequency of interaction with friends, neighbors, and acquaintances in several types of activities. These data were then used to determine if LTA families substituted non-kin for kin relationships.

Both the kin and non-kin relations of the 1200 husbands and wives were further classified by the types of persons involved. These coparticipants[1] were also classified by source, i.e., it was determined if the coparticipant was first met through family and kin, in the neighborhood, at work, through voluntary associations, etc. These cross-tabulations allowed a further check on the hypothesis that the LTA families may substitute neighborhood relationships for kinship ties.

The information on the coparticipants in the family social world made possible an assessment of kinship, the neighborhood, and work as foci for the husband's and wife's separate social networks. The effect of welfare dependency on the social linkage between work and the husband's local social world was then determined.

Neighborhood Stability

Table 3-4 in Chapter 3 gives the number of residence changes that the sample families have made in the last two years, and Table 3-5 shows the number of months that a family have resided in their present neighborhood. We might

---
[1]The terms "participant" and "coparticipant" are used interchangeably in this chapter.

expect that a family making frequent residence changes and frequent changes of neighborhood would make fewer acquaintances in the neighborhood than a family with a stable residence pattern. Table 5-1 shows the number of families in the neighborhood known to each respondent.

If the indexes of residence stability and number of acquaintances in the neighborhood are rank ordered for the subgroups in the sample, the relationship between the two dimensions can be determined. No correlation is shown when the cases are classified by dependency status. When they are classified by geographic location, the San Jose cases show lowest residential and neighborhood stability and lowest knowledge of neighbors, whereas the Valley cases show the reverse. If classified by ethnic status, black families show highest residential stability and most knowledge of neighbors. These results indicate that neighborhood stability operates to determine social participation in the neighborhood only when the cases are classified by geographic location. In other words, there appears to be a general relationship between residential stability and knowledge of neighbors for families living in San Jose or in the San Joaquin Valley, but this relationship is overridden when ethnic and dependency factors are taken into account.

The number of persons that a family knows in its neighborhood is a quite limited indicator of social interaction within a neighborhood. Another and possibly more adequate index can be constructed by comparing the relative frequency of a family's neighborhood relationships to kinship relations and to friendships made at work. This measure can be called a neighborhood utilization index. If the subgroups of the sample are rank ordered for this index and for the indexes of neighborhood stability, the relationship between the two dimensions can be ascertained. The only subgroup ranking the same on both dimensions is the San Jose group, which shows low use of the neighborhood and low neighborhood residential stability.

With the exception of the San Jose cases, we conclude that length of residence in the neighborhood seems to be a minor factor in determining the use of the neighborhood as a base for developing non-kin social relations.

Frequency of Interaction

In our study of patterns of mutual aid, our interest focused on those largely unplanned and spontaneous acts whereby one individual or family helps another. Mutual aid covers a wide range of activities, from such trivial and routine things as borrowing a cup of sugar from a neighbor to more critical events such as help in the case of accidents or illnesses. Either the giving or receiving of mutual aid by one of the sample families (outside the context of a formal organization) was treated as equal. Table 5-2 shows the distribution of crisis mutual aid relationships for the 1200 families. The median number of such mutual aid relationships was 2.3 for the 893 families involved. The five types of crisis mutual aid (emergencies) involved: birth, moving, accidents, police and courts.

Table 5-1
Percent of Husbands Who Know One or More Neighbors and Median Number of Families Known

Families Known	Cases Classified by Dependency				Cases Classified by Area					Cases Classified by Ethnicity				
	NOA	STA	LTA	Total	S.F.	S.J.	VAL.	L.A.	Total	Black	Span.	White	Other	Total
Those knowing one or more families in their neighborhood	87.8	84.8	82.3	85.2[1]	83.3	80.3	93.3	83.7	85.2[1]	82.6	84.5	88.0	86.4	85.2[1]
Median number of families known	5.0	5.3	5.3	5.2[2]	5.4	4.3	6.7	4.8	5.2[2]	5.8	4.4	5.7	5.0	5.2[2]

[1] N = 1200 families.
[2] N = 1023 families; those knowing one or more families in their neighborhood.

Table 5-2
Percentage Distribution of Families by Number of Crisis Mutual Aid Relationships in the Last Twelve Months[1] and Median Number of Relationships

Number of Mutual Aid Relationships	Cases Classified by Dependency				Cases Classified by Area					Cases Classified by Ethnicity				
	NOA	STA	LTA	Total	S.F.	S.J.	VAL.	L.A.	Total	Black	Span.	White	Other	Total
All mutual aid relationships	100.0	100.0	100.0	100.0[2]	100.0	100.0	100.0	100.0	100.0[2]	100.0	100.0	100.0	100.0	100.0[2]
0	29.1	23.3	25.3	25.6	16.7	25.0	32.3	28.3	25.6	23.1	30.2	23.2	16.3	25.6
1	28.8	29.9	33.8	30.3	27.2	27.3	28.3	38.3	30.3	33.5	28.0	30.0	34.8	30.3
2	23.2	26.1	25.3	25.0	32.7	24.0	20.4	23.1	25.0	28.8	22.5	24.8	25.6	25.0
3	13.6	13.8	11.0	13.2	15.7	14.3	13.7	9.0	13.2	11.2	13.6	14.5	11.6	13.2
4	3.8	4.6	2.5	3.9	4.7	6.7	3.0	1.3	3.9	2.8	3.9	4.5	7.0	3.9
5 or more	1.5	2.3	2.1	2.0	3.0	2.7	2.3	0.0	2.0	0.6	1.8	3.0	4.7	2.0
Median number of mutual aid relationships	2.3	2.3	2.1	2.3[3]	2.4	2.4	2.3	1.9	2.3[3]	2.2	2.3	2.3	2.3	2.3[3]

[1] The five types of crisis mutual aid (emergencies) involved: birth, moving, accidents, police, and courts.
[2] N = 1200 families. The participants involved with the 1200 families equaled 1746 persons.
[3] N = 893 families, the respondents engaging in one or more crisis mutual aid relationships.

Each type was counted only once. Thus, *five* was the maximum frequency that could be reported. Differences between the cases when classified by dependency are negligible. When classified by geographic location, the Los Angeles cases show the lowest median.

The number of friendships formed by the husbands of our sample families, and the frequency of contact with these friends is an obvious and vital dimension of non-kin social relations. The questionnaire provided space for each informant to list three friends. Questions were asked about frequency of contact with friends, types of activities, and how the friend was first met. Table 5-3 shows the distribution of friends for the 1200 husbands. Only 7.5% of the husbands listed no friends, and over 66% listed three friends. There were no significant differences between subgroups in the median number of friends listed.

Table 5-4 provides data on how often friends were seen. On the average, these men see their friends slightly more often than once a week, and if they listed two or three friends, they tend to see each one of them with equal frequency. We cannot infer equal intensity in these friendship relations, as the meaning of friendship varies from one person to another. At the same time, we can note the high degree of similarity in the friendship interaction behavior of the husbands regardless of their dependency status, ethnic status, or geographic location.

An additional subject concerned the participation of informants in voluntary associations. Table 5-5 shows the number of associations to which these 1200 men belonged. Forty-one percent did not belong to any organization. Of those who did belong to an organization, the vast bulk belonged to only one.

Table 5-6 provides data on the kinds of organizations joined by the respondents. Of the 59% who did have membership in organizations, some three-quarters belonged only to a church. The Spanish-speaking cases showed the highest concentration of memberships in a religious organization.

Table 5-7 shows that the median attendance at organizational meetings (times per year per organization) is approximately once per week. While the Spanish-speaking cases are high in church membership, in rate of attendance they fall almost exactly at the overall group median.

If the data on mutual aid relationships, friends, and organizational participation are combined as a set of indexes, we can determine whether the lowered participation of the LTA cases with kin is balanced out by a relatively high rate of interaction with non-kin. If the LTA cases show the highest rates of interaction on the 12 indexes given in Table 5-8, we can conclude that they do not show any pattern of social withdrawal.

Table 5-8 shows that the LTA group occupies a middle position on these indexes. The NOA group still shows the same pattern of highest interaction rates that was manifested in their relationships with kin, and the STA cases are the low group. Thus, LTA husbands only partially substitute non-kin for kin relations for they do not show up as the high group in interaction rates. If the indexes of interaction for both kin and non-kin relationships are combined, the NOA group has the highest interaction, the STA occupies a middle position, and

Table 5-3
Percentage Distribution of Husbands by Number of Friends [1]

Number of Friends	Cases classified by Dependency				Cases classified by Area					Cases classified by Ethnicity				
	NOA	STA	LTA	Total	S.F.	S.J.	VAL.	L.A.	Total	Black	Span.	White	Other	Total
All friends	100.0	100.0	100.0	100.0[2]	100.0	100.0	100.0	100.0	100.0[2]	100.0	100.0	100.0	100.0	100.0[2]
No friends	7.9	6.8	8.4	7.5	7.7	8.0	4.7	9.7	7.5	6.6	8.4	7.5	4.5	7.5
One friend	5.9	7.4	10.1	7.4	7.0	8.0	6.0	8.7	7.4	5.4	8.0	8.5	6.8	7.4
Two friends	15.1	16.6	13.5	15.5	10.0	16.7	20.3	15.0	15.5	7.9	17.7	18.8	18.2	15.5
Three friends	71.1	69.2	68.0	69.6	75.3	67.3	69.0	66.6	69.6	80.1	65.9	65.2	70.5	69.6

[1] The interview schedule allowed space for a maximum of three friends to be listed. Only friends who were visited are included in this table.
[2] N = 1200 husbands.

Table 5-4
Percent of Husbands Who Listed Friends, and Median Number of Visits

Interaction with Friends	Cases Classified by Dependency				Cases Classified by Area					Cases Classified by Ethnicity				
	NOA	STA	LTA	Total	S.F.	S.J.	VAL.	L.A.	Total	Black	Span.	White	Other	Total
First Friend														
Those who did list a first friend	92.3	93.3	92.0	92.7[1]	92.3	92.0	96.7	90.0	92.7[1]	93.4	91.8	92.7	97.7	92.7[1]
Median number of visits per year	68.4	58.1	59.7	59.6[2]	59.6	55.6	58.0	73.1	59.6[2]	62.6	59.6	60.0	62.7	59.6[2]
Second friend														
Those who did list a second friend	86.0	86.2	81.4	85.2[3]	84.0	84.7	90.0	81.7	85.2[3]	86.7	84.3	84.0	93.2	85.2[3]
Median number of visits per year	60.7	55.4	57.3	56.6[4]	58.8	53.0	55.6	69.0	56.6[4]	61.7	54.4	59.5	54.1	56.6[4]
Third Friend														
Those who did list a third friend	71.7	70.2	67.5	70.2[5]	75.0	69.3	70.0	66.3	70.2[5]	79.4	66.4	67.0	70.5	70.2[5]
Median number of visits per year	62.7	55.0	58.0	59.5[6]	57.0	52.5	57.0	58.5	59.5[6]	62.8	54.1	58.4	54.0	59.5[6]

[1] N = 1200 husbands.
[2] N = 1113 husbands, those who did visit first friend.
[3] N = 1200 husbands.
[4] N = 1022 husbands, those who did visit second friend.
[5] N = 1200 husbands.
[6] N = 842 husbands, those who did visit third friend.

Table 5-5
Percentage of Husbands by Number of Organizational Memberships

Number of Organizations	Cases Classified by Dependency				Cases Classified by Area					Cases Classified by Ethnicity				
	NOA	STA	LTA	Total	S.F.	S.J.	VAL.	L.A.	Total	Black	Span.	White	Other	Total
All organizations	100.0	100.0	100.0	100.0[1]	100.0	100.0	100.0	99.9	100.0[1]	100.0	100.0	100.0	100.0	100.0[1]
0 Organizations	36.6	45.6	39.1	41.4	34.7	32.0	53.7	45.2	41.4	43.9	24.6	58.5	36.4	41.4
1 Organization	48.5	45.7	51.9	47.9	46.3	56.1	40.6	48.7	47.9	41.0	66.2	32.7	52.3	47.9
2 Organizations	11.2	6.9	6.4	8.2	13.7	10.5	4.0	4.4	8.2	10.6	6.9	7.8	6.8	8.2
3 Organizations	3.7	1.8	2.6	2.5	5.3	1.4	1.7	1.7	2.5	4.5	2.3	1.0	4.5	2.5

[1] N = 1186 husbands; NR = 14 (1.2%).

Table 5-6
Percent of Husbands' Memberships by Type of Organization

Type of Organization	Cases Classified by Dependency				Cases Classified by Area					Cases Classified by Ethnicity				
	NOA	STA	LTA	Total	S.F.	S.J.	VAL.	L.A.	Total	Black	Span.	White	Other	Total
All organizations	100.0	100.0	100.0	100.0[1]	100.0	100.0	100.0	100.0	100.0[1]	100.0	100.0	100.0	100.0	100.0[1]
Religious	79.7	79.7	82.6	80.3	72.7	82.5	86.1	81.5	80.3	70.4	90.7	72.7	61.5	80.3
Other	20.3	20.3	17.4	19.7	27.3	17.5	13.9	18.5	19.7	29.6	9.3	27.3	38.5	19.7

[1] N = 670 husbands, those belonging to one or more organizations. NR = 25.

Table 5-7
Percent of Husbands Participating in One or More Organizations and Median Attendance per Year

Organizational Participation	Cases Classified by Dependency				Cases Classified by Area					Cases Classified by Ethnicity				
	NOA	STA	LTA	Total	S.F.	S.J.	VAL.	L.A.	Total	Black	Span.	White	Other	Total
Those attending one or more organizations	57.9	51.1	57.4	54.2[1]	60.7	62.7	43.7	51.3	54.2[1]	52.8	71.8	36.2	61.4	54.2[1]
Median attendance (times per year, per organization)	51.9	51.2	50.2	51.5[2]	30.9	40.2	53.1	51.7	51.5[2]	52.3	51.7	27.7	30.9	51.5[2]

[1] N = 1200 husbands.
[2] N = 650 husbands, those who did attend meetings.

Table 5-8
Subgroups Showing Highest and Lowest Scores on 12 Indexes of Non-Kinship Social Relations

Indexes	Cases Classified by Dependency		Cases Classified by Area		Cases Classified by Ethnicity	
	High	Low	High	Low	High	Low
Percent of husbands knowing one or more families in neighborhood	Tied Ranks		VAL	S.J.	Tied Ranks	
Median number of families known in neighborhood[2]	Tied Ranks		VAL	S.J.	Black	Spanish
Percent of families having engaged in one or more crisis mutual aid relationships	STA	NOA	S.F.	VAL	Spanish	Black
Median number of crisis mutual aid relationships in last 12 months[3]	Tied Ranks		S.F. S.J.	L.A.	Tied Ranks	
Percent of husbands listing one or more friends	STA	LTA	VAL	L.A.	Black	Spanish
Median number of husband's friends (upper limit of 3)[4]	Tied Ranks		Tied Ranks		Tied Ranks	
Husbands' median visits per year with first friend	NOA	STA	L.A.	S.J.	Tied Ranks	
Husbands' median visits per year with second friend	Tied Ranks		L.A.	S.J.	Tied Ranks	
Husbands' median visits with third friend	NOA	STA	L.A.	S.J.	Black	Spanish
Percentage of husbands belonging to one or more organizations	NOA	STA	S.J.	VAL	Spanish	White
Percent of husbands attending meetings at least once per year	NOA	STA	S.J.	VAL	Spanish	White
Husbands' median attendance at organizations[5]	Tied Ranks		VAL	S.F.	Black	White

[1] If the difference between the scores of the high and low subgroup was 10% or less, the subgroups were defined to have "tied ranks." The 10% criterion was obtained by taking 10% of the score recorded for all the cases. For example, 85% of the cases listed knowing a family in the neighborhood. The difference between the value of the highest and lowest group (classified by dependency) is less than 8.5%; therefore, it is called "tied ranks."

the LTA group is lowest. In purely quantitative terms, then, the LTA group shows a pattern of social withdrawal by comparison with the other families in the sample.

It should also be noted that differences in the frequency of non-kin interaction show up for blacks, who are the high group by contrast with white families, who are the lowest ethnic group in interaction rates. Patterned differences in the social participation of families are not shown when the cases are classified by geographic location. When the indexes of interaction for both kin and non-kin are combined, the largest differences occur when the cases are classified by dependency, the range of differences is less when the cases are classified by geographic status, and the smallest differences in interaction rates are found when the families are classified by ethnic status.

Classification of Husband and Wife Social Relations by Type and Source of Coparticipants

The quantitative analysis of non-kin social relations has indicated that the lowered kinship support of the LTA families is not compensated for by a proportionate increase in non-kin social relations. Does this social withdrawal occur with reference to the neighborhood, friends made at work, or participation in voluntary associations? Furthermore, we may ask whether this withdrawal occurs equally for the wife and the husband. Analysis of the types and sources of coparticipants in the separate social worlds of husband and wife makes possible some limited conclusions in answering these questions. These procedures will allow us to determine if work declines in the contribution it makes to the husband's social world as the period of his welfare dependency lengthens.

Previous studies such as Komarovsky's *Blue Collar Marriage* (1964) have indicated that kin and non-kin relations are not used in the same way by men and women. In identifying the separate social networks of the husband and wife, it seemed fairly clear that crisis mutual aid involving matters of birth, death, and illness tends to revolve around a mother's role.

The data on crisis mutual aid were classified first by type of participants (see Table 4-7 in Chapter 4). For each subgroup in the table, relatives are utilized most frequently, friends are second and neighbors third. The sources where these participants were first met, while similar in certain respects, are not identical with the types of persons involved. For example, a neighbor may have been first met at work. Table 5-9 shows the sources where coparticipants were first met. These sources are classified as work, neighborhood, home and relatives, and other. The last category covers such sources as school, voluntary associations, or military service.

It can be seen that home and relatives are the most important source for coparticipants in crisis mutual aid, the neighborhood is second, and the remaining two sources are of much less significance. The data substantiate the

Table 5-9
Percentage Distribution of Persons Involved in Family Crisis Mutual Aid Relationships by Source

Sources Where First Met	Cases Classified by Dependency				Cases Classified by Area						Cases Classified by Ethnicity				
	NOA	STA	LTA	Total	S.F.	S.J.	VAL.	L.A.	Total		Black	Span.	White	Other	Total
All sources	100.0	100.0	100.0	100.0[1]	100.0	100.0	100.0	100.0	100.0[1]		100.0	100.0	100.0	100.0	100.0[1]
Work	7.9	8.5	6.5	7.9	7.5	11.0	8.9	3.9	7.9		5.7	9.0	9.6	0.0	7.9
Neighborhood	34.4	34.0	41.8	35.6	37.1	25.0	32.6	49.2	35.6		45.0	26.2	36.1	40.0	35.6
Home and relatives	51.5	48.8	45.6	49.0	47.0	52.1	52.4	44.4	49.0		42.0	57.3	46.8	51.7	49.0
Other	6.2	8.7	6.1	7.5	8.4	11.9	6.1	2.5	7.5		7.3	7.5	7.5	8.3	7.5

[1] N = 1356 participants involved with the 1200 families; NR = 390.

Table 5-10
Percentage Distribution of Persons Involved in Men's Routine Mutual Aid Relationships by Type of Participant[1]

Types of Participants	Cases Classified by Dependency				Cases Classified by Area						Cases Classified by Ethnicity				
	NOA	STA	LTA	Total	S.F.	S.J.	VAL.	L.A.	Total		Black	Span.	White	Other	Total
All types of participants	100.0	100.0	100.0	100.0[2]	100.0	100.0	100.0	100.0	100.0[2]		100.0	100.0	100.0	100.0	100.0[2]
Friend	49.5	47.1	47.0	47.9	50.7	50.4	42.3	48.1	47.9		56.4	50.4	40.5	36.4	47.9
Relative	23.2	28.6	25.6	26.3	24.5	26.9	33.0	20.8	26.3		20.7	26.7	30.0	27.3	26.3
Neighbor	21.5	18.7	19.8	19.8	18.6	16.6	19.7	24.3	19.8		17.0	18.1	22.3	30.7	19.8
Minister	1.0	4.6	0.0	0.8	0.7	0.4	1.4	0.8	0.8		0.9	0.3	1.2	1.1	0.8
Other	4.8	1.0	7.6	5.2	5.5	5.7	3.6	6.0	5.2		5.0	4.5	6.0	4.5	5.2

[1] The five types of men's routine mutual aid involved: household repairs, money borrowed, rides to work, car repairs, and other.
[2] N = 2483 participants involved with the 1200 families.

findings of Komarovsky and others that kinship relations predominate in the social networks of lower-class wives.

To obtain data on the husbands that would parallel the facts on crisis mutual aid, questions were asked about certain routine types of mutual aid directly related to the male role. These items were: help in fixing automobiles, household repairs, rides to work, and borrowing small sums of money. Table 5-10 shows the distribution of these male routine mutual aid activities classified by type of coparticipants. It can be seen that friends occupy the first rank, accounting for 47.9% of the coparticipants; relatives are second in importance and neighbors third.

When these mutual aid relationships are classified by source of participant, additional facts are brought to light. It could well have been the case that most of the husband's coparticipants in mutual aid relationships were first met through the husband's relatives. Table 5-11 shows that this is not the case. The neighborhood is the most important source for participants in routine mutual aid, home and relatives second, and work is third. Quite similar findings are reflected in the data on the source of the husband's friends. Table 5-12 shows that the neighborhood is the source for 50% of the husband's friends, work is the second most important source and family is third.

One additional element aids in delineating differences in husband's and wife's social networks. Table 5-13 shows the types of activities engaged in by the husband with his friends, and is directly comparable with the data on activities with relatives (see Table 4-6 in Chapter 4). Only 8% of the husband's activities with friends were defined as ritual, whereas 18% of family activities with kin were classified as ritual. We may guess that these family relationships with relatives involve either the wife by herself, or the husband and wife jointly, but not the husband by himself.[2] Whereas kinship is of first importance to wives and

---

[2] The tables on type and source of participants in non-kin social relations can be used as a check on the conclusion that the LTA cases show over-all lowered social participation. In Tables 4-9, 5-9, 5-10, 5-11, and 5-12, the total interaction described in each table was defined as 100% and this total was distributed by type of participant or source of participant. In four out of five cases where the LTA group was low in the utilization of relatives, it was high in the use of neighbors or the neighborhood. This balancing of neighborhood as a substitute source for lowered use of the kinship system does not mean that the LTA families thereby manifest the same *frequency* of social relations as the NOA families, but rather that lowered use of kin was partly compensated for by relatively heavier use of the neighborhood and neighbors as sources for social relations.

Much the same type of analysis can be made in the case of the Spanish-speaking families. The Spanish-speaking cases showed the lowest interaction rates with kin. They occupied the middle rank in interaction with non-kin. It was expected that the importance of kinship among Spanish-speaking families would have been reflected in higher rates of interaction, but the tables in Chapter 4 did not show this. Could it be the case that *proportionately* the interaction of Spanish-speaking families is concentrated with kin, even though the aggregate rate of interaction is not as high as the other ethnic groups? Tables 5-9 through 5-12 do not show this to be the case. Taking the total interaction of the Spanish-speaking families as 100%, they do not show a disproportionate concentration of their relationships to be with kin when compared with the other two ethnic groups.

Table 5-11
Percentage Distribution of Persons Involved in Men's Routine Mutual Aid Relationships by Source

Sources Where First Met	Cases Classified by Dependency				Cases Classified by Area					Cases Classified by Ethnicity				
	NOA	STA	LTA	Total	S.F.	S.J.	VAL.	L.A.	Total	Black	Span.	White	Other	Total
All sources	100.0	100.0	100.0	100.0[1]	100.0	100.0	100.0	100.0	100.0[1]	100.0	100.0	100.0	100.0	100.0[1]
Work	24.1	20.4	21.1	21.7	20.3	26.8	19.5	21.2	21.7	24.1	26.0	16.2	23.8	21.7
Neighborhood	42.7	45.9	46.1	45.0	42.1	39.4	47.6	50.3	45.0	41.9	42.0	49.3	48.7	45.0
Home and relatives	27.3	27.7	26.6	27.3	28.9	25.8	31.0	23.2	27.3	24.0	27.1	30.2	25.0	27.3
Other	5.9	6.0	6.2	6.0	8.7	8.0	1.9	5.3	6.0	10.0	4.9	4.3	2.5	6.0

[1]N = 2282 participants involved with the 1200 families; NR = 201.

Table 5-12
Percentage Distribution of Husbands' Friends by Source

Source Where First Met	Cases Classified by Dependency				Cases Classified by Area					Cases Classified by Ethnicity				
	NOA	STA	LTA	Total	S.F.	S.J.	VAL.	L.A.	Total	Black	Span.	White	Other	Total
All sources	100.0	100.0	100.0	100.0[1]	100.0	100.0	100.0	100.0	100.0[1]	100.0	100.0	100.0	100.0	100.0[1]
Work	28.9	28.3	20.5	27.0	24.1	30.3	30.9	22.4	27.0	22.7	32.6	25.3	20.0	27.0
Neighborhood	48.7	47.6	59.3	50.2	50.3	43.6	52.8	54.2	50.2	51.3	44.8	53.8	61.7	50.2
Through family	17.4	14.4	12.7	15.1	18.4	14.0	12.9	14.9	15.1	17.2	17.1	11.6	11.3	15.1
Other	5.0	9.7	7.5	7.7	7.2	12.1	3.4	8.5	7.7	8.8	5.5	9.3	7.0	7.7

[1]N = 2966 friends listed by the 1200 husbands.

Table 5-13
Percentage Distribution of Husbands' Relationships with Friends by Type of Activities

Types of Activities	Cases Classified by Dependency				Cases Classified by Area					Cases Classified by Ethnicity				
	NOA	STA	LTA	Total	S.F.	S.J.	VAL.	L.A.	Total	Black	Span.	White	Other	Total
All activities	100.0	100.0	100.0	100.0[1]	100.0	100.0	100.0	100.0	100.0[1]	100.0	100.0	100.0	100.0	100.0[1]
Mutual aid	20.2	22.0	21.1	21.2	28.5	19.7	20.5	13.1	21.2	22.8	17.9	22.4	28.1	21.2
Recreation	65.4	64.4	68.5	65.4	53.7	65.0	71.1	76.8	65.4	60.3	69.2	66.6	61.1	65.4
Ritual	8.3	8.4	6.1	8.0	12.4	6.5	5.5	6.0	8.0	10.9	7.4	6.2	6.0	8.0
Organizational	6.1	5.2	4.3	5.4	5.4	8.8	2.9	4.1	5.4	6.0	5.5	4.8	4.8	5.4

[1] N = 4124 relationships with friends.
 If all 1200 husbands had each listed three friends, and if all four types of activities had been engaged in with friends, N would equal 14,400.

the neighborhood second, the neighborhood appears to be the most significant source for men's social relations, with family and kin of second importance (closely followed by work). Voluntary associations, school, and other institutions are of minor significance as sources for participants in either the husband's or the wife's social life.

The Primacy of Kinship and the Family's Local Social World

Because kinship functions to maintain the *unity* of the family over time, it has been ranked as the most important element in the over-all family social network even though it has greater significance for wives than for husbands. We can conclude that the reduction in kinship ties of the LTA families probably affects wives more directly than it does husbands.

The neighborhood is significant as a source of social relations, first because it is significant for both the husband's and the wife's social networks. In addition, it also functions as an ecological focus for a wide range of both kin and non-kin social relationships. The term neighborhood does not adequately connote the significance that a local ecological area has for these low-income families. The emphasis on informality of social relationships, and upon contacts with neighbors, physically close kin, and others leads to the conception that a major focus of these families' lives is within a local social world. For lower-class families, the importance of kinship for the family social network and the significant focus on a local social world have been reported in a number of recent studies (Komarovsky, 1964; Bernard, 1964; Hodges, 1964; Besner, 1965; Gans, 1965; W. Miller, 1965; and Rainwater, 1959).

Work and Its Relation to the Husband's Local Social World

The differentiation of the various sources of coparticipants in the husband's social world makes possible some assessment of how work, welfare dependency, and the husband's local social world may be interconnected.

Of the husband's coparticipants in routine mutual aid, 21.7% were first met at work. Of his friends, 27% were first met at work, and 7.9% of the persons involved in family crisis mutual aid were first met at work (see Tables 5-11, 5-12, and 5-9). The focus of the husband's mutual aid activities, of family crisis mutual aid, and of the husband's activities with friends is within his local social world. The figures just cited show that a significant proportion of the coparticipants in these activities were first met at work. Thus, there is a *systemic* linkage between the husband's work world and his social world. Some significant proportion of persons first met at his place of work subsequently become involved in his local social world.

If welfare dependency is associated with family social withdrawal, we can surmise that this withdrawal would affect the husband's social network. Tables 5-9, 5-11 and 5-12 indicate a decrease in coparticipants derived from work. While this decrease is small, it supports the conclusion that loss of work and attendant welfare dependency reduces the husband's participation in his local social world. The husband's social withdrawal is due not only to the loss of sociability in the work setting itself, but also to loss of associates first met at work who had been subsequently drawn into his local social world.

Summary

Residential and neighborhood stability was found to be of minor significance as a determinant of neighborhood interaction except in the case of the families living in San Jose.

Analysis of the frequency of non-kin social relations of the 1200 families indicates that the LTA families do not effectively substitute for lowered social participation with relatives by a proportionate increase in non-kin relationships.

Classification of the husband's and wife's social networks by type and source of coparticipants led to the following conclusions:

1. kinship relations are first in importance in the family social network;
2. the weakening of kinship ties among the LTA families probably affects the wife's social network more directly than that of the husband's;
3. the focus of both husband's and wife's social networks is within a "local social world";
4. work is a significant source for coparticipants in the husband's social network;
5. a systemic linkage exists between the husband's work world and his social world;
6. some significant proportion of persons first met by the husband at work are subsequently involved in his local social world; and
7. work as a source for coparticipants in the husband's social network shows a decline as welfare dependency increases. Thus, the LTA husband shows the same pattern of small but systematic withdrawal from his social network that was found to be true for family relationships with relatives.

Section III:
Economic Characteristics of the Cases

6 Level of Living and Economic Security

In this chapter and in the one that follows, a picture will be drawn of the economic and material level of living that characterizes the 1200 families in our sample. The topics covered in this chapter deal with matters of current income, household possessions, automobiles, coverage by public programs related to economic security, debt, credit, family foresight practices, and housing. These various subjects can be looked on as indexes of the ways that families allocate their economic resources. In Chapter 7, the occupational bases that generate the family's financial resources will be analyzed.

Where feasible, brief comparisons will be made between the characteristics of our sample and the characteristics of the low-income population as reported in other studies. In addition, comparisons will be made with two studies on the life style of low-income families during the depression of the 1930s. The first of these is E. Wight Bakke's two-volume report on unemployed families in New Haven, and the other is John McConnell's study, *The Evolution of Social Classes*.[1] Comparison of low-income families with regard to savings, debts, and housing in the 1930s and the 1960s allows some conclusions about possible changes in level of living and economic security of this low-income stratum. Furthermore it can be ascertained if there has been a change in the pattern as well as in the level of living with regard to matters such as family foresight practices.

A variety of meanings can be attached to facts concerning the level of living and economic security of a family. For example, material items (i.e., household possessions) have to be linked with matters of credit and debt in order to see an overall pattern that gives significance to the notion of a standard or level of living. Level of living also reflects opportunities and expectations, and thus demands some treatment of a family's past as well as its future in order to understand its present economic position. This pattern, extending over time, constitutes the level of living element in a family's life style.

---

[1] McConnell's study was also done in New Haven and was based in significant degree on a sample survey of some 2008 New Haven workers (the survey was in 1931 and again in 1933). This same sample was *one* of several data sources used by Bakke in his research on unemployed workers. The two authors' descriptions of this sample population are not redundant, as each chose to classify the cases in ways appropriate to his research goals. Taken together, the two studies complement each other in providing detailed descriptions of low-income families in New Haven during the 1930s, and provide opportunity for some significant comparisons with the characteristics of the 1200 families reported on in this study.

Table 6-1
Average Income of Families for Last 12 Months[1]

Family Income	Cases Classified by Dependency				Cases Classified by Area					Cases Classified by Ethnicity				
	NOA	STA	LTA	Total[2]	S.F.	S.J.	VAL.	L.A.	Total[2]	Black	Span.	White	Other	Total[2]
Median income in dollars	3,682	3,190	3,068	3,306	3,586	3,364	3,009	3,330	3,306	3,489	3,351	3,162	3,083	3,306
Mean income in dollars[3]	3,679	3,263	3,099	3,367	3,658	3,453	2,958	3,399	3,367	3,475	3,419	3,220	3,403	3,367

[1] In addition to husband's earnings, family income includes welfare payments, unemployment compensation payments, earnings of children and of wife where so reported by the husband.
[2] N = 1200 families.
[3] Standard deviations for the three dependency groups are: NOA, $1,400; STA, $1,359; and LTA, $1,100.

Current Income

Table 6-1 provides data on the median income of the various subgroups of the sample. The median annual income for the past 12 months for the sample families was $3,306, with a median family size of 6.8 persons. Figure 6-1 shows per capita income (median) by family size for the 1200 families. The median per capita income for a three-person family is $700, declining to a per capita figure of $400 for families with ten or more members. The indexes given in this chapter present a rough picture of how this income level is utilized to produce a given level of living in terms of material possessions and economic security. The collected data do not cover a wide enough range of items to allow an analysis of a total family budget. Since the evaluation and construction of budgets is a major activity of public welfare workers, the analysis of level of living here was directed toward problems of economic security.

Table 6-1 also indicates some significant differences in current annual income, with the NOA cases showing a 20% higher income than the LTA cases. Families in the San Joaquin Valley show a lower income level than any of the three other areas, and a similar differential occurs between ethnic groups, with the black cases showing the highest median and the white cases the lowest.[2] We can expect that these differentials in income will be associated with differences in level of living, and can also determine whether there are significant changes in the pattern as well as level of living for the various subgroups.

Material Possessions

The survey of a family's material goods was restricted to the items included in Table 6-2 and focused on household possessions, thus it did not cover such vital matters as type and quantity of food, clothing, or medicines. Despite these limitations, the data in Table 6-2 provide some clues to overall level of living and to differences between subgroups.

American civilization is heavily oriented to technical and mechanical things, and none more so than with reference to household activities. This emphasis is reflected in the high percentage of families who own TV sets, radios, and cars (89%, 87%, and 70%, respectively). These facts point to obvious differences in life style between poverty groups in the United States and the poor of other nations. At the same time, the possible inference that other mechanical household aids are owned by an equally large percentage of the sample families is gainsaid by the data in Table 6-2. With the exception of refrigerators, such is

---

[2] Because the black cases were disproportionately concentrated in San Francisco, and this city shows the highest income level of any of the geographic areas, the higher income of the black group may be due in large measure to geographic location. The same argument cannot be made, however, for the white cases since they were not disproportionately concentrated in the Valley area which shows the lowest median income of the four sample areas.

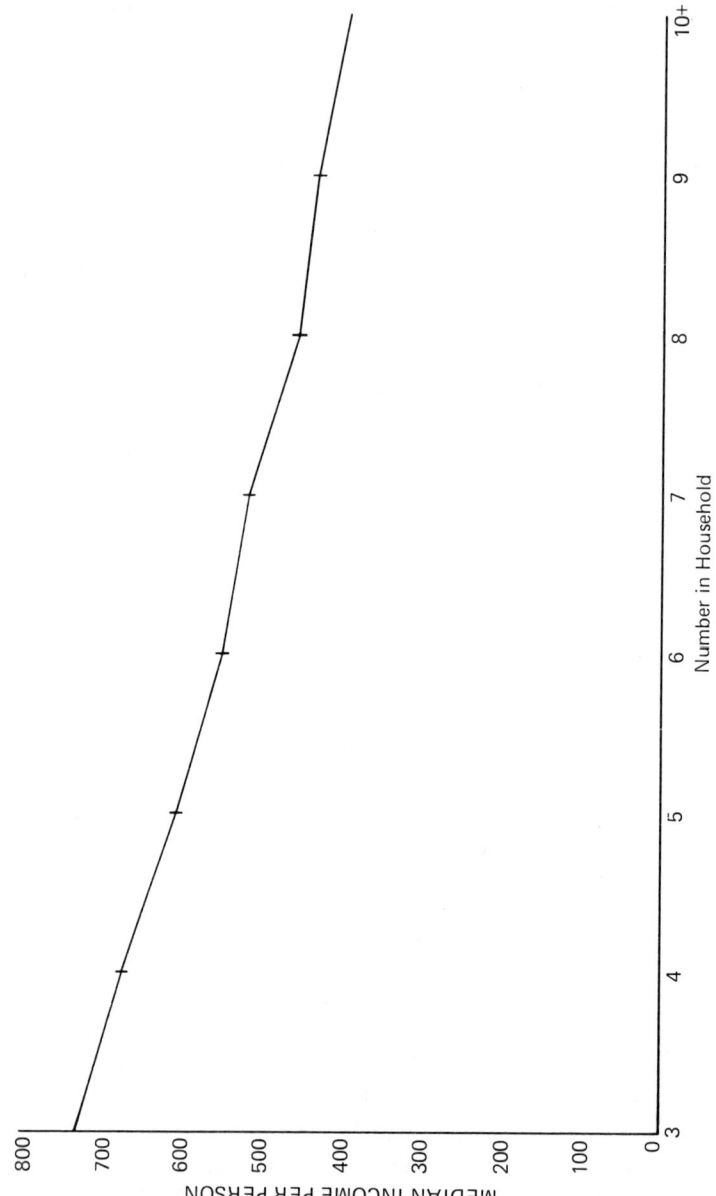

Figure 6-1. Median Income per Person by Household Size for Sample Families. (N=1200 families).

Table 6-2
Percent of Families Having Specified Types of Household Possessions, Including Automobiles

Household Possessions	Cases Classified by Dependency				Cases Classified by Area						Cases Classified by Ethnicity				
	NOA	STA	LTA	Total	S.F.	S.J.	VAL.	L.A.	Total		Black	Span.	White	Other	Total
Radio	89.6	87.0	86.5	87.8[1]	91.3	89.7	82.3	88.0	87.8[1]		91.5	92.0	82.0	72.7	87.8[1]
Telephone	59.0	43.1	45.5	48.8[2]	67.0	54.0	32.7	41.0	48.8[2]		60.4	44.3	44.5	47.7	48.8[2]
Television	87.2	88.2	95.7	89.4[3]	90.0	91.6	81.3	94.6	89.4[3]		91.7	90.6	85.1	93.1	89.4[3]
Vacuum cleaner	33.9	24.9	24.1	27.7[4]	33.0	34.3	21.3	22.1	27.7[4]		26.3	21.1	36.0	27.3	27.7[4]
Washer	47.4	44.5	44.5	45.4[5]	54.5	45.0	26.3	56.0	45.4[5]		49.2	48.1	40.4	38.6	45.4[5]
Washer and dryer	5.9	4.0	1.3	4.1[6]	4.0	6.7	3.3	2.3	4.1[6]		2.2	3.4	6.3	4.5	4.1[6]
Sewing machine	47.8	41.1	37.9	42.7[7]	36.7	45.1	46.8	42.0	42.7[7]		32.1	52.2	40.2	47.7	42.7[7]
Refrigerator	86.9	90.3	89.8	89.1[8]	90.0	88.5	91.6	86.3	89.1[8]		93.6	87.2	87.7	88.4	89.1[8]
Sofa	89.7	89.2	89.0	89.4[9]	93.3	86.8	84.6	92.7	89.4[9]		94.6	86.5	88.0	93.0	89.4[9]
Encyclopedia	24.0	20.7	21.1	21.9[10]	26.7	24.0	17.7	19.1	21.9[10]		27.6	16.4	23.5	20.5	21.9[10]
Bible	37.8	36.1	31.2	35.7[11]	42.7	22.0	53.0	25.1	35.7[11]		47.0	26.1	36.5	43.2	35.7[11]
Bookcase	36.7	30.4	30.4	32.4[12]	37.0	35.7	28.0	29.1	32.4[12]		38.4	25.5	35.3	34.1	32.4[12]
Newspaper subscriber	39.8	37.3	36.3	37.9[13]	52.3	32.0	37.0	30.3	37.9[13]		50.0	25.9	39.5	56.8	37.9[13]
Automobile	79.5	73.2	50.0	70.4[14]	49.3	87.5	86.3	59.3	70.4[14]		55.1	76.2	77.2	67.4	70.4[14]
Auto (1961 or newer)	12.8	3.4	0.4	5.9[15]	4.7	7.1	7.0	4.7	5.9[15]		4.5	7.8	3.8	16.3	5.9[15]

[1] N = 1200 families; NR = 3 (0.3%).
[2] N = 1200 families; NR = 16 (1.3%).
[3] N = 1200 families; NR = 7 (0.6%).
[4] N = 1199 families; NR = 1 (0.1%).
[5] N = 1197 families; NR = 3 (0.3%).
[6] N = 1197 families; NR = 3 (0.3%).
[7] N = 1184 families; NR = 16 (1.3%).
[8] N = 1193 families; NR = 7 (0.6%).
[9] N = 1193 families; NR = 7 (0.6%).
[10] N = 1199 families; NR = 1 (0.1%).
[11] N = 1199 families; NR = 1 (0.1%).
[12] N = 1199 families; NR = 1 (0.1%).
[13] N = 1200 families.
[14] N = 1189 families; NR = 11 (0.9%).
[15] N = 840 families; those who owned an automobile.

not the case. Telephones, vacuum cleaners, washing machines and sewing machines (taken individually) are items missing in over 50% of the households. While we can assume that families *use* the mechanical items they have in their households, we cannot necessarily conclude that they *own* them. In a large number of cases (though undetermined in this survey), repossessions take place, with a resulting ebb and flow of material items available for use. The data in Table 6-2 probably represent the average number of items available for use by the sample of 1200 families.

A marked inconsistency in the use of material objects is found if the TV, radio, and automobile ownership are compared to items related to reading—encyclopedias, Bibles, bookcases, and newspapers. On the average, these items are owned by only about one third of the families. Reading is one of the vital media for the diffusion of values from the larger society, and is obviously highly restricted in this group by comparison with TV watching. This inconsistency suggests a split in the commitment of these low-income families to values of the larger society and therefore in their linkage to it. It suggests that these families are isolated in certain important ways from the outside world, whereas in certain other specific ways, they are very much in contact.

Differences between subgroups of the sample can best be seen by identifying the group with the highest and lowest level of ownership for each item. Table 6-3 presents the results of such a classification. The NOA cases are high on nine out of fifteen indexes and the LTA group are low on eight. A strong pattern is shown by geography, with the rural Valley area showing lowest levels of ownership for eight out of fifteen indexes, with San Francisco being high on six. Ethnic differences are not quite as marked, with the black cases ranking highest on seven out of fifteen indexes, while the Spanish-speaking cases are low on five items.

Within this general pattern of differences, some discrepancies can be noted. Valley families are high in automobile ownership though they are low in income, presumably because the use of automobiles is a necessity for work, whereas in the case of San Francisco this is less true. The Valley cases, the LTA cases, and the Spanish-speaking cases show the highest percentage of families who own sewing machines. It seems plausible that these families compensate for lowered income by making some of their own clothes, though this interpretation offers no explanation of why ownership of sewing machines is not uniformly high for the entire sample of low-income households.

The last item in Table 6-2 casts some light on the often repeated statement that welfare families squander their money on new and expensive cars. Twelve percent of the NOA families have cars newer than a 1961 model, whereas less than 1% of the LTA families own such late model vehicles.

Economic Security and Foresight Practices

Historically, the poor have had only kin members to fall back on for security in old age. The analysis of kinship functions already given has indicated that today

Table 6-3
Subgroups Showing Highest and Lowest Scores for Material Possessions

Indexes	Cases Classified by Dependency		Cases Classified by Area		Cases Classified by Ethnicity	
	High	Low	High	Low	High	Low
Percent of families having a radio	Tied Ranks[1]		S.F.	VAL	Black	White
Percent of families having a telephone	NOA	STA	S.F.	VAL	Black	Spanish
Percent of families having a television	Tied Ranks		S.J.	VAL	Tied Ranks	
Percent of families having a vacuum cleaner	NOA	LTA	S.J.	VAL	White	Black
Percent of families having a washing machine	Tied Ranks		S.F.	VAL	Black	White
Percent of families having both a washing machine and a dryer	NOA	LTA	S.J.	VAL	White	Black
Percent of families having a sewing machine	NOA	LTA	VAL	S.F.	Spanish	Black
Percent of families having a refrigerator	Tied Ranks		Tied Ranks		Tied Ranks	
Percent of families having a sofa	Tied Ranks		Tied Ranks		Tied Ranks	
Percent of families having a set of encyclopedia	NOA	LTA	S.F.	VAL.	Black	Spanish
Percent of families having a Bible	NOA	LTA	VAL.	S.J.	Black	Spanish
Percent of families having a bookcase	NOA	LTA	S.F.	VAL	Black	Spanish
Percent of families having a subscription to a newspaper	Tied Ranks		S.F.	S.J.	Black	Spanish
Percent of families having an automobile	NOA	LTA	S.J.	S.F.	White	Black
Percent of families having an automobile, 1961 or newer	NOA	LTA	S.J.	S.F.	Tied Ranks	

[1] If the difference between the scores of the high and low subgroup was 10% or less, the subgroups were defined to have "tied ranks." The 10% criterion was obtained by taking 10% of the score recorded for all the cases. For example, 88% of the cases listed radios. The difference between the value of the highest and lowest group (classified by dependency) is less than 8.8%; therefore, it is called "tied ranks."

kin members are a very meager resource for potential aid to the sample families in their old age. One major resource that offers an alternative to support by kin is the federal government's Old Age and Survivors Insurance program. Table 6-4 shows that 83% of the husbands specify that they are covered by social security. This high figure is in contrast to the low coverage of 30% in the case of wives. As with material possessions, the NOA group is high in coverage and the LTA group is low. The high percentage of Valley families who affirm social security coverage is unexpected, and no plausible explanation could be given concerning possible bias or errors in these respondents' answers. This particular finding contradicts all the other evidence concerning the economic status of these rural people and therefore must necessarily be considered as suspect.

Unemployment compensation is another program of the state and federal government aimed at alleviating short-run distress caused by unemployment. Table 6-5 provides data on these families who have drawn such compensation at least once in their work history.

The table reflects two factors whose effects can be at least partially separated analytically. On the one hand, it is highly plausible that some portion of these families have never worked on jobs that are covered by unemployment compensation. On the other hand, at least some portion of these families have never been unemployed or have not been unemployed long enough to be recipients of unemployment compensation benefits. The rural Valley cases show the lowest percent of husbands having received benefits, and this is easily explainable by lack of coverage under the law. The LTA cases show highest use of benefits, and this undoubtedly reflects their higher unemployment rate. The average figure of 41% with benefit experience probably points to the low coverage for the entire group by comparison with the federal government's social security program.

Turning from social security to other sources of support in old age, Table 6-6 indicates that only 18.7% of the families expect to have *any other source of economic support*. Over three-fourths of the 18.7% expecting to receive old age support report that the source will be some form of pension, leaving only a tiny handful who look to savings as a resource.

The low percentage of families who expect to receive pensions arises from a number of sources, including lack of continuity in employment, as well as from employment in types of work where pensions are not included as a part of fringe benefits. It could also be expected then that the husbands of these families would *not* have been in union jobs. Table 6-7 indicates that 56% of the husbands have belonged to at least one union on at least one job. To understand the meaning of this figure, we need also to know about continuity of union experience. Table 6-7 shows the number of jobs where workers have had union status and indicates that most of them have only been covered on one job. If we also look at the number of jobs these husbands have had in the last three years (Table 7-7, Chapter 7), it is clear that characteristically they do not remain on the same job from one year to the next.

These tables make it clear that the 56% of husbands with union experience

Table 6-4
Percent of Husbands and Wives with Social Security Coverage

Eligibility Class	Cases Classified by Dependency				Cases Classified by Area					Cases Classified by Ethnicity				
	NOA	STA	LTA	Total	S.F.	S.J.	VAL.	L.A.	Total	Black	Span.	White	Other	Total
Husbands														
All eligibility categories	100.0	100.0	100.0	100.0[1]	100.0	100.0	100.0	100.0	100.0[1]	100.0	100.0	100.0	100.0	100.0[1]
Husband will be eligible	85.8	85.6	72.5	83.0	80.9	82.7	91.1	77.7	83.0	83.7	79.6	85.9	84.2	83.0
Husband will not be eligible	3.7	4.1	8.6	4.9	6.0	3.9	3.1	6.5	4.9	5.3	4.1	5.2	7.9	4.9
Husband does not know if he will be eligible	10.5	10.3	18.9	12.1	13.1	13.4	5.8	15.8	12.1	11.0	16.3	8.9	7.9	12.1
Wives														
All eligibility categories	100.0	100.0	100.0	100.0[1]	100.0	100.0	100.0	100.0	100.0[1]	100.0	100.0	100.0	100.0	100.0[1]
Wife will be eligible	32.8	29.8	27.0	30.2	28.1	34.5	32.4	25.8	30.2	27.9	29.7	31.9	36.8	30.2
Wife will not be eligible	40.2	44.8	46.4	43.6	44.9	34.2	47.9	48.0	43.6	50.2	36.9	44.9	52.6	43.6
Husband does not know if wife will be eligible	27.0	25.4	26.6	26.2	27.0	31.3	19.7	26.2	26.2	21.9	33.4	23.2	10.6	26.2

[1] N = 1089 marital pairs. The husbands provided the answers concerning both themselves and their wives. NR = 111 (9.3%).

Table 6-5
Percent of Husbands Who Have Ever Drawn Unemployment Compensation during Their Work History

Experience under Unemployment Compensation	Cases Classified by Dependency				Cases Classified by Area					Cases Classified by Ethnicity				
	NOA	STA	LTA	Total	S.F.	S.J.	VAL.	L.A.	Total	Black	Span.	White	Other	Total
Those who did draw unemployment compensation	31.3	45.7	49.5	41.8[1]	47.8	47.1	26.4	45.5	41.8[1]	42.9	37.7	45.6	38.5	41.8[1]

[1] N = 1092 husbands; NR = 108 (9.0%).

Table 6-6
Percent of Families Expecting Pensions or Other Monies on Retirement

Retirement Income	Cases Classified by Dependency				Cases Classified by Area					Cases Classified by Ethnicity				
	NOA	STA	LTA	Total	S.F.	S.J.	VAL.	L.A.	Total	Black	Span.	White	Other	Total
Those listing some sources of income	26.4	16.0	12.2	18.7[1]	26.1	19.1	9.0	20.5	18.7[1]	22.6	15.3	18.8	22.7	18.7[1]
All sources of income	100.0	100.0	100.0	100.0[2]	100.0	100.0	100.0	100.0	100.0[2]	100.0	100.0	100.0	100.0	100.0[2]
Pension	76.0	82.1	74.1	78.2	73.3	79.3	78.5	77.0	78.2	78.9	82.3	74.1	80.0	78.2
Money	6.7	4.2	6.5	5.7	4.8	12.1	3.6	1.7	5.7	4.2	7.4	4.9	10.0	5.7
Other	17.3	13.7	19.4	16.1	15.9	8.6	17.9	21.3	16.1	16.9	10.3	21.0	10.0	16.1

[1] N = 1195 families; NR = 5 (0.4%).
[2] N = 230. Sources of income listed by 223 families. Seven cases listed two sources of income.

have not experienced *continuity* of union status. These men have been in jobs that reach up into the world of union status, but this experience has been episodic rather than continuous. These facts all sustain the view that economic security deriving from unions and collective bargaining is very limited for this group. The lowered rate of union experience among Valley cases reflects obvious differences between rural and urban labor markets.

Table 6-8 shows that 9% of the 1200 families have savings. This fact about the *current economic* situation of the families is quite consistent with their prediction concerning savings as a resource for retirement income. The pattern of differences in this table is consistent with that shown in the other tables that have been presented. The NOA cases, the urban cases, and the black cases tend to show the highest percent engaging in foresight practices, and the LTA cases, the rural cases, and the Spanish-speaking cases tend to be lowest.

Table 6-8 can be compared directly with the data concerning low-income workers in New Haven during the 1930s. Bakke (1940) reports that 74% of 200 unemployed families who were studied intensively had some savings. The occupational data on these families show some one-third to be skilled workers thus, the cases are not directly comparable to our sample. However, McConnell (1942) reports on that occupational segment of the 2008 unemployed persons sample labeled "common labor," and gives a figure of 40.8% who had savings. Returning to the sample of 200 persons described in Bakke's volume, the percent of families with savings shows large differences when the cases are classified by ethnic status. The comparison leads to the surprising conclusion that unemployed lower-class families in New Haven during the depression era actually had more security from savings (though the average amount of savings was not given) than is true of our 1964 sample of 1200 families. Furthermore, differences between New Haven Italians and "Americans" in the practice of savings were larger than the differences between black, white, and Spanish-speaking cases in the present study.[3]

The number of families covered by insurance is not markedly different from the facts about savings. One fourth of the families have life insurance policies. The median value of these policies is $5,131. The same pattern of differences between subgroups is found in this table.

Burial insurance is a specialized type of policy that has historically been significant to low-income groups. Table 6-10 shows that some 6% of the families have this type of coverage. The reader will note that purchase of this type of insurance is most frequent among blacks.

Checking accounts (Table 6-11) show the low degree to which these people use banks, with only 11% making use of this type of institution. Exactly the same pattern is manifested in the use of credit unions, with only 7% indicating any such experience.

---

[3] In Caplowitz's study, *The Poor Pay More* (1963), he found that the level of savings and debts were significantly related to ethnic status of his respondents.

Table 6-7
Percent of Husbands with Union Jobs and Number of Union Jobs

Union Jobs	Cases Classified by Dependency				Cases Classified by Area					Cases Classified by Ethnicity				
	NOA	STA	LTA	Total	S.F.	S.J.	VAL.	L.A.	Total	Black	Span.	White	Other	Total
Those having one or more union jobs	58.8	55.8	54.7	56.6[1]	71.4	71.5	28.2	55.0	56.6[1]	57.5	58.3	54.1	54.8	56.6[1]
All union jobs	100.0	100.0	100.0	100.0[2]	100.0	100.0	100.0	100.0	100.0[2]	100.0	100.0	100.0	100.0	100.0[2]
One job	47.6	38.7	50.4	43.9	37.3	36.4	48.8	60.0	43.9	43.6	42.5	45.5	47.8	43.9
Two jobs	32.6	28.1	28.5	29.7	29.2	31.1	26.8	30.0	29.7	28.2	34.4	25.4	30.4	29.7
Three jobs	10.6	16.5	8.9	13.0	14.6	18.4	6.1	7.5	13.0	12.7	14.2	12.0	13.0	13.0
Four or more jobs	9.2	16.7	12.2	13.4	18.9	14.1	18.3	2.5	13.4	15.5	8.9	17.1	8.8	13.4

[1] N = 1167 husbands; NR = 33 (2.8%).
[2] N = 660 husbands.

Table 6-8
Percent of Families with Savings and Median Amount of Savings

Family Savings	Cases Classified by Dependency				Cases Classified by Area					Cases Classified by Ethnicity				
	NOA	STA	LTA	Total	S.F.	S.J.	VAL.	L.A.	Total	Black	Span.	White	Other	Total
Those having some savings	15.1	7.0	3.8	9.0[1]	14.3	8.3	6.7	6.7	9.0[1]	12.7	7.0	7.7	13.6	9.0[1]
Median savings in dollars	264	89	95	217[2]	175	150	250	299	217[2]	175	150	275	350	217[2]

[1] N = 1200 families.
[2] N = 108 families, those who had savings.

Table 6-9
Percent of Families with Life Insurance by Size of Policy and Median Amount of Insurance[1]

Life Insurance (amount in dollars)	Cases Classified by Dependency				Cases Classified by Area					Cases Classified by Ethnicity				
	NOA	STA	LTA	Total	S.F.	S.J.	VAL.	L.A.	Total	Black	Span.	White	Other	Total
Those with some life insurance	41.7	20.6	14.1	25.9	40.4	21.5	15.9	26.5	25.9	38.4	21.2	22.2	27.9	25.9
All amounts of life insurance	100.0	100.0	100.0	100.0[2]	100.0	100.0	100.0	100.0	100.0[2]	100.0	100.0	100.0	100.0	100.0[2]
1 – 299	1.4	2.7	0.0	1.7	0.0	3.2	4.4	1.4	1.7	1.0	2.2	1.2	8.3	1.7
300 – 599	2.0	2.7	3.1	2.4	2.7	0.0	6.7	1.4	2.4	6.7	0.0	0.0	0.0	2.4
600 – 899	2.0	1.8	0.0	1.7	1.8	0.0	0.0	4.2	1.7	1.0	2.2	2.3	0.0	1.7
900 – 2999	27.9	32.1	50.0	32.0	33.5	29.0	48.9	21.1	32.0	31.7	34.9	31.4	16.7	32.0
3000 – 5999	25.2	26.8	15.6	24.7	23.9	32.3	11.1	28.2	24.7	20.2	30.4	24.4	25.0	24.7
6000 – 8999	4.8	8.9	12.5	7.2	8.0	8.1	2.2	8.5	7.2	10.6	6.7	4.7	0.0	7.2
9000 & over	36.7	25.0	18.8	30.3	30.1	27.4	26.7	35.2	30.3	28.8	23.6	36.0	50.0	30.3
Median (in dollars)	5457	4875	2750	5131	5156	4857	2100	5700	5131	5154	4300	5385	7999	5136

[1] N = 1125 families; NR = 75 (6.3%).
[2] N = 291 families, those who have coverage.

Table 6-10
Percentage of Families with Burial Insurance and Median Amount of Insurance

Burial Insurance	Cases Classified by Dependency				Cases Classified by Area					Cases Classified by Ethnicity				
	NOA	STA	LTA	Total	S.F.	S.J.	VAL.	L.A.	Total[1]	Black	Span.	White	Other	Total[1]
Those with some burial insurance	8.1	7.0	4.8	6.9[1]	9.4	4.8	8.7	4.8	6.9[1]	15.2	3.9	4.1	4.5	6.9[1]
Median amount (in dollars)	775	1292	1583	1260[2]	1591	1200	650	1400	1260[2]	1333	1100	1400	700	1260[2]

[1] N = 1171 families; NR = 29 (2.4%).
[2] N = 81 families, those who have burial insurance.

Table 6-11
Percent of Husbands with a Checking Account or Membership in a Credit Union

Bank and Credit Union	Cases Classified by Dependency				Cases Classified by Area					Cases Classified by Ethnicity				
	NOA	STA	LTA	Total[1]	S.F.	S.J.	VAL.	L.A.	Total[1]	Black	Span.	White	Other	Total[1]
Those having checking accounts	18.1	9.8	3.9	11.3	12.5	12.8	10.6	9.4	11.3	10.2	7.0	16.5	14.6	11.3
Those belonging to credit unions	12.0	6.1	1.3	7.1	11.8	6.6	3.1	6.7	7.1	11.2	5.9	5.6	2.4	7.1

[1] N = 1176 husbands; NR = 24 (2.0%).

Debts

As expected, the data regarding the percent of families with debts are the exact reverse of the data on savings. Some 76% have debts with a median value of $649. In this table, the LTA group shows the lowest percent (57.4%) having debts of any of the subgroups.

Holmes' (1965) report on expenditures of low-income families, based on the federal government's Consumer Expenditure Survey, indicates that the average deficit of low-income families ranged from $285 for urban families to $160 for rural nonfarm families. Thus, our sample families show a more impoverished condition than low-income families in general. While the data collected on the sample families did not allow a computation of net worth, it seems likely that a large percent of the cases fall within the 12% of the nation's low-income families whose net worth is less than zero (*Federal Reserve Bulletin*, 1964).

Table 6-13 indicates that 58% of the 1200 families do some purchasing from second-hand stores.

The data on gifts from relatives (Table 4-12), already presented in the chapter on kinship relations, indicate that only about one-ninth of the families receive any support from this source.

Housing

Costs of housing show the median payment to be $66 per month. The major difference between groups is the lower housing cost ($45) for families in the San Joaquin Valley. The proportion of annual income spent on rent (or mortgage payments) by the 1200 families was 23.9%. Holmes (1965) reports (based on the nation's Consumer Expenditure Survey) 23.7% of the low-income family's income was expended for total housing costs (shelter, fuel, light, refrigeration, and water). Taking into account the discrepancy between rent and total housing cost, we can conclude that the 1200 families pay more proportionately for housing costs than low-income families in general. In W.L. Warner's comprehensive study of Yankee City (1941) in the early 1930s, he reports that among lower lower-class families some 20% of the family budget was spent for housing.

As expected, only a small percent of families (12.9) own their own homes. The pattern of home owernship reverses the rural-urban differences shown in the other tables. San Francisco cases show lowest home ownership (3.5%) and Valley cases the highest (26%). The median number of rooms occupied by these families shows only small variations.

Home ownership for the nation's low-income families (Holmes, 1965) is 47%, while ownership for the urban segment of this group is 37%. McConnell's report on New Haven indicates that some 24.9% of unemployed common laborers owned their own homes during the early 1930s. Again, by comparison with the low-income population of the nation and by comparison with a sample of families living in New Haven during the depression, our sample of 1200 families show a lower level of economic security.

Table 6-12
Percent of Families with Debts and Median Amount of Debt

Measures of Debt	Cases Classified by Dependency				Cases Classified by Area					Cases Classified by Ethnicity				
	NOA	STA	LTA	Total	S.F.	S.J.	VAL.	L.A.	Total	Black	Span.	White	Other	Total
Those having debts	81.6	81.1	57.4	76.5[1]	70.8	81.5	86.6	67.3	76.5[1]	74.1	79.1	77.4	61.4	76.5[1]
Median debts (in dollars)	836	620	475	649[2]	554	850	599	524	649[2]	550	709	636	875	649[2]

[1] N = 1194 families; NR = 6 (0.5%).
[2] N = 914 families, those having debts (including a mortgage debt).

Table 6-13
Percent of Families Purchasing from Second-Hand Stores

Use Made of Second-Hand Stores	Cases Classified by Dependency				Cases Classified by Area					Cases Classified by Ethnicity				
	NOA	STA	LTA	Total	S.F.	S.J.	VAL.	L.A.	Total	Black	Span.	White	Other	Total
Those buying from second-hand stores	46.2	66.2	59.9	58.4[1]	56.7	56.7	70.7	49.7	58.4[1]	50.0	54.5	69.5	56.8	58.4[1]

[1] N = 1198 families; NR = 2 (0.2%).

Table 6-14
Family Median Monthly Payments for Housing[1]

Monthly Housing Costs	Cases Classified by Dependency				Cases Classified by Area					Cases Classified by Ethnicity				
	NOA	STA	LTA	Total	S.F.	S.J.	VAL.	L.A.	Total	Black	Span.	White	Other	Total
Median payments (dollars)	69.3	63.7	66.2	66.1	69.2	85.1	45.6	66.8	66.1	64.8	67.8	66.2	65.5	66.1

[1]N = 1070 families; NR = 130 (10.8%), includes both those paying rent and those making mortgage payments.

Table 6-15
Percent of Families Owning Their Own Homes and Median Number of Rooms in House, for Both Renters and Owners

Home Ownership and Size	Cases Classified by Dependency				Cases Classified by Area					Cases Classified by Ethnicity				
	NOA	STA	LTA	Total	S.F.	S.J.	VAL.	L.A.	Total	Black	Span.	White	Other	Total
Those owning own home	20.6	11.3	4.0	12.9[1]	3.5	14.9	26.0	6.8	12.9[1]	9.6	14.7	13.6	11.9	12.9[1]
Median number of rooms in house	5.2	4.9	5.0	5.1[2]	5.1	5.4	4.9	5.1	5.1[2]	5.2	4.9	5.1	4.4	5.1[2]

[1]N = 1157 families; NR = 43 (3.6%).
[2]N = 1130 families; NR = 70 (5.8%).

Interpretation of Findings

If the various facts and comparisons presented in the tables are placed together, certain general characteristics concerning level of living and economic security are overwhelmingly evident. First among these is the inconsistency in communication between this group and the larger society. This is suggested by the ownership of material possessions that relate to communication media. By and large, these families appear to be isolated from the world of reading and all that it implies for participation in the larger society, though the opposite is true with reference to TV and radio.

The second conclusion is that these families have little or no cushion to take care of the economic crises of unemployment except for unemployment compensation. Many of them are in jobs not covered by this program. As a result, their level of living must necessarily rise and fall around the average described in the tables.

The third conclusion is that they do not make use of institutions such as banks, credit unions, or insurance companies. In this regard, the sample families show the same orientation as the lower-class workers studied by McConnell (1942) in the 1930s.

The fourth conclusion is that the federal government's program of social security is the one single source of income for old age security. Taken as a group, these families have no savings at present, expect to have none in the future, are not covered by employer or union pension schemes, and cannot look to significant help from relatives. The pattern is one of chronic economic insecurity coupled with a lack of control over their own economic fortunes.

The brief comparisons made to the low-income population of the nation indicate that in economic security, the sample families are not only below a "poverty line," but that they share with certain other groups the lowest position in the socioeconomic order. While the comparisons made between our sample and unemployed families during the depression have been quite limited, and refer only to the study of one community, the points of comparison have been quite sharply defined. These limited comparisons suggest that there has been little, if any, increase in economic security for families living at this bottom socioeconomic level, except through the development of government programs.

It is important to differentiate between changes in the number and kind of material items possessed by low-income families in the 1930s and 1960s, and changes in their economic security. As stated earlier in the chapter, ownership of automobiles, TV sets, and radios reaches the 80 and 90% level among the sample cases. Undoubtedly, a smaller proportion of low-income families in New Haven in the 1930s had automobiles, radios, or such items as refrigerators. But the significant comparison concerns questions of economic security, and the data suggest that the only significant changes have been through the mechanism of government programs (OASI and unemployment insurance).

Within the general pattern that has been described, there are significant differences for the various subgroups within the sample. It has already been

Table 6-16
Subgroups Showing Highest and Lowest Scores for Economic Security

Indexes	Cases Classified by Dependency		Cases Classified by Area		Cases Classified by Ethnicity	
	High	Low	High	Low	High	Low
Percent of husbands specifying Social Security coverage	NOA	LTA	VAL.	L.A.	Tied Ranks[1]	
Percent of families listing some retirement funds	NOA	LTA	S.F.	VAL.	Black	Spanish
Percent of husbands having one more more union jobs	Tied Ranks		S.J.	VAL.	Tied Ranks	
Percent of families with savings	NOA	LTA	S.F.	L.A. VAL.	Black	Spanish
Percent of families with life insurance	NOA	LTA	S.F.	VAL.	Black	Spanish
Median amount of life insurance[2]	NOA	LTA	S.F.	VAL.	Black	Spanish
Percent of families having burial insurance	NOA	LTA	S.F.	S.J.	Black	Spanish
Percent of families having a checking account	NOA	LTA	S.F.	VAL.	White	Spanish
Percent of families belonging to a credit union	NOA	LTA	S.F.	VAL.	Black	White
Percent of families without debts	LTA	NOA	L.A.	VAL.	Tied Ranks	
Percent of families owning their own home	NOA	LTA	VAL.	S.F.	Spanish	Black

[1] If the difference between the scores of the high and low subgroups was 10% or less, the subgroups were defined to have "tied ranks." The 10% criterion was obtained by taking 10% of the score recorded for all the cases. For example, 83% of the cases listed "Social Security Coverage." The difference between the value of the highest and lowest groups (classified by dependency) is less than 8.3%; therefore, it is called "tied ranks."

[2] For those families having life insurance.

pointed out that in level of material possessions the NOA cases, the urban cases, and the black cases are highest, and that the LTA cases, the rural cases, and the Spanish-speaking cases are the lowest. Table 6-16 shows the rank order of the subgroups for 12 indexes of economic security. These same groups show up in exactly the same rank order. While the differences by ethnic groups are not as strong as by geography and dependency, a pattern is still evident.

In evaluating these differences, it is important first to recognize the designation of a high and a low group refers to variations within a common condition. For example, the dependency group having the highest percentage of persons who expect to receive retirement income other than social security is the NOA subgroup (26.4%) in contrast to the low group, the LTA cases, with 12.2%. Similarly, 15% of the NOA cases have some savings in contrast to 3% for the LTA cases. While the differences between the high and the low group may be as much as 200 or 300%, the high group still shows a level of living that is characterized by economic insecurity and lack of control over their life chances.

The findings that dependency and the rural-urban dimension are axes for the patterning of differences in a family's level of living and economic security are hardly surprising, as many other studies have shown similar results. It is somewhat surprising to report that Spanish-speaking families show lower levels of living and less economic security than black families.

One way to consider the similarities and differences among these sample families in level of living and economic security is to recognize how different they are from those above them in socioeconomic status. In a society dedicated both to a rising standard of living and to economic security buttressed by unions, employer fringe benefits, private savings, life insurance, home ownership, and ownership of stocks and bonds, these families occupy a position where they are on the outside looking in. Their low living level and economic insecurity represent massive economic handicaps. These economic handicaps constitute a way of life with economic insecurity at its very center. Certain groups, the LTA cases, the rural cases, and the Spanish-speaking cases stand out as the most severely handicapped within the sample of 1200 families.

When the pattern of differences in level of living and economic security of the various subgroups is compared with differences in income, there is a high correlation, except that whites show the lowest median income but do not show the greatest handicap in measures of economic security. With this exception, the groups with the highest median income show the greatest economic security, and those with lowest incomes the least security. It seems plausible, then, that income level is the greatest single determinant of economic security and of material life style. Before drawing this conclusion, however, it is important to look at certain facts that qualify this argument.

The first qualification is that the rural cases show the lowest income of the geographic groups, but do not show the lowest ownership of items related to reading. The second qualification is that ownership of sewing machines (a relatively high-cost item) is inversely related to income. The third point is that when classified by ethnic status, the subgroup showing the lowest income (whites) does not turn out to be the group showing the lowest level of economic security, particularly with reference to foresight practices. This position is filled by the Spanish-speaking group.

These considerations indicate the possibility that cultural patterns of the three ethnic groups may tend at certain points to override income differences. It will be remembered that Bakke's findings point to the importance of ethnicity as a factor associated with the practice of savings, and Caplowitz's recent study points to the same conclusion.

To ascertain more fully the function of income in determining material life style and the economic security of these low-income families, we can turn to the analysis of the occupational sources that generate the workers' income.

If the general findings of this chapter hold true, we should find that the occupational level of the subgroups in the sample should be closely correlated with income level, and income level, as has just been demonstrated, is correlated with material level of living and foresight practices. In Chapter 7, the discussion will center not only on the occupational history of the family breadwinner, but on his income history as well. If income dictates the material aspects of life style. this correlation should hold true not only for a family's current income level but for past income as well.

7 The World of Work

Whatever else may be said about low-income families, their condition clearly arises from the way they are linked to the world of work. Type of occupation, changes in occupation, changes in jobs, continuity of employment, and variation in wage rates are all matters that must be described in some detail to understand how these families generate a given level of income.

The method used to achieve this end was to obtain from each of the 1200 husbands a work history starting with his present employment status and extending back in time to the first job he held.

The detailed information that was needed proved to be quite difficult to obtain. Respondents who had held many jobs within the last several years had difficulty recalling with any accuracy the details of each job, including how long it lasted, what the pay rate was, whether or not it was a union job, and the specific work that was performed. By the same token, persons with several unemployment periods had difficulty remembering the length of each period. In general, the respondent's report tended to become less accurate as he went back in time, and particularly so if his work history extended over ten, fifteen, or twenty years. Consequently, the data concerning past job experience and unemployment are somewhat crude, and not highly reliable. Undoubtedly, the extent of unemployment is underrepresented in terms of length and number of periods, as well as the number of jobs that were held. Despite these difficulties, major trends can be discerned; and, in comparing subgroups within the total sample, the biases we have described are probably randomized. In judging the overall effect of the unreliability in reporting, it is evident that, if anything, the position of these workers in the job world is an even more disadvantaged one than is portrayed by the statistics presented in this chapter.

Occupational Status

The 1200 workers were first asked to specify their usual occupation. Table 7-1 presents the answers given to this question. The predominant occupations are low-skilled and low-status jobs. Only 15.6% of the cases fall in skilled, clerical, and sales occupational categories.

The self-definition of one's occupation is only one estimate of an occupational career, and tends to be biased toward reporting that occupation which is highest on the skill and status ladder. Consequently, the job history of each worker was summarized to provide an estimate of the occupational level

Table 7-1
Percent of Husbands in Each Major Occupational Group (usual occupation)[1]

Major Occupational Group	Cases Classified by Dependency				Cases Classified by Area					Cases Classified by Ethnicity				
	NOA	STA	LTA	Total	S.F.	S.J.	VAL.	L.A.	Total	Black	Span.	White	Other	Total
All occupational groups	100.0	100.0	100.0	100.0[2]	100.0	100.0	100.0	100.0	100.0[2]	100.0	100.0	100.0	100.0	100.0[2]
Professional & managerial	1.5	1.2	2.5	1.6	3.0	1.7	0.7	1.3	1.6	2.8	0.2	2.3	0.0	1.6
Clerical & sales	7.1	5.4	4.2	5.8	11.3	2.7	0.7	8.3	5.8	8.2	2.0	8.3	2.3	5.8
Service	11.7	9.6	16.5	11.7	21.0	5.3	5.3	15.0	11.7	20.3	8.9	6.5	25.6	11.7
Agricultural	17.9	27.0	15.6	21.8	3.7	20.7	57.7	5.0	21.8	8.9	30.0	21.8	32.6	21.8
Skilled	13.0	8.4	8.9	10.0	12.7	11.3	3.7	12.0	10.0	7.6	8.9	12.8	11.6	10.0
Semiskilled	23.2	19.8	19.8	20.9	19.7	19.0	16.3	29.0	20.9	21.8	17.5	25.0	14.0	20.9
Unskilled	25.3	28.4	32.4	28.2	28.3	39.3	15.7	29.3	28.2	30.4	32.3	23.5	14.0	28.2

[1] Classified by the *Dictionary of Occupational Titles*.
[2] N = 1198 husbands; NR = 2 (.2% persons who were never employed).

characteristic of his entire working experience. Table 7-2 presents the results of this classification.

Some 83% of the 1200 husbands have worked primarily in unskilled and semiskilled jobs, and this statistic corresponds rather well with the figures about these workers' self-definition of their usual occupation.

Still another way of looking at occupational histories is in terms of movement up and down the occupational ladder. Miller (1964) in his studies of occupational careers indicates that a person's starting job and final job may be vastly different in skill and status. Upper-middle-class persons may start work at low-status jobs, but such work represents only a temporary trial period that changes rapidly. By contrast, lower-class workers' careers show much less movement up and down the occupational ladder. They start work at jobs that are low in skill and status and tend to remain at this level throughout their working lives.

In order to determine such trends, the job history of each husband was summarized in terms of movement on the occupational ladder. Table 7-3 presents the results of this type of classification. Seventy-nine percent of the 1200 husbands showed a stationary position in occupational level. Some 6% showed upward occupational mobility, and a corresponding percent a downward movement. Taken together, the three tables on occupational classification indicate that the lifetime position of these men in the world of jobs is that of low skill and fixed status.

Employment Continuity

A second measure of the life chances of workers concerns the continuity of their jobs. The reader will remember that one-half of the sample families were current welfare cases, hence the data on current unemployment of husbands reflect this fact of sampling. Table 7-4 shows the current employment status of the husbands and Table 7-5 of wives. Table 7-5 shows that only 11% of the wives are currently employed.

A more significant measure of employment continuity was derived from a summary of each worker's unemployment history. Table 7-6 shows that 88% of the husbands have been unemployed at some time. The median number of times unemployed was 2.1, and the median amount of aggregate unemployment was 9.6 months. Though biased due to underreporting, the figures in Table 7-6 make clear the fact that unemployment is endemic to the entire group.

Another measure of employment continuity is reflected in job changes over time. Table 7-7 presents data on the number of job changes made within the last three years. Forty-one percent of these husbands have had more than two jobs within the last three years. Two-thirds have had more than one job during this same period. Thus, lack of continuity in employment is also bound up with frequent changes of job.

It can be expected that concentration of these workers in seasonal work in

Table 7-2
Percent of Husbands in Each Job-History Type

Job History Type	Cases Classified by Dependency				Cases Classified by Area					Cases Classified by Ethnicity			
	NOA	STA	LTA	Total	S.F.	S.J.	VAL.	L.A.	Total	Black	Span.	White	Other	Total
Total Classified	100.0	100.0	100.0	100.0[1]	100.0	100.0	100.0	100.0	100.0[1]	100.0	100.0	100.0	100.0	100.0[1]
All unskilled, combination of semiskilled and unskilled	70.8	82.4	83.4	78.9	76.6	81.1	85.1	73.1	78.9	83.5	86.2	68.6	65.9	78.9
All semiskilled	11.0	4.0	5.4	6.5	9.3	4.6	4.0	8.0	6.5	5.6	4.9	8.2	14.6	6.5
Combinations of semiskilled, unskilled and skilled work	8.8	8.1	5.4	7.8	6.6	9.6	6.2	8.7	7.8	7.3	4.4	11.4	12.2	7.8
All skilled	4.4	2.4	4.5	3.4	2.8	2.9	2.2	5.9	3.4	1.3	2.9	6.1	0.0	3.4
Other[2]	5.0	3.1	1.3	3.4	4.7	1.8	2.5	4.3	3.4	2.3	1.6	5.7	7.3	3.4

[1] N = 1132; NR = 68 (5.7%).
[2] Other: Because of the small frequencies involved, persons with some clerical or professional experience were combined with persons with all clerical or all professional experience.

Table 7-3
Percent of Husbands in Each Occupational Mobility Pattern[1]

Mobility Pattern	Cases Classified by Dependency				Cases Classified by Area					Cases Classified by Ethnicity				
	NOA	STA	LTA	Total	S.F.	S.J.	VAL.	L.A.	Total	Black	Span.	White	Other	Total
All patterns	100.0	100.0	100.0	100.0[2]	100.0	100.0	100.0	100.0	100.0[2]	100.0	100.0	100.0	100.0	100.0[2]
Upward	9.5	5.0	5.0	6.5	8.0	9.6	4.6	3.9	6.5	6.5	7.3	5.5	7.3	6.5
Downward	4.6	6.9	6.9	6.1	10.9	6.4	2.5	4.9	6.1	8.2	4.9	6.0	4.9	6.1
Stationary	77.2	80.9	80.3	79.6	70.6	74.8	89.7	82.8	79.6	77.4	82.7	77.5	82.9	79.6
Erratic	8.7	7.2	7.8	7.8	10.5	9.2	3.2	8.4	7.8	7.9	5.1	11.0	4.9	7.8

[1]The categories upward and downward refer to patterned changes in the respondent's job history; e.g., from a semiskilled to a skilled level. "Erratic" signifies change in occupational level without patterned direction.

[2]N = 1125 husbands; NR = 75 (6.3%).

Table 7-4
Percentage Distribution of Husbands by Current Employment Status

Current Employment Status	Cases Classified by Dependency				Cases Classified by Area					Cases Classified by Ethnicity				
	NOA	STA	LTA	Total[1]	S.F.	S.J.	VAL.	L.A.	Total[1]	Black	Span.	White	Other	Total[1]
Total classified	100.0	100.0	100.0	100.0	100.0	100.0	100.0	100.0	100.0	100.0	100.0	100.0	100.0	100.0
Unemployed	19.8	48.1	73.8	44.1	50.3	53.9	26.7	45.0	44.1	45.0	41.3	47.2	33.3	44.1
Part-time employment	5.2	8.2	1.7	5.9	2.7	4.1	14.4	2.7	5.9	3.5	4.7	9.6	2.4	5.9
Full-time employment	75.0	43.7	24.5	50.0	47.0	42.0	58.9	52.3	50.0	51.5	54.0	43.2	64.3	50.0

[1]N = 1179; NR = 21 (1.8%).

Unemployed includes undetermined and those persons on public assistance engaged in "work relief" or training programs.

Table 7-5
Percentage Distribution of Wives by Current Employment Status[1]

Current Employment Status	Cases Classified by Dependency				Cases Classified by Area						Cases Classified by Ethnicity			
	NOA	STA	LTA	Total[2]	S.F.	S.J.	VAL.	L.A.	Total[2]	Black	Span.	White	Other	Total[2]
Total classified	100.0	100.0	100.0	100.0	100.0	100.0	100.0	100.0	100.0	100.0	100.0	100.0	100.0	100.0
Unemployed	88.0	87.0	94.5	88.8	87.3	87.9	87.9	92.0	88.8	87.9	89.8	87.9	93.2	88.8
Part-time employment	4.3	4.9	3.0	4.3	6.7	3.7	5.7	1.3	4.3	5.1	3.4	4.8	4.5	4.3
Full-time employment	7.7	8.1	2.5	6.9	6.0	8.4	6.4	6.7	6.9	7.0	6.8	7.3	2.3	6.9

[1] All data derived from husband's answers.
[2] N = 1197; NR = 3 (0.3%). The data do not allow differentiation between wives who are seeking employment and are therefore unemployed, and those wives who are not seeking employment and are, therefore, "not in the labor force."

Table 7-6
Unemployment of Husbands for Entire Job History by Percent Unemployed, Longest Period, Number of Periods, and Total Months

Unemployment History	Cases Classified by Dependency				Cases Classified by Area					Cases Classified by Ethnicity				
	NOA	STA	LTA	Total	S.F.	S.J.	VAL.	L.A.	Total	Black	Span.	White	Other	Total
Percent of those who have been unemployed	70.5	95.0	99.6	88.0[1]	89.0	95.2	85.5	82.3	88.0[1]	85.7	87.2	92.2	74.4	88.0[1]
Median number of months of unemployment for longest unemployment period	6.8	5.6	12.1	6.1[2]	8.6	6.1	4.1	7.3	6.1[2]	7.5	3.9	6.2	.3	6.1[2]
Median number of times unemployed	1.9	2.3	1.9	2.1[3]	1.9	2.0	3.6	1.7	2.1[3]	1.9	2.3	2.2	1.9	2.1[3]
Median number of months unemployed	6.1	9.1	18.9	9.6[4]	12.1	9.2	7.9	10.1	9.6[4]	12.3	7.9	9.3	7.5	9.6[4]

[1] N = 1186 husbands; NR = 14 (1.2%).
[2] N = 1044 husbands, those cases reporting one or more periods of unemployment (minimum one month).
[3] N = 1041 husbands, those cases reporting one or more periods of unemployment.
[4] N = 1040 husbands, those cases reporting one or more periods of unemployment.

both the agricultural and nonagricultural sectors may well contribute to the lack of employment continuity that has just been described. Table 7-8 presents data on this topic. Some 42% of the cases have had seasonal jobs within the last three years, and of these persons, some 56% have had two or more seasonal jobs within this same period.

Wage History

If these workers at the bottom of the occupational ladder are fixed in status and characterized by lack of continuity in employment, it follows that their earning power when expressed in wage rates would also be low. It could be the case, however, that their earning power fluctuates and that they have held jobs with relatively high wage rates for limited periods, even though such jobs may not have been classified as skilled. The data on the wage histories of the sample cases offer an answer to this question. Viewed in terms of their job histories, the minimum and maximum wages (translated into a monthly figure) of the respondents show considerable variation, ranging from $262 per month to $365 (Table 7-9). The median monthly income for the job of longest duration in the work history was $323. If these figures are multiplied by 12, the derived hypothetical annual income ($3,876) can be compared to the group's current median annual income (last 12 months) of $3,306.

If the annual earnings of the 1200 cases were at the minimum level of their past earning, they would equal $3,144, some $152 below their current income. If, on the other hand, their annual income were at the maximum level of past earnings, their income would be $4,380, some $1,074 above the current figure. If current earnings were equal to wages earned during the job of longest duration, annual income would be $3,876, or $570 above what was actually earned during the last 12 months.[1]

Even though these workers have been employed at given times in jobs at wage levels that would hypothetically raise their annual income by one-third, such employment is not characteristic of their work histories. Furthermore, their work histories are characterized by chronic unemployment. Consequently, the long-run level of their past annual income is a product both of the average low wage level at which they are employed and of the lack of continuity in employment.

**Differences in Occupational Status, Employment
Continuity and Wage History**

As with the other topics that have been treated, the relative position of the subgroups in occupational status, employment continuity, and earning power

---

[1] None of the income data was adjusted for inflation since this would have necessitated classifying all monthly incomes by the particular year in which they were earned.

Table 7-7
Percentage Distribution of Husbands by Number of Jobs in the Last Three Years[1]

Number of Jobs	Cases Classified by Dependency				Cases Classified by Area					Cases Classified by Ethnicity				
	NOA	STA	LTA	Total	S.F.	S.J.	VAL.	L.A.	Total	Black	Span.	White	Other	Total
All jobs	100.0	100.0	100.0	100.0	100.0	100.0	100.0	100.0	100.0	100.0	100.0	100.0	100.0	100.0
One job	38.5	25.7	42.7	32.9	38.3	33.1	22.5	37.0	32.9	35.4	38.0	24.6	39.0	32.9
Two jobs	31.3	22.6	26.5	26.2	26.7	29.7	20.1	27.9	26.2	27.1	27.0	25.4	19.5	26.2
Three jobs	12.8	17.9	17.8	16.2	15.6	17.5	12.4	17.9	16.2	16.7	16.0	16.8	9.8	16.2
Four or more jobs	17.4	33.8	13.0	24.7	18.4	19.7	45.0	17.2	24.7	20.8	19.0	33.2	31.7	24.7

[1] Of the 1200 cases, 1057 (88.0%) had one or more jobs in the last three years; 56 (4.7%) were unemployed during this period; and 87 (7.3%) were undeterminable cases.

Table 7-8
Percentage Distribution of Husbands by Number of Seasonal Jobs in the Last Three Years

Number of Seasonal Jobs	Cases Classified by Dependency				Cases Classified by Area					Cases Classified by Ethnicity				
	NOA	STA	LTA	Total	S.F.	S.J.	VAL.	L.A.	Total	Black	Span.	White	Other	Total
Those with seasonal jobs	32.1	51.3	35.0	41.8[1]	28.2	55.1	69.4	17.0	41.8[1]	30.1	46.7	46.8	34.1	41.8[1]
All seasonal jobs	100.0	100.0	100.0	100.0[2]	100.0	100.0	100.0	100.0	100.0[2]	100.0	100.0	100.0	100.0	100.0[2]
One job	44.2	40.7	57.1	44.3	57.9	50.6	27.2	65.3	44.3	55.4	45.5	38.4	28.6	44.3
Two jobs	26.7	18.2	29.9	22.2	19.3	26.9	19.0	24.5	22.2	20.7	27.5	17.5	21.4	22.2
Three jobs	10.8	14.5	3.9	11.9	10.8	12.8	13.6	4.1	11.9	10.9	12.2	12.4	7.1	11.9
Four jobs	6.7	12.0	2.6	9.1	8.4	3.2	16.3	2.0	9.1	6.5	5.3	13.0	28.6	9.1
Five jobs	4.2	5.5	6.5	5.3	3.6	2.6	8.7	4.1	5.3	4.3	4.2	7.3	0.0	5.3
Six or more jobs	7.4	9.1	0.0	7.2	0.0	3.9	15.2	0.0	7.2	2.2	5.3	11.4	14.3	7.2

[1] N = 1130; NR = 70 (5.8%).
[2] N = 472, those husbands having one or more seasonal job in the last three years.

can be best seen if the low and high groups are indicated. The ranked position of the subgroups on 13 indexes is given in Table 7-10. Certain obvious patterns emerge by dependency and geography, whereas the rank order of ethnic groups shows only a minor pattern.

The NOA group shows slightly higher occupational status, greater stability in employment,[2] and greater stability in earning power than either the STA or LTA cases. The STA and LTA cases show more oscillation in earning power, having as a group earned at some time in their work histories both higher and lower wages than the NOA respondents.

The differences between the Valley subgroup and the three urban areas are clear, with the rural cases showing lower occupational status, somewhat less continuity of employment, and lower earning power both in the past and in the present.

A separate classification of the work histories showed that some 10.9% of the 1200 cases have shifted from rural to urban jobs, whereas only 1.8% have shifted from urban to rural job patterns. The differences in occupational status, employment continuity, and earning power between the rural and urban sectors of California's labor market offer an obvious explanation of why urban workers do not tend to seek jobs in the rural sector.

When the cases are classified by ethnic status, no equally clear pattern of differences emerges except for a minor pattern indicating the Spanish-speaking group to be low in occupational status and earning power. The wage data show the earning power of Spanish-speaking cases to be low historically, though the white group is lowest in terms of present income.

Correlation of Occupational Level, Income Level, and Level of Living

The differences in the work histories of the 1200 husbands show occupational, wage, and employment differences that look much like the pattern found for level of living and family economic security. For example, the Long-Time Aid cases and the rural cases show the same handicapped position. In Chapter 6, analysis of a family's level of living led to the conclusion that income level appeared to be the key factor associated with several aspects of level of living. By comparing the occupational and employment histories of these men with the data on family level of living, it will be possible to see what subgroups are characteristically low or high on each of these indexes.

In Table 7-11, the data on level of living are separated into three indexes labeled material possessions, reading, and economic security and foresight practices. Also in Table 7-11, the category of income is considered in terms of

---

[2]The indexes on unemployment are somewhat confounded by the age differential between the dependency groups. The median age of the LTA cases is some four years greater than the other two groups, and hence, their exposure to possible unemployment has been longer.

Table 7-9
Husband's Minimum and Maximum Median Wage during Last Three Years, and Median Wage for Job of Longest Duration

Measures of Monthly Wage in Dollars	Cases Classified by Dependency				Cases Classified by Area					Cases Classified by Ethnicity				
	NOA	STA	LTA	Total	S.F.	S.J.	VAL.	L.A.	Total	Black	Span.	White	Other	Total
Median maximum wage for last three years	373	385	332	365[1]	355	408	317	344	365[1]	372	347	380	407	365[1]
Median minimum wage for last three years	301	247	245	262[2]	314	273	219	255	262[2]	293	251	245	265	262[2]
Median wage for job of longest duration (from the entire job history)	332	317	365	323[3]	359	348	248	319	323[3]	335	309	326	343	323[3]

[1] N = 1125 husbands; NR = 75 (6.3%).
[2] N = 1115 husbands; NR = 85 (7.1%).
[3] N = 1086 husbands; NR = 114 (9.3%).

Table 7-10
Subgroups Showing Highest and Lowest Scores on 13 Indexes of Socioeconomic Status

Indexes	Cases Classified by Dependency		Cases Classified by Area		Cases Classified by Ethnicity	
	High	Low	High	Low	High	Low
A. Occupation[1]						
Socioeconomic level of husband's usual occupation	NOA	STA	S.F.	VAL.	Black	Spanish
Socioeconomic level of husband's occupational history	NOA	STA	L.A.	VAL.	White	Black
Husband's occupational mobility pattern	NOA	STA LTA	S.F.	VAL.	Black	White

B. Employment Continuity

						Tied Ranks²	
Percent of husbands who have never been unemployed	NOA	LTA	L.A.	S.J.	Tied Ranks²	
Median number of months of unemployment for longest unemployment period³	NOA	LTA	VAL.	S.F.	Spanish	Black
Median number of times unemployed for entire job history³	NOA	STA	L.A.	VAL.	Black	Spanish
Median number of months unemployed for entire job history³	LTA	LTA	VAL.	S.F.	Spanish	Black
Percent of husbands belonging to a union on one or more jobs	NOA	LTA	S.J.	VAL.	Tied Ranks	
Median number of jobs in last three years⁴	Tied Ranks	STA	S.F.	VAL.	Spanish	White
Percent of persons having one or more seasonal jobs	LTA	STA	L.A.	VAL.	Black	White

C. Wage History

Median maximum wage for last three years	NOA	STA	S.J.	VAL.	White	Spanish
Median minimum wage for last three years	STA	LTA	S.F.	VAL.	Black	White
Median wage for job of longest duration (from entire job history)	NOA	LTA	S.F.	VAL.	Black	Spanish

¹ If the *distribution* of the husbands usual occupation is considered from the viewpoint of socioeconomic level (Table 7-1), it is clear that a higher proportion of NOA cases are concentrated in higher socioeconomic occupations than is true of the STA cases. The same reasoning was used in creating the other two indexes dealing with the subject of occupations.

² If the difference between the scores of the high and low subgroup was 10% or less, the subgroups were defined to have "tied ranks." The 10% criterion was obtained by taking 10% of the score recorded for all the cases. For example, 12% of the cases listed never being unemployed. The difference between the value of the highest and lowest group (classified by dependency) is less than 1.2%; therefore, it is called "tied ranks."

³ For those cases who have experienced unemployment.

⁴ For those who have had more than one job in the last three years.

income history and current income, i.e., income for the last 12 months. Finally, the data on occupational status were combined into one index. Thus, Table 7-11 contains a set of indexes that allows us to compare subgroups of the sample for occupational level, income level, and three aspects of income expenditures.

The reader should recognize that in comparing subgroups within the sample, we are dealing with cases that have already been matched in several ways for socioeconomic status. By comparison with the full spectrum of socioeconomic positions in the general society, these cases represent a slice from the bottom of the socioeconomic ladder and consequently look very much alike. At the same time, the subgroups of the sample show small but significant differences in income level and occupational status. Given the facts of the original attempt to hold socioeconomic status constant, it could well be expected that small variations between subgroups in average income and occupation would be accounted for by differences in ethnic status.

The data in Table 7-11 present an answer to this hypothesis and also allow us to infer the relative importance of dependency status, rural-urban status, and ethnic status as factors affecting the economic characteristics of these families, whether it be the consumption or production aspects of their lives.

Let us consider first the proposition that occupation determines income and that income determines level of living. When the cases are classified by dependency status and the high and low groups indicated for each index, we find that with one exception (income history) the relationship holds true. When the cases are classified by geography, and the three urban areas (San Jose, San Francisco, and Los Angeles) are compared to the Valley cases, the relationship between occupation, income, and level of living holds true except for the index of reading. However, when the cases are classified by ethnic status, the ordering relationship between occupation, income and level of living is no longer clearly evident.

A slightly different view of the table produces the same conclusions. If we reason that income is the single best index of socioeconomic status and therefore predicts occupational level and level of living, we find that this holds true for the cases when classified by dependency, and holds true when the cases are classified by rural-urban status. However, when the cases are classified by ethnic status, income is not a good predictor of occupation and level of living.

The inference is clear that for these low-income families, dependency status is the most powerful factor affecting the ordering of occupation, income, and certain aspects of level of living. Rural-urban status is the second most powerful factor ordering the relationship between these three variables, and ethnicity is the least powerful. It is important to make clear that significant functions of ethnicity in modern life are not being denied.[3] No inference can be drawn from the argument just given that significant cultural differences are not found among

---

[3] The argument given here is not inconsistent with that presented by Gordon (1964), in which he argues for the function of ethnicity in defining choice of participants in interpersonal relations.

the black, white, and Spanish-speaking groups. Indeed, the very label "Spanish-speaking" signifies the fact of an important cultural difference from the dominant society. Nevertheless, when the cases were matched for socioeconomic status, small patterned differences in mode of labor force participation, in income level, and in aspects of level of living did not correlate highly with ethnic status.

In effect, it appears that the elements making up the dependency variable override the elements involved in ethnic status insofar as employment, income, and certain aspects of level of living are concerned. It must be emphasized that we are dealing with small differences in socioeconomic position after the 1200 cases have been initially matched for socioeconomic status. It is rather obvious that the general socioeconomic position of all blacks in California when compared to the position of all whites is not the subject matter that we are analyzing.

If other ethnic groups were included in the analysis, and in particular those groups such as the Chinese population that show considerable poverty, it might be that elements such as income and occupation when classified by the ethnic factor would override the ordering effects associated with the dependency factor. If such were the case, we would find that income level, occupational level, and level of living for low-income Chinese would show no relationship to the welfare dependency condition, for the simple reason that few if any of the cases would show any welfare dependency experience.

In utilizing job histories as a base for analyzing the relationship of these low-income workers to the world of work, we have necessarily focused on the past and have tended to emphasize that aspect of a worker's life that predates the welfare dependency experience itself. Another dimension that reflects the linkage between the worker and world of work is that of the job-finding process. In the questions that were asked about barriers and aids to finding work, the focus was on the present and thus reflects not only the worker's previous job experience but whatever welfare dependency experience he may have had. A third dimension centers on the reactions of workers to the work experience itself. Questions were asked about the worker's likes and dislikes on his current job, or on the last job he had held. For some workers, these questions referred to their current employment, but for those currently on public assistance, the referent was to some point in the past when they were last employed. In the section that follows, the respondents' reports about the job-finding process, and about their reactions to work itself, tend to focus on the present circumstances in a worker's life though not exclusively so in all cases.

Barriers to Employment

The data presented so far deal with the objective position of 1200 low-income workers in the labor market, and provide a description of the life chances of a worker somewhat independent of his interpretation of the situation. The answers to questions about job-finding and the work experience itself cover two separate but interrelated areas, i.e., facts and feelings.

In some instances, facts and feelings can be checked against each other. For example, we can expect that blacks will mention racial discrimination as a barrier to employment, whereas whites will not. Thus, the attitudes that are displayed, when coupled with objective data about life chances, serve to enlarge the understanding of how these men are linked to the world of work.

Though no objective data were available concerning the health of these families, some 31% stated that ill health was a handicap to one or more of the family members. Table 7-12 indicates that there is a gradient of increasing health problems, with the NOA families showing the least handicap and the LTA families the largest. The same pattern holds for the health of husbands. The Los Angeles cases and the white cases show the same higher levels of health problems as the LTA group.[4]

In Table 7-13, the barrier to employment that looms as outstanding in the minds of these men is the lack of skill and training (47.8%). The second greatest barrier is that of the distance traveled to find work, the third most important is low pay, and the fourth perceived handicap is that of age.

When the various answers are compared with known facts about the objective position of the various subgroups, there is a surprisingly high correlation. The higher age level of the LTA husbands is reflected in the percent listing this handicap. Blacks mention job discrimination much more often than Spanish-speaking families do. The Valley cases mention low pay most frequently and see unionism as less of a barrier to employment. They also mention barriers to apprenticeship less often and reflect the reality that apprenticeship has little relevance to agricultural jobs. Spanish-speaking respondents mention language difficulties most frequently. A final check shows that the LTA cases see themselves as having more trouble in finding work—all of which fits the reality of their unemployment condition.

When the items in Table 7-13 are evaluated to see what subgroups mentioned the largest number of difficulties, it was found that the LTA group was high on ten out of 17 items, whereas the NOA group was low in perceived barriers to employment on 14 out of 17 items. The self-evaluation of each group seems to fit the relative difference in their actual employment condition.

As with the LTA cases, it could be expected that the rural cases would reflect their handicapped position by seeing more barriers to employment than the urban cases. The data do not support this expectation—the San Jose cases were high in mention of barriers and the Los Angeles cases were low. When classified by ethnicity, it could be expected that whites would see the fewest barriers to

---

[4] A similar question was asked about health but at a different place in the questionnaire and with reference to the husband's health only. These results given in Table 7-13 are not identical with the data in Table 7-12. The rank order of groups by dependency and ethnicity is the same. However, San Jose rather than Los Angeles is the high group by geographic classification of the cases.

Table 7-11
Subgroups Showing Highest and Lowest Scores on 6 Indexes Related to Income Production and Expenditures

Indexes[1]	Cases Classified by Dependency		Cases Classified by Area		Cases Classified by Ethnicity	
	High	Low	High	Low	High	Low
Current income	NOA	LTA	S.F.	VAL.	Black	White
Income history	Tied Ranks		S.J.	VAL.	White	Spanish
Reading	NOA	LTA	Tied Ranks		Black	Spanish
Material possessions	NOA	LTA	S.F. S.J.	VAL.	Tied Ranks	
Economic security and foresight practices	NOA	LTA	S.F.	VAL.	Black	Spanish
History of occupational status	NOA	STA	S.F.	VAL.	Tied Ranks	

[1]The index of current income is taken directly from the medians given in Table 6-1. The index of income history is based on the measures provided in Table 7-9. The items comprising the two indexes of reading and of material possessions are contained in Table 6-2. The index of economic security and foresight practices is comprised of items taken from Tables 6-4 through 6-12. The index of occupational status is taken from items contained in Tables 7-1 through 7-3.

Table 7-12
Percentage of Family Members Whose Work of Schooling is Limited by Illness or Injury[1]

Family Health Conditions	Cases Classified by Dependency				Cases Classified by Area						Cases Classified by Ethnicity				
	NOA	STA	LTA	Total	S.F.	S.J.	VAL.	L.A.	Total		Black	Span.	White	Other	Total
All families	100.0	100.0	100.0	100.0[2]	100.0	100.0	100.0	100.0	100.0[2]		100.0	100.0	100.0	100.0	100.0[2]
Families with no ill members	79.1	66.7	58.1	69.0	72.3	70.4	69.2	64.6	69.0		75.6	74.6	56.7	79.5	69.0
Husband, ill health	9.7	17.2	26.2	16.5	10.7	17.3	12.8	25.3	16.5		11.4	14.0	24.3	9.1	16.5
Wife, ill health	1.5	5.1	5.5	4.0	4.7	4.3	4.3	2.7	4.0		5.1	3.6	3.8	2.3	4.0
Children, ill health	7.6	8.2	6.8	7.8	9.3	6.0	9.7	6.0	7.8		5.7	6.1	11.3	6.8	7.8
Other, ill health	2.1	2.8	3.4	2.7	3.0	2.0	4.0	1.4	2.7		2.2	1.7	3.9	2.3	2.7

[1]Where more than one member of the family was listed, the first person listed was chosen to be included in the table. Thus, the base for the table is 1200 families.
[2]N = 1199 families; NR = 1 (0.1%).

Table 7-13
Percent of Husbands Listing Difficulties in Getting a Job

Types of Difficulties	Cases Classified by Dependency				Cases Classified by Area					Cases Classified by Ethnicity				
	NOA	STA	LTA	Total	S.F.	S.J.	VAL.	L.A.	Total	Black	Span.	White	Other	Total
Had to stand in line too long	11.8	17.6	15.1	15.2^1	13.8	28.1	15.7	3.4	15.2^1	8.3	20.0	15.7	13.6	15.2^1
Age problem	14.7	19.9	28.0	19.8^2	18.5	28.5	12.7	19.5	19.8^2	8.9	20.4	27.9	18.2	19.8^2
Can't get into union	6.1	13.1	16.5	11.5^3	24.0	10.5	5.0	6.4	11.5^3	16.1	9.4	10.3	9.1	11.5^3
Pay too low	16.6	25.6	14.3	20.4^4	21.3	30.1	26.7	3.7	20.4^4	13.9	23.8	22.6	13.6	20.4^4
Only swing or graveyard shift available	2.6	1.8	2.1	2.1^5	2.0	4.4	1.7	0.3	2.1^5	2.2	2.5	1.8	0.0	2.1^5
Takes days just to find a few hours work	16.4	27.3	19.4	19.4^6	22.1	28.5	32.1	6.0	19.4^6	15.9	24.4	26.1	9.3	19.4^6
Had to travel too far in looking for work	18.2	26.3	19.8	22.3^7	20.3	26.7	27.0	15.4	22.3^7	16.9	26.4	23.0	15.9	22.3^7
Transportation costs too high	14.3	21.6	17.3	18.3^8	10.7	22.7	26.3	13.7	18.3^8	12.1	18.0	23.6	20.4	18.3^8
No money for union initiation fees	4.4	17.6	18.1	15.0^9	22.0	19.5	11.3	7.3	15.0^9	16.1	15.7	13.5	13.6	15.0^9

Do not know anyone in area because I'm new here	11.7	7.9	7.2	9.0^{10}	9.3	16.1	6.7	4.0	9.0^{10}	5.4	12.1	8.8	6.8	9.0^{10}
Can't get into apprentice program	7.1	13.5	15.6	11.8^{11}	15.1	19.3	5.7	7.3	11.8^{11}	8.6	14.1	12.5	6.8	11.8^{11}
Ethnic or racial discrimination	12.5	12.8	16.9	13.5^{12}	24.7	12.3	6.0	11.0	13.5^{12}	29.2	13.9	2.0	2.3	13.5^{12}
Ill health (self)	8.4	17.0	28.3	16.4^{13}	13.0	20.4	14.0	18.3	16.4^{13}	11.1	13.2	24.5	13.6	16.4^{13}
Ill health (family member)	1.0	2.8	3.8	2.4^{14}	3.3	2.3	2.7	1.3	2.4^{14}	1.6	2.0	3.3	4.5	2.4^{14}
Lacks skill and/or training	36.2	53.4	53.6	47.8^{15}	42.3	56.3	48.0	44.7	47.8^{15}	36.4	51.6	53.5	40.9	47.8^{15}
Language barrier	3.1	2.3	4.6	3.0^{16}	3.7	3.7	1.7	3.0	3.0^{16}	0.9	4.8	2.5	4.5	3.0^{16}
No car	0.5	0.4	0.4	0.4^{17}	0.3	0.3	0.3	0.7	0.4^{17}	0.0	0.2	1.0	0.0	0.4^{17}
Lack of education	4.1	3.2	4.6	3.8^{18}	4.3	2.0	3.3	5.3	3.8^{18}	2.2	3.9	4.3	9.1	3.8^{18}
Other	14.3	20.3	18.1	17.9^{19}	23.3	20.4	9.3	18.7	17.9^{19}	20.5	14.8	19.8	13.6	17.9^{19}
Little or no trouble	31.9	14.0	5.5	18.2^{20}	19.0	19.4	13.7	20.7	18.2^{20}	14.9	23.5	15.3	15.9	18.2^{20}

[1] $N = 1189$
[2] $N = 1189$
[3] $N = 1195$
[4] $N = 1195$
[5] $N = 1196$
[6] $N = 1196$
[7] $N = 1199$
[8] $N = 1199$
[9] $N = 1198$
[10] $N = 1198$
[11] $N = 1199$
[12] $N = 1199$
[13] $N = 1199$
[14] $N = 1200$
[15] $N = 1200$
[16] $N = 1200$
[17] $N = 1200$
[18] $N = 1200$
[19] $N = 1200$
[20] $N = 1199$

employment. However, the Spanish-speaking group is high (most barriers) and the black cases low (least barriers).

These various facts indicate that in certain respects, a direct connection exists between objective conditions and the perception of such conditions. In the case of the Valley families who show high handicaps by contrast with urban families, self-perception only partially reflects these objective conditions. A number of factors may intervene between objective condition and subjective evaluation, such as resignation, a sense of defeat, apathy, etc. It is frequently argued, for example, that the rising expectations of blacks create an increased sensitivity to the barriers that block them. Thus, we would expect the black cases to place the heaviest emphasis on barriers to employment. However, the data in Table 7-13 do not support this theory.

A number of explanations might be given for these results. It may be that it is black leadership and the mobile black population who vocally express dissatisfaction, whereas the people who were included in our sample are neither leaders nor mobile. They are the group with the least chance for socioeconomic mobility. This may affect their assessment of their situation.

Given the complexities of psychological situations that may make people's attitudes diverge from objective elements in their situation, the most frequent pattern to be seen in the self-evaluation of these families is the tendency to interpret their objective condition with considerable accuracy. Lack of skill appears to be the dominant barrier to employment as these men evaluate their situation.

Sources of Aid in Finding Jobs

Many viewpoints have been expressed about how low-income workers go about searching for work including the belief that they really don't make any effort to find work at all. While the data in Table 7-14 do not throw any light on this latter point, they do provide some evidence from workers themselves concerning the search for jobs.

The source used by the largest percentage of respondents in the search for employment is the State Employment Service (62%), and according to these men, their use of this agency is current. The second most frequent use is of want ads (60%); the third source, friends (45%); the fourth, unions (27%); and the fifth is past or present employers (20%).

As with the subject of barriers to employment, it is possible to compare the respondents' statements about job-finding with certain objective conditions of their socioeconomic environment. The Valley cases could be expected to make infrequent use of unions as a mechanism in job-finding, and this expectation is borne out by their answers. Similarly, the expectation that San Francisco cases would show the most frequent use of unions is affirmed. Based on the analysis of the respondents' social life given in Chapter 5, a gradient of declining use of friends could be expected when the cases are classified by dependency; and the data in Table 7-14 support this hypothesis. Where seasonality in employment is high, we might expect that employers would be less significant as an aid in employment, and the data show the Valley cases to be low in the use of this source by comparison with the urban areas. Equally so, use of want ads in the Valley might be expected to be low, and such is the case.

The NOA cases show the lowest use of the State Employment Service when compared with the other two dependency groups, and this may well be due to their greater continuity of employment and less frequent change of jobs. In general, the informants' statements about the use made of various aids in finding jobs seem to correspond with known conditions of their environment.

Frequency of use does not correspond to the importance that a given agency or source may have. Consequently, the respondents were asked to rank the importance of the various sources of aid in job finding The results are given in Table 7-15. The rank order from first to sixth in importance was as follows: self-help, friends, employment service, unions, want ads, and relatives. The figures in the table indicate that the importance or value attached to various ways of finding jobs is spread over several sources rather than being concentrated in one channel, such as friends or relatives. It should also be noted that relatives are low in significance (8.1%) as an aid in the job-finding process (confirming this particular limitation of kinship functions as described in Chapter 4).

Perhaps the most important pattern in the rankings of the respondents is the fact that individual and interpersonal sources of aid in finding work are first and second in importance.[5] The remaining sources of aid are all impersonal in character, with the exception of relatives. In Chapters 4 and 5, the conclusion was drawn that the social world of the sample families is a local social world characterized by informal relationships. This same attribute is manifested in the channels that are rated as important in finding work.

In looking at the job-finding process, we can guess about the relative importance of ethnic status. Friends constituted the second most important source of aid in finding jobs. While no questions were asked of the respondents concerning the ethnic status of their friends, it is safe to assume that the vast majority of a man's friends were of the same ethnic group as himself. It is plausible, then, that a major aspect of the job-finding process takes place within the confines of ethnic group relationships.

Orientations to the Work Experience Itself

Table 7-16 and 7-17 are based on those qualities of the work experience that were spontaneously mentioned by the respondents in answer to a general question about their likes and dislikes on either present or past jobs. The two tables show clearly that pecuniary elements in work are of transcendent importance; statements about money are mentioned most often—whether it be

---
[5] Bakke's (1940) analysis of the job-finding process points toward the same conclusion as does the BLS Study of the unemployed reported on by Kalish (1966).

Table 7-14
Percent of Husbands Using Various Sources of Aid in Finding Jobs

Sources of Aid	Cases Classified by Dependency				Cases Classified by Area					Cases Classified by Ethnicity				
	NOA	STA	LTA	Total	S.F.	S.J.	VAL.	L.A.	Total	Black	Span.	White	Other	Total
Union Membership	22.7	31.3	28.2	27.9[1]	38.0	34.6	18.6	20.3	27.9[1]	30.0	27.2	27.5	22.7	27.9[1]
All periods	100.0	100.0	100.0	100.0[2]	100.0	100.0	100.0	100.0	100.0[2]	100.0	100.0	100.0	100.0	100.0[2]
Before 1940	0.0	1.7	1.6	1.2	2.6	0.0	0.0	1.6	1.2	2.1	1.7	0.0	0.0	1.2
1940 – 1950	9.0	2.8	10.4	6.0	7.0	2.9	8.9	6.6	6.0	5.3	2.5	10.9	0.0	6.0
1950 – 1960	18.0	22.3	22.4	21.2	18.4	16.3	26.8	29.5	21.2	23.2	17.5	21.8	40.0	21.2
Since 1960	61.8	54.2	50.7	55.5	55.3	60.6	51.8	50.8	55.5	53.6	65.0	46.4	60.0	55.5
Undetermined	11.2	19.0	14.9	16.1	16.7	20.2	12.5	11.5	16.1	15.8	13.3	20.9	0.0	16.1
Aid from Friends	46.9	46.7	39.2	45.3[3]	44.7	44.0	49.2	43.3	45.3[3]	44.6	44.8	46.4	45.5	45.3[3]
All circumstances	100.0	100.0	100.0	100.0[4]	100.0	100.0	100.0	100.0	100.0[4]	100.0	100.0	100.0	100.0	100.0[4]
Present job only	31.0	13.9	12.9	19.5	26.1	19.7	17.7	14.6	19.5	17.7	24.4	15.1	25.0	19.5
Several jobs	65.2	80.1	81.7	75.3	67.2	75.0	80.3	78.5	75.3	76.6	68.5	82.7	65.0	75.3
All jobs	3.8	6.0	5.4	5.2	6.7	5.3	2.0	6.9	5.2	5.7	7.1	2.2	10.0	5.2
Past or Present Employers	16.0	24.6	15.6	20.0[5]	17.6	26.6	22.0	14.0	20.0[5]	17.7	15.6	27.2	15.9	20.0[5]
All periods	100.0	100.0	100.0	100.0[6]	100.0	100.0	100.0	100.0	100.0[6]	100.0	100.0	100.0	100.0	100.0[6]
Before 1940	0.0	1.4	0.0	0.8	0.0	1.3	1.5	0.0	0.8	0.0	1.4	0.9	0.0	0.8
1940 – 1950	0.0	0.7	8.1	1.7	0.0	3.8	0.0	2.5	1.7	1.8	1.4	1.8	0.0	1.7
1950 – 1960	15.9	10.6	16.2	12.9	24.5	7.5	6.1	19.0	12.9	21.4	5.8	11.0	42.9	12.9
1960 and after	76.2	66.0	51.4	66.3	60.4	64.9	78.8	57.1	66.3	60.7	69.7	67.9	57.1	66.3
Undetermined	7.9	21.3	24.3	18.3	15.1	22.5	13.6	21.4	18.3	16.1	21.7	18.4	0.0	18.3

	1	2	3	4	5	6	7	8	9	10	11	12	13	14
Employment Service	42.7	71.7	73.0	62.5^{7}	62.4	64.3	63.2	59.9	62.5^{7}	59.7	60.8	67.1	56.8	62.5^{7}
All periods	100.0	100.0	100.0	100.0^{8}	100.0	100.0	100.0	100.0	100.0^{8}	100.0	100.0	100.0	100.0	100.0^{8}
Before 1955	6.6	2.5	2.3	3.3	3.8	3.6	1.1	5.0	3.3	4.8	3.0	3.0	0.0	3.3
1955 – 1959	8.4	3.7	2.9	4.6	6.5	4.2	4.8	2.8	4.6	5.3	3.4	4.9	8.0	4.6
1960 or since	84.4	91.6	93.1	90.4	88.6	88.6	92.0	92.2	90.4	89.4	91.0	90.6	88.0	90.4
Yes, but not date specified	0.6	2.2	1.7	1.7	1.1	3.6	2.1	0.0	1.7	0.5	2.6	1.5	4.0	1.7
Want Ads	49.9	63.1	70.0	60.2^{9}	60.5	65.1	38.8	76.4	60.2^{9}	56.1	53.3	71.6	54.5	60.2^{9}
Organizations, Lodge, Church or Similar	4.3	9.5	5.9	7.1^{10}	9.0	7.0	7.7	4.7	7.1^{10}	5.4	6.6	8.8	9.1	7.1^{10}
Minister or Other Person Who Wasn't Exactly a Friend	3.8	6.3	8.1	5.8^{11}	9.4	5.3	3.7	5.0	5.8^{11}	6.0	5.9	5.8	4.5	5.8^{11}
Self-Help	10.4	13.3	14.7	12.6^{12}	18.0	14.3	13.0	5.3	12.6^{12}	11.0	7.5	19.0	18.1	12.6^{12}

[1] $N = 1199$ husbands; NR = 1 (0.1%).
[2] $N = 335$ husbands; those who claimed a union had been of some help at some time.
[3] $N = 1199$ husbands; NR = 1 (0.1%).
[4] $N = 543$ husbands; those who did get aid from friends.
[5] $N = 1198$ husbands; NR = 2 (0.2%).
[6] $N = 241$ husbands; those who listed aid from past and present employers.
[7] $N = 1196$ husbands; NR = 3 (0.3%).
[8] $N = 748$ husbands; those who did use the Employment Service.
[9] $N = 1196$ husbands; NR = 4 (0.3%).
[10] $N = 1198$ husbands; NR = 2 (0.2%).
[11] $N = 1199$ husbands; NR = 1 (0.1%).
[12] $N = 1197$ husbands; NR = 3 (0.3%).

Table 7-15
Percentage Distribution of Husbands' Statements Concerning the Most Important Ways of Getting a Job[1]

Sources of Job Information	Cases Classified by Dependency				Cases Classified by Area					Cases Classified by Ethnicity				
	NOA	STA	LTA	Total	S.F.	S.J.	VAL.	L.A.	Total	Black	Span.	White	Other	Total
All Sources	100.0	100.0	100.0	100.0	100.0	100.0	100.0	100.0	100.0	100.0	100.0	100.0	100.0	100.0
Employment service	12.2	17.1	18.2	15.8	13.6	16.2	18.2	14.9	15.8	14.9	15.4	16.6	16.9	15.8
Job training	3.6	4.0	3.9	3.9	5.4	4.5	1.7	4.0	3.9	4.5	4.2	3.1	3.9	3.9
Friends	21.8	19.1	18.2	19.8	18.8	18.8	22.7	18.6	19.8	20.3	20.2	18.5	24.7	19.8
Relatives	11.1	7.6	4.5	8.1	9.1	7.9	10.0	5.6	8.1	8.0	9.1	7.3	7.8	8.1
Organizations	0.9	1.5	0.7	1.2	1.7	0.9	0.7	1.5	1.2	1.8	0.7	1.3	1.3	1.2
Want ads	9.6	9.4	14.5	10.4	8.4	10.5	4.0	18.7	10.4	6.9	10.1	13.2	7.8	10.4
Unions	10.7	10.5	10.9	10.6	16.0	15.5	4.7	6.8	10.6	14.3	12.1	7.4	5.2	10.6
Employers	5.7	6.0	5.2	5.7	4.7	7.3	9.3	1.7	5.7	5.3	4.9	6.7	7.8	5.7
Other[2]	24.5	24.8	23.9	24.5	22.3	18.4	28.7	28.2	24.5	24.0	23.3	25.9	24.6	24.5

[1]From a list of nine items, each respondent was asked to list the three most important sources of aid to him in getting jobs. The 1200 husbands gave 2350 answers. There were 1250 "no" responses.
[2]This category includes those specifying "self-help."

Table 7-16
Positive Characteristics of Work, Rank Ordered by Percent of Husbands Listing Each Characteristic[1]

Job Likes	Cases Classified by Dependency				Cases Classified by Area					Cases Classified by Ethnicity				
	NOA	STA	LTA	Total	S.F.	S.J.	VAL.	L.A.	Total	Black	Span.	White	Other	Total
Provides a living (money)	40.6	41.9	37.3	40.5	35.7	40.3	59.3	26.8	40.5	37.7	39.4	41.8	61.4	40.5
Friendships/association with nice people	22.7	22.9	22.4	22.8	29.0	22.3	24.3	15.3	22.8	22.8	21.1	23.5	31.8	22.8

	Cases Classified by Dependency				Cases Classified by Area					Cases Classified by Ethnicity				
	NOA	STA	LTA	Total	S.F.	S.J.	VAL.	L.A.	Total	Black	Span.	White	Other	Total
Interesting experience, purposeful	19.4	17.9	17.7	18.3	18.7	16.3	18.7	19.7	18.3	15.2	16.1	23.5	15.9	18.3
Security	19.1	10.5	8.9	13.0	18.7	9.7	12.7	11.0	13.0	13.9	11.6	12.0	29.5	13.0
Brings self-respect	8.7	9.5	8.4	9.0	10.7	8.0	14.7	2.7	9.0	6.3	8.6	10.5	18.2	9.0
Fills the day	8.4	9.5	8.4	8.9	6.3	13.7	11.3	4.3	8.9	5.1	11.8	8.5	11.4	8.9
Chance for advancement	9.2	4.6	4.6	6.1	7.7	5.7	5.7	5.3	6.1	7.6	5.2	5.5	9.1	6.1
High status prestige	0.5	1.9	3.0	1.7	2.3	2.3	1.0	1.0	1.7	1.9	1.8	1.5	0.0	1.7

[1] N = 1200 husbands. Each row constitutes a separate answer for the 1200 respondents.

Table 7-17
Negative Characteristics of Work, Rank Ordered by Percent of Husbands Listing Each Characteristic[1]

Job Dislikes	Cases Classified by Dependency				Cases Classified by Area					Cases Classified by Ethnicity				
	NOA	STA	LTA	Total	S.F.	S.J.	VAL.	L.A.	Total	Black	Span.	White	Other	Total
Pay inadequate	25.3	25.4	20.8	24.4	19.7	21.7	37.7	18.7	24.4	18.7	25.7	27.3	27.3	24.4
Dull, boring, exhausting	9.2	11.0	8.9	10.0	8.0	13.7	7.0	11.3	10.0	8.9	10.2	10.8	9.1	10.0
No chance for advancement	9.7	11.7	5.5	9.8	6.3	6.7	21.3	5.0	9.8	6.3	9.5	12.8	11.4	9.8
Job insecurity	6.6	11.4	7.2	9.0	6.0	7.7	18.4	4.0	9.0	10.1	10.0	7.5	4.5	9.0
Forces association with people one does not like	4.1	4.7	4.6	4.5	5.7	5.3	2.0	5.0	4.5	4.1	3.2	6.3	4.5	4.5
Low status, no prestige	2.6	3.0	2.1	2.7	2.7	2.7	4.0	1.3	2.7	2.8	2.3	3.0	2.3	2.7
Uninteresting	2.6	2.5	2.1	2.4	1.3	2.7	3.7	2.0	2.4	1.6	3.0	2.5	2.3	2.4
Reduces self-respect	0.8	2.6	2.5	2.0	2.3	2.3	2.0	1.3	2.0	2.5	1.6	1.8	4.5	2.0

[1] N = 1200 husbands. Each row constitutes a separate answer for the 1200 respondents.

in positive or negative terms. The second most frequent topic on the side of positive statements concerns interpersonal relations. Friends and positive human relationships at work were the focus of the respondents' comments. On the negative side, the statements referred to boredom, exhaustion, and dullness—all matters that have to do with the personal reaction of these men to their work condition.[6]

Several differences in the answers of the various subgroups fit the known conditions of their work environment or job histories. In terms of positive responses to the work situation, the LTA cases mentioned the security that work provided less often than the NOA cases. In terms of dislikes about the work situation itself, the inadequacy of pay is mentioned almost twice as often by the Valley cases when compared with the other geographic areas. Job insecurity was mentioned almost three times as often by Valley cases as by the urban respondents. A final comparison concerns both positive and negative statements about the chance for advancement. The group responding most frequently to this aspect of work, whether in a positive or negative vein, was the NOA cases, and the group responding least often was the LTA cases. It is clear that advancement on the job is a matter of greater significance to the NOA cases than it is to the Long-Time Aid group.

In bringing together the husbands' statements about barriers and aids in the job-finding process and their reactions to work itself, certain key points stand out that add to the conclusions derived from the analysis of the husbands' work histories. Ill health, lack of skill and training, and age were seen by these men as key barriers to employment. Variation in the use of friends and relatives as aids in finding work is still another important point. It was also possible to look at the total responses of each subgroup on the question about barriers to employment to ascertain which subgroup saw the most and least barriers to finding jobs. In terms of likes and dislikes on the job, a differential concern with opportunities for advancement showed up as a significant issue.

If these seven issues are listed in terms of the subgroups that ranked highest and lowest in frequency of response, we can ascertain if the husbands' answers are patterned by dependency status, geographic status, or ethnic status. On all seven indexes, it was found that the NOA group ranked low and the LTA group ranked high. For the three dependency groups, the NOA cases mentioned ill health least often, listed lack of training least often, indicated age as a barrier least often, listed fewer barriers to work (in the aggregate), made the most frequent use of friends and relatives in job-finding i.e., showed *the lowest* social withdrawal, and mentioned advancement on the job most frequently (whether positively or negatively). When the cases were classified by geography, there was no such clear pattern, but for the ethnic subgroups, whites were high on five of seven points and blacks were low on six of the seven issues.

---

[6]These conclusions about the meaning of work for lower lower-class workers are consistent with a number of other studies, particularly Friedmann and Havighurst (1962), Morse and Weiss (1962), Bakke (1940), McConnell (1942), Miller and Form (1964), and Komarovsky (1964).

We can draw the same conclusion that was made in the case of the work history data. In terms of perceived handicaps in the search for work and in response to work itself, dependency is the most important—though not the only—factor surrounding the relationship of these men to the world of work.

Summary and Interpretation of Economic Characteristics

The data on the work histories of the 1200 husbands show their occupational status to be predominantly that of unskilled and semiskilled workers and furthermore show them to be fixed in status. Their low wages coupled with lack of continuity in employment point to the economic insecurity that is endemic to the entire group.

In level of living, the median per capita income of the family varies from $700 per person for a three-person family to $400 per capita for families with ten or more members. In terms of income and occupational history, this group shows much the same disadvantaged position in the past that they manifest in the present.

It seems evident that this sample of families is close to the bottom of the present low-income population in the United States. When matched with a comparable sample of workers during the 1930s, they show little if any difference in economic security. The data on savings, insurance, and other foresight practices indicate that they have little or no cushion to protect themselves from unemployment and have no prospect of economic security in old age except for the federal government's old-age insurance program.

In their linkage to the larger society, these people show only a minor usage of financial institutions that are characteristically utilized by middle-class families. Data on onwership of TV and of items related to reading indicate that their primary connection to the larger society is via TV and not by means of the printed word.

Their mode of finding jobs focuses on interpersonal relations, though they also make use of institutions such as the State Employment Service. Some 31% of these families indicated illness that impedes one or more members in their work or schooling. In the search for work, the chief barrier that they see to employment is a lack of skill and training. Other important barriers are low pay and problems associated with age.

In all these characteristics, small but patterned differences emerge when the subgroups of the sample are compared. If each of these characteristics is considered as a scale indicating a greater or lesser degree of economic handicap, the subgroups can be ranked as occupying a high or low position with reference to each characteristic. It was found that certain groups consistently ranked high and low in handicaps. This patterning or correlation of the differences between subgroups was strongest when the cases were classified by dependency status, less strong when classified by rural-urban status, and least when classified by ethnic status. The NOA group was characteristically low in handicaps by contrast with the high handicapped position occupied by the LTA groups. The rural cases showed more economic handicaps than the cases from the three urban areas. A minor pattern indicated more handicaps for the Spanish-speaking cases and fewer handicaps for the black subgroup.

Section IV:
The Orientation of the Cases

8 Psychological Dependency and Anomie

The topic of this chapter is the orientation of our respondents to the world about them. The issue involved is whether or not their general orientation or subjective outlook is in any way connected with welfare dependency, rural-urban status, or ethnic status. Are these families characteristically defeated and apathetic or are they rebellious and resentful of their life conditions? Are they impulse-dominated or puritanical in outlook? Is their general orientation a homogeneous one, or are there wide variations in their outlook depending on their ethnic or welfare dependency status?

In attempting to characterize a person's general orientation to his world, the range of possible subjects to be investigated seems almost endless. In Chapter 10, a systematic framework designed to measure the *central* elements in a person's value system has been adapted for use with the sample families. In this chapter, two *specific* subjects have been selected for investigation. The first subject is that of psychological dependency and the second is that of anomie.

Psychological dependency was chosen as a topic of investigation first because of the widespread belief that it is a cause of welfare dependency. Secondly, investigation of this dimension requires a consideration of the viewpoint that the individual's orientation to his world is in significant degree a product of his personality. His personality, in turn, is primarily a product of childhood experience.

The essential quality of dependency is that of reliance on others. It implies a relationship where one receives but does not give in return. Psychological dependency thus signifies lack of reciprocity in interpersonal relations. The dependent person may appear to rebel against being subjected to control by others, but his reliance on others is the underlying and dominant motif of his interpersonal relationships.

The first attitude scale was chosen to measure the husband's psychological dependency. A second scale was chosen to measure intergenerational tendencies toward psychological dependency within a family. Husbands were asked questions relating to dependency in their children and questions about how closely they were tied to their own parents. To extend the analysis of the dependency dimension, the husbands were asked additional questions about taking responsibility for their children.

The second topic is that of anomie. As such, the subject of anomie refers to a most general orientation of the individual toward his world—an orientation that is diffused throughout all the particular attitudes that makes up his subjective outlook. The anomic individual feels himself to be in a state of normlessness, i.e., that he is not governed by rules, and that he is lacking attachment to any groups within society.

From the sociological point of view, anomie is a product of social disorganization or rapid social change. The individual's feelings of anomie are, presumably, a product of his current social environment. Thus, feelings of anomie could be expected to change as one's social environment changes. According to the theory, the degree of anomic feelings expressed by the 1200 husbands should reflect their current social and economic conditions. If we stress the strong kinship ties and informal social relations that seem to characterize the life of low-income families, we might expect the respondents to show a low level of anomie. On the other hand, the lack of control over their own economic fortunes and the lack of achievement and recognition by the larger society may result in strong feelings of anomie. It can also be argued that the social withdrawal manifested by the LTA cases would create strong feelings of anomie. The anomie test is an attitude scale made up of questions drawn from previously published work and additional questions made up for this study.

Appendix B contains a detailed discussion of how the various items in the attitude scales were chosen, and also lists the questions that were contained in the questionnaire. The Appendix also contains a description of the scoring procedure that was used and includes the tables that were developed to test the significance of the difference between the mean scores of the subgroups of the sample.

The attitude items were scored on a five-point scale ranging from strongly disagree to strongly agree, and with assigned numerical values from minus two to plus two. Table 8-1 presents the average score for each subgroup for each attitude scale. The higher the score, the higher an individual's psychological dependency. An average score of zero places an individual at the midpoint of the scale. An average score of +2 represents the highest degree of dependency, and a score of −2 the lowest degree. The anomie items were scored in the same way.

The data in Table 8-1 indicate, in the main, that the husband's attitudes are on the high side of the scales measuring dependency and anomie. Without comparative data from other socioeconomic groups, the location of the attitudes of the overall sample on a scale ranging from minus two to plus two has little significance. Consequently, the major analysis in the chapter will necessarily be devoted to a comparison of differences or similarities in the attitudes of the subgroups of the sample.

Psychological Dependency and Intergenerational Influences

The items used to measure the husband's psychological dependency were drawn from an unpublished doctoral dissertation by Lamphere (1953). The questions used in the Lamphere scale were first classified by subject matter. All those questions that ask about the respondent's feelings were classified under the heading of dependency feelings. Those questions that ask about specific actions were classified as dependency behavior. These two categories were further subdivided by the acceptability of the questions. A panel of judges reviewed each question. If the question centered on a subject matter (either feelings or behavior) that would be viewed positively by the public, it was classified as acceptable. Conversely, if the judges thought that the subject matter of a question would evoke a negative public reaction, it was classified as unacceptable. The terms acceptable and unacceptable do not refer to the reliability or validity of a question, but only to the presumed public attitude toward it. The questions were classified in this manner in an effort to eliminate a "public" bias in answering questions, namely the tendency for respondents to give a positive answer about those elements of their own feelings and behavior that are publicly acceptable, and to give negative answers concerning aspects of their own feelings or behavior that receive a negative public evaluation. Assuming this constant difference in the way respondents will respond to the questions, we can evaluate the answers that were obtained.

The average score for the total sample on the "unacceptable" dependency items (−.46) was lower than on those items labeled "acceptable" dependency (+1.11), thus confirming the expectation that they tend to disagree with items classified as "unacceptable." With the exception of this uniformity, the subgroups of the sample differed widely in their responses to the questions.

These differences fall into readily identifiable patterns when the subgroups showing highest and lowest scores are tabulated. These results are given in Table 8-2 and indicate systematic differences in psychological dependency (as measured by these tests) when the cases are classified by welfare experience and by ethnic status. The NOA group is consistently low and the LTA groups consistently high on these tests. The Spanish-speaking cases show equally high scores and the white cases low scores.

These first results point to a pattern which is sustained in all the other attitude tests, and immediately forces recognition that in matters of subjective orientation ethnicity is as important a factor as dependency. Stated in another way, we can say that a high psychological dependency score is correlated not only with a long experience on public assistance, but also with status in a Spanish-speaking ethnic group. When classified by geographic location, the cases do not show a consistent pattern of responses by rural-urban status.

One difference between the orientation of the LTA cases and the Spanish-speaking cases should be noted. The LTA group is high on both unacceptable dependent behavior and on acceptable feelings of dependency, whereas the Spanish-speaking group is not so high on acceptable feelings of dependency.

The attitude items measuring the husbands' orientation toward their children and the husbands' orientation toward their own parents were drawn from the Parental Attitude Research Instrument constructed by Schaefer and Bell (1958). The scale labeled "dependency on family of orientation" was designed to measure how closely an adult feels tied to his own parents. It asks how much he depends upon his own parents and to what extent he may consider his ties to

Table 8-1
Mean Scores of Respondents on 14 Attitude Scales[1]

Attitude Scale	Cases Classified by Dependency				Cases Classified by Area					Cases Classified by Ethnicity				
	NOA	STA	LTA	Total[2]	S.F.	S.J.	VAL.	L.A.	Total	Black	Span.	White	Other	Total
Dependency feeling scale	.17	.19	.28	.20	.16	.32	.18	.15	.20	.17	.36	.06	.19	.20
Dependency acceptable feeling scale	.90	.96	.97	.94	.93	.92	.97	.93	.94	1.03	.93	.89	.97	.94
Dependency unacceptable feeling scale	−.56	−.58	−.42	−.54	−.60	−.32	−.60	−.63	−.54	−.70	−.22	−.77	−.58	−.54
Dependency behavior scale	.42	.44	.54	.45	.36	.50	.53	.42	.45	.42	.59	.34	.39	.45
Dependency acceptable behavior scale	1.30	1.27	1.30	1.29	1.19	1.25	1.41	1.29	1.29	1.29	1.32	1.24	1.28	1.29
Dependency unacceptable behavior scale	−.47	−.39	−.23	−.38	−.48	−.25	−.35	−.46	−.38	−.46	−.15	−.56	−.50	−.38
Total acceptable dependency scale	1.10	1.12	1.37	1.11	1.06	1.10	1.17	1.11	1.11	1.16	1.12	1.06	1.13	1.11
Total unacceptable dependency scale	−.51	−.48	−.32	−.46	−.54	−.28	−.47	−.55	−.46	−.58	−.18	−.67	−.54	−.46
Dependency on family of orientation - P.A.R.I. scale	.28	.28	.49	.32	.33	.36	.34	.27	.32	.33	.52	.12	.09	.32
Fostering child dependency - P.A.R.I. scale	.96	1.09	1.16	1.06	1.03	.99	1.25	1.03	1.06	1.15	1.28	.76	.87	1.06

Autonomy of child - P.A.R.I. scale	.19	.30	.48	.30	.44	.23	.12	.40	.30	.61	.06	.30	.42	.30
Child acceptance of responsibility	.83	1.01	.93	.94	.97	.96	.98	.92	.94	1.06	.88	.90	.85	.94
Anomie scale	-.11	.01	.18	.01	.04	.01	-.01	-.02	.01	.02	.24	-.23	-.26	.01
Gildea Responsibility Scale	.10	.08	.02	.08	-.06	.17	.14	.06	.08	-.12	.23	.05	.32	.08

[1] Attitude Scale scoring formula:

Where:
- a = scoring weights 2, 1, 0, -1, -2
- n = number of persons per group
- m = number of items per scale
- j = jth item in scale
- i = ith score per item

[2] Mean N of Entire Series = 1182.3 persons.

Table 8-2
Subgroups Showing High and Low Scores on Psychological Dependency Scales

Dependency Scales	Cases Classified by Dependency		Cases Classified by Area		Cases Classified by Ethnicity	
	High	Low	High	Low	High	Low
Dependency feeling scale	LTA	NOA	S.J.	L.A.	Spanish	White
Dependency acceptable feeling scale	LTA	NOA	VAL.	S.J.	Black	White
Dependency unacceptable feeling scale	LTA	STA	S.J.	S.F. VAL.	Spanish	White
Dependency behavior scale	LTA	NOA	VAL.	L.A.	Spanish	White
Dependency acceptable behavior scale	Tied Ranks[1]		VAL.	S.F.	Spanish	White
Dependency unacceptable behavior scale	LTA	NOA	S.J.	S.F.	Spanish	White
Total acceptable dependency scale	LTA	NOA	VAL.	S.F.	Black	White
Total unacceptable dependency scale	LTA	NOA	S.J.	L.A.	Spanish	White

[1] Tied ranks were determined as follows:: Using the appropriate value in Appendix Table B-4, we defined the difference between the low and high group as "tied ranks" if it was greater than the 5% level of significance. If two groups had scores at one end of the continuum from low to high, and there was only a chance difference between these two scores, but better than chance difference between them and the contrasting high or low score, then these two scores were recorded in the table. If as many as three scores were no better than a chance difference apart, then all the scores were defined as tied ranks.

them as transcendent over his ties to his own wife and children. Three questions from the Schaefer and Bell attitude scale were chosen.

Table 8-3 shows the rank order position of the subgroups on this test as well as on two tests concerned with the children of these families. The high and low groups by dependency and ethnicity are the same as were identified by the first set of tests.

The second scale, included in Table 8-3, is labeled "autonomy of the child." This scale is intended to measure the father's stated desire for his child to maintain his own independence and to learn by experience. The third scale reported on in Table 8-3 is constructed to measure the tendency of parents to foster dependency in their children.

When the high and low groups are compared on these two tests, the NOA cases scored low both in their tendency to create autonomy in their children and in their tendency to induce dependency. Conversely, the LTA husbands score high in the tendency to develop autonomy in their children at the same time that they tend to foster dependency. The Spanish-speaking cases scored low in autonomy of the child and high in tendency to foster dependency in their children. This finding indicates an important difference between the Spanish-speaking and the LTA cases.

If the results of the items chosen from Lamphere's scales and the PARI instrument are combined two clear patterns emerge. The first of these has already been noted, namely, that differences between ethnic groups form consistent patterns, and these differences are as large as the difference between the cases when classified by dependency status. The Spanish-speaking husbands show high reliance on their own parents, foster dependency in their children, and show high psychological dependency themselves as measured by the test scores. The white cases show just the opposite pattern. The pattern of scores for the LTA cases looks much like the Spanish-speaking cases, but with two major differences. First, the Spanish-speaking families did not show as high a level of dependent feelings as did the LTA families. Second, the Spanish-speaking families, according to the husbands' responses, foster dependency in their children but are also low in their demands that the child achieve autonomy, whereas the LTA families demand both autonomy and dependence from their children. These variations indicate that family dynamics in the Long-Time Aid families and the Spanish-speaking families are significantly different.

The second pattern is the tendency within the subgroups of the sample for intergenerational continuity in degree of psychological dependency. The husband's description of his relationship to his parents resembles his description of his relationship to his own children and, in turn, resembles his description of himself. A rather considerable caution needs to be exercised in treating these answers as fully accurate accounts of actual happenings, for the statements are all being made by one individual at one time in response to a questionnaire. The possibility is always present that he is projecting himself into each situation and reading into the past what his present feelings are, even though the past and the present may be different.

Taking into account the complicating effects that may arise from the projective tendencies of the respondents, it still seems plausible that the husband's reports reflect the quality of his relationships to his own parents and to his own children. The respondent's answers refer, then, not to episodes or events, but to the developmental character of a family relationship as it has taken place and is taking place. The quality of these relationships has been labeled "psychological dependency."[1] However, the consequences of such dependency in the adult conduct of the 1200 husbands do not necessarily imply welfare or financial dependency. Rather, the quality of psychological dependency appears to be correlated with *both* ethnic status and welfare dependency experience.

Responsibility and Child-Rearing

The first scale measures the parent's feelings about handling responsibility for his or her children, and is drawn from work done by Gildea (1961) who found that these items discriminated between persons of middle- and lower-class status. Gildea states that the items measure a feeling of "potency." Mothers who felt that they were capable of taking charge of their own children successfully rated high in potency.

The second scale consists of three questions utilized in Shannon's study of assimilation of immigrants to Racine, Wisconsin (reported in Shannon and Krass, 1964). The three questions ask whether or not the parent feels that his children are less obedient, less respectful, and less willing to face hardships today than children were in the old days.

The results of administering these two scales are given in Table 8-4. The items from the Gildea scale do not show significant differences between dependency groups, but there are significant differences on both scales for the cases when classified by geography and ethnicity. It is interesting to note that the Spanish-speaking husbands show the strongest feelings of self-responsibility for their children, as well as feeling that their children are capable of taking responsibility. The blacks fall at the other end of both scales, considering their children to be less responsible and feeling themselves less potent in handling responsibility for their children.

The scores of the Spanish-speaking group on these two scales aid in interpreting the meaning of this group's high psychological dependency scores. The emphasis by the Spanish-speaking husbands on child responsibility and valuation of the child's ability to accept responsibility indicates that what might otherwise be called psychological dependency may in its behavioral consequence constitute interdependency insofar as family interpersonal relations are concerned.

---

[1] A further discussion of the Lamphere scale based on his factor analysis can be found in Appendix B.

Anomie

The anomie scale contains two items from Shannon's questionnaire, items from a questionnaire by Himelson and Takagi (1963), and new items made up for this particular study. The questions relate to the five attributes of anomie postulated by Srole (1956). These are (1) community leaders are detached and indifferent to one's needs; (2) the social order is fickle, unpredictable, and disorderly, and gives little direction to one's life or the lives of others; (3) people are regressing from the goals they have already reached; (4) there is a loss of meaning of internal group norms, values, and goals; and (5) personal relations are no longer supportive.

It might have been expected that the rural valley cases would show lower anomie scores and higher psychological dependency scores than the respondents living in urban areas. If such rural-urban gradient existed, the San Jose cases would occupy a position somewhere between the Valley cases at the low end of the scale and the San Francisco and Los Angeles cases at the high end of the scale.[2] When the rank order positions of the geographic groups were compared (Tables 8-2 through 8-5), no such pattern emerged. Rather, the San Jose cases occupied a relatively high position in psychological dependency and in anomie. In the main, this effect can be accounted for by the overrepresentation of Spanish-speaking cases in this geographic area. Over and above this confounding factor, an additional potential explanation for the high anomie scores of the San Jose cases may be found in the fact that this city has grown rapidly from an agricultural service center to a city with a diversified economic base.

Turning to the dependency and ethnic classifications of the cases, we note that Table 8-5 indicates the high and low subgroups on the scale. The LTA and Spanish-speaking cases hold the same high position as on the previous scales that have been discussed, and the NOA and white cases show the same low average scores. Thus, the anomie scores predict LTA status and Spanish-speaking status equally well. In the case of the Spanish-speaking subgroup, the characteristics of Latin-American cultures with their strong Catholicism, traditionally strong kinship ties, and tight-knit social organization are the antitheses of the social conditions that presumably produce anomie. Either the social life of the Spanish-speaking people in our sample has become completely different from its cultural origins, or the anomie test is measuring something other than it is supposed to measure.

These results make it quite clear that the meaning of the anomie scores and the psychological dependency scores must be interpreted in terms of the ethnic cultures with which the respondents are identified. A full interpretation of these test results requires that the tests be standardized for the respective ethnic populations. If the cases had not been classified by ethnic status, this important

---

[2] In the discussion of an index of rural-urban status (see Chapter 3), it was concluded that the Santa Clara County cases are somewhat less urban than San Francisco or Los Angeles cases.

Table 8-3
Subgroups Showing High and Low Scores on Scales of Intergenerational Dependency and Child Autonomy

Scales	Cases Classified by Dependency		Cases Classified by Area		Cases Classified by Ethnicity	
	High	Low	High	Low	High	Low
Dependency on family of orientation- P.A.R.I. scale	LTA	NOA			Spanish	White
Fostering dependency - P.A.R.I. scale	LTA	STA	VAL.	S.J.	Spanish	White
Autonomy of child - P.A.R.I. scale	LTA	NOA	S.F.	VAL.	Spanish	White

Table 8-4
Subgroups Showing High and Low Scores on Scales of Child and Parent Responsibility

Scales	Cases Classified by Dependency		Cases Classified by Area		Cases Classified by Ethnicity	
	High	Low	High	Low	High	Low
Child acceptance of responsibility	NOA	STA	S.F.	VAL.	Spanish	Black
(Gildea) Adult responsibility for children	Tied Ranks		S.J. VAL.	S.F.	Spanish	Black

Table 8-5
Subgroups Showing High and Low Scores on the Anomie Scale

Scale	Cases Classified by Dependency		Cases Classified by Area		Cases Classified by Ethnicity	
	High	Low	High	Low	High	Low
Anomie Scale	LTA	NOA	S.F.	L.A.	Spanish	White

qualification would not have been apparent. The function of ethnicity in patterning the orientation of the low-income workers in our sample is in contrast to the findings in the previous chapters. Where measures of kin and non-kin social relations were involved, and where occupation and income facts were concerned, the dependency factor and the rural-urban factor appeared to be the most powerful determinants of the respondent's life style. When the subjective reaction of these men is tapped, the important determinants become ethnic status and welfare dependency status.

The Significance of Dependency

In analyzing the various relationships that have been found, we will discuss the dependency factor first and then the ethnic factor. The data on psychological dependency support the theory that personality factors contribute to the general outlook of the respondents. At the same time, the scores on the anomie test indicate that the current social conditions experienced by these men also contribute to differences in their outlook.

At one end of the range of variation are the LTA family members who manifest the greatest psychological dependency and the highest degree of anomie, whereas the NOA cases show the least psychological dependency and alienation. If we reflect at all on the objective condition of our respondents' lives as described in the preceding chapters, we cannot be surprised at the overall view they have of the world about them.

On the face of things, it might appear that the orientation of these men is the simple mirror image of their socioeconomic environment, but the test data do not lead to this single simple conclusion. While the outlook of a person can be seen as a reaction to his current life circumstances, his subjective viewpoint may also be thought of as a contributor to the circumstances in which he lives. In this case, the individual's orientation tends to be, in part, the determiner of his current condition.

The test data that have been presented indicate that the respondent's orientation or subjective viewpoint is a combined product of present life conditions and of personality characteristics stemming from early experience. The data point to an interactive or feedback effect in which certain aspects of personality—namely, psychological dependency—interact with a range of economic, social, and medical handicaps in the adult life of the individual. The interaction of these factors coupled with extended welfare dependency experience produces a sense of hopelessness and defeat that is manifested in the high anomie scores of the Long-Time Aid cases.

One additional piece of evidence from the attitude test data provides a clue to the effects that the public assistance experience itself may have on those who become welfare cases. Most of the attitude items in the questionnaire that discriminate between dependency groups fall into one of two patterns. The first of these patterns is an upward or downward progression of scores from the NOA

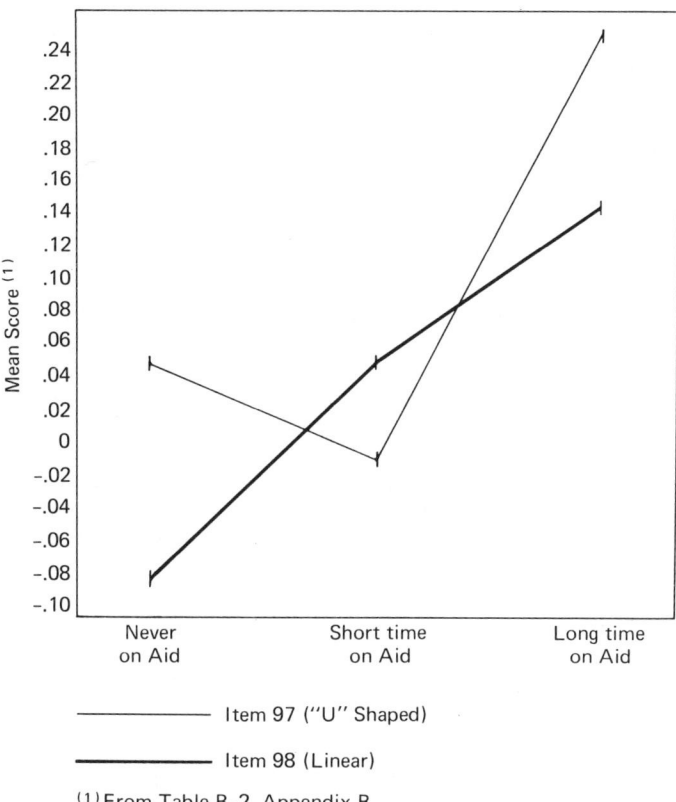

Figure 8-1. Scores of Respondents by Dependency Status for Questionnaire Items 97 and 98.

cases to STA to the LTA cases, in which the relationship is linear. The second pattern is a U or inverted U-shaped distribution in which the scores of the STA cases fall well above or below a straight line connecting the NOA and LTA scores. Items 97 and 98 have been plotted in Figure 8-1 to illustrate such relationships. Out of forty attitude items, only five did not show one of these two patterns. Eighteen of the attitude items showed a U-shaped distribution and seventeen were linear in form. The U-shaped distributions tended to be concentrated in the items related to the anomie scales and the linear distributions were characteristic of the psychological dependency scales.

The U-shaped distributions suggest the possibility that the onset of welfare dependency constitutes a disturbing factor in the orientations of the respondents, causing stronger reactions than would otherwise be expected. While these responses may be those of current STA cases who will eventually become LTA cases, the U-shaped distributions suggest that adjustments to the onset of public assistance are in part a product of the welfare experience itself.

The Significance of Ethnicity

While the scores of the cases, when classified by ethnic status, do not negate the interpretation that has just been given, they do render it more complex. In this connection, it should be noted first that the psychological dependency scores of the Spanish-speaking cases show the same continuity between generations that was found for the LTA cases. Thus, the conclusion that early experience affects present orientation remains unchanged when the cases are classified by ethnicity.

The meaning of the psychological dependency scores is different, however, for the Spanish-speaking subgroup than for the LTA cases. It was noted earlier in the chapter that there was a consistency in the child training practices of the Spanish-speaking cases. That is, while they fostered dependency in their children, they did not also simultaneously demand that their children develop autonomy. In actual conduct, the consequences of psychological dependency in the Spanish-speaking family seem to be translated into family and possibly into kinship interdependency. The evidence in Chapter 4 would indicate that kinship bonds operate as a source of support to lower-class families rather than as a handicap. Thus, the psychological dependency of the Spanish-speaking families takes on its meaning in a somewhat different kind of social system than is true for the white or black families.

It is true that the data in Chapter 4 did not show the Spanish-speaking group to have stronger kinship bonds than the other two ethnic groups, despite the expectation that such differences would be found. Consequently, it might appear that the argument presented here for a strong sense of family ties negates the data on kinship. However, the attitude questions concerning the dependency of our respondents on their parents did not involve other kin members, but only these two key members of the respondent's nuclear family of orientation. Hence, the data on kinship bonds and the scores on the psychological dependency scales reported in this chapter are not actually inconsistent with each other if the argument about strong family ties is limited to members of the nuclear family.

Much the same argument can be made about the high anomie scores of the Spanish-speaking respondents. At the same time that these people manifest high anomie scores in their answers to attitude questions, they also have a positive view of the abilities of their children to accept responsibility. Coupled with the strong solidarity of their nuclear family, it would appear that the Spanish-speaking respondents manifest a high degree of suspicion and mistrust of outsiders and of the larger community. This interpretation is consistent with the results of a recent study of Bay Area Mexican families.[3]

---

[3] Margaret Clark, *Health in the Mexican-American Culture* (Berkeley: University of California Press, 1959).

Using this interpretation of the attitude data on the Spanish-speaking cases, it can be expected that within this ethnic group, a correlation would still be found between psychological dependency and anomie with increasing welfare dependency experience. However, the degree of such psychological dependency and the feelings of powerlessness and loss of attachment, as measured by attitude tests, would be higher than in LTA cases drawn from the white or black low-income group. A preliminary cross-tabulation of some questionnaire items indicated that this hypothesis is upheld.

Still another factor is reflected in the scores of the Spanish-speaking group. Their average scores on the attitude items tend to be least like the white subgroup. This indicates the persistence of a cultural heritage that is reflected in the orientation of these Spanish-speaking people that distinguishes them from both middle- and lower-class Anglos, even though they manifest many of the same handicaps that characterize all the members of the lower-class sample.

The black respondents did not manifest a high degree of dependence on parents and occupied a middle position on the scale between the Spanish-speaking and the white populations. Their judgments of their children indicated a harsh evaluation of them, and they showed the highest scores on fostering autonomy in their offspring. They showed the lowest scores in their feelings about coping with responsibility for their children.

While the general pattern of responses for the blacks, fell in a middle position between the white and Spanish-speaking cases, it was also true on some test items they showed the highest scores and on others the lowest. This tendency to oscillate in the level of their answers was greater than was true for either of the other two ethnic groups, and may be a reflection of the marginal status of blacks in American society today. The black cases did show higher anomie scores than the white cases, which again could be a reflection of their minority status. There is, of course, no question about the added handicaps of segregation and discrimination experienced by these black families in addition to the handicaps they share by virtue of their low income and lower-class status. However, these added handicaps were not reflected in anomie scores as high as the LTA cases. Nor were the psychological dependency scores of the blacks as high as the scores of the LTA group. It may well be that vital elements in the orientation or subjective outlook of the blacks were not adequately tapped through the measurement of psychological dependency and anomie. The most that can be said here is that the added handicaps faced by lower-class blacks were not clearly reflected in the test items on the questionnaire.

The white cases showed the lowest degree of psychological dependency and of anomie of the three ethnic groups. These results are in keeping with the fact that they are members of the dominant cultural and racial group of the United States. The white subgroup fell between the Spanish-speaking and black group in their tendencies to foster autonomy in their children and in their feelings about taking responsibility for their children. These findings suggest that, in their relationships with their children, the white families manifest less family solidarity than Spanish-speaking families, but more solidarity than the black families.

The data on the social-psychological orientation of the 1200 cases show clearly that ethnic identification is a factor as strong as, or even stronger than, the welfare dependency experience in shaping the outlook of the respondents. The test data also indicate that present circumstances and personality factors are intertwined in producing the high psychological dependency and the sense of defeat, hopelessness and powerlessness that characterize the outlook of the LTA cases.

If the ethnic factor is important in matters of subjective outlook and in family dynamics, we can expect this same factor to be equally important in structuring husband-wife roles within the family. If the dependency factor is a more powerful determinant, we will then find larger differences between the dependency groups than will be true when the cases are classified by ethnicity.

Husband-Wife Roles within the Family

In the previous chapters, the data on social and economic characteristics of the 1200 cases have shown that mode of participation in the labor force and mode of participation with kin, friends and acquaintances in a local social world are connected with welfare dependency. These subjects all center on matters outside the limits of the family unit. The first discussion of internal family processes as they may relate to the behavior and attitudes of the respondents has been in the previous chapter. This chapter deals directly with one aspect of family organization and functioning as it relates to the husband's and wife's orientations.

In order to more fully understand the internal workings of family life among these low-income households, questionnaires were administered to 150 wives of the families in the San Francisco sample and 150 wives from the sample families in San Jose. In the husband's questionnaire, a major focus was on his work history. In the women's questionnaire, this was replaced by a focus on family relations and child-rearing practices. The major portion of the section on family relations consisted of open-ended questions. The answers to these questions were then classified and analyzed by content analysis to determine if the same conclusions would be drawn as in the case of the men's questionnaire. These data are reported on in Chapter 10. The data on child-rearing practices are not being utilized for this study. The section of the women's questionnaire devoted to specific questions concerning husband-wife roles provided the data reported on in this chapter.

The specific question to be raised in this chapter concerns possible shifts in the husband's and wife's roles within the family as a function of welfare dependency experience. Such shifts may involve obvious changes, such as the performance of family tasks, or may involve more subtle changes in the interpersonal relations of family members with reference to matters such as respect, authority, and power. The questions that were asked of the wives largely focused on matters of the division of labor within the household, i.e., the definition of those tasks defined as the wife's responsibility, those tasks defined as the husband's responsibility, and those considered to be joint. It was recognized that shifts in interpersonal relations between husband and wife might take place, but with no apparent changes in the division of labor within the household. Thus, the data in this chapter on husband-wife roles are somewhat limited in meaning. If shifts in the division of labor within the family are correlated with dependency status, some clear inferences can be made about the orientations of husbands and wives. If such shifts are not manifested, we still cannot be sure that changes have not occurred in interpersonal relations within the family.

Longitudinal Studies of Unemployment and Family Organization

Because of the limitations of our data, a brief summary will be given of the case studies reported by E. Wight Bakke (1940), Ruth Cavan and Katherine Ranck (1938), and Mirra Komarovsky (1940). These longitudinal studies of family life, unemployment, and welfare dependency were carried out during the depression era and remain the classic sources for analyzing the relationship between preunemployment family patterns of living as they relate to changes in family living resulting from unemployment and dependency. Based upon this summary, comparisons can be made between our findings and those of Bakke, Cavan and Ranck, and Komarovsky.

Bakke's case studies of twenty-four families over an eight-year period during the depression era led to the formulation of a theory of stages in family adjustment to unemployment and welfare dependency. These stages involve the concepts of equilibrium, unstable equilibrium, disorganization, and readjustment. He points out first that internal changes in family life and response to loss of work are associated with external changes:

Another observation concerning the journey of the families through these several stages is relevant. The economic changes are accompanied by social changes in family and community relationships. The two are closely related and react upon each other [p. 176, 1940].

Bakke states that as a family moves through this set of stages, few changes occur in the division of labor, but shifts take place in the relative power and authority of husband and wife. Psychological practices of rationalization are used by both husband and wife in coping with these changes. The wife tends to assume a larger degree of control over managing and planning and tends to have control over money. Family ritual declines, and Bakke suggests that there may be increasing health problems.

For these twenty-four cases, Bakke found that readjustment did not take place unless the family head was able to obtain work relief. He makes the hypothesis that family breakup follows the stage of disorganization unless the husband's role in the family can be stabilized by work relief. He states:

The job of the head of the family provides not only an income but a social role for which there is no adequate substitute in a working class culture.

Cavan and Ranck's study (1938) of 100 families resulted in much the same general conclusions as Bakke's. They state that a family's reaction to the crisis of unemployment and relief status rests on family organization in the past and susceptibility to disturbance, the type of economic impact experienced, the necessity of requesting relief, and the family modes of coping with crisis in the past. A number of types of adjustment were found, including denial that a crisis existed, acceptance by the husband of dependency status, change in husband-wife roles, and various attempts at escape. The mechanisms of escape included daydreaming, contemplation of suicide, living in the past, absorption in religion, ill health, and actual suicide. A brief summary of their findings is given as follows:

It is characteristic of the families that were well organized before the depression that other crises do not complicate the situation, and of the families that were disorganized before the depression, that crises either supersede the depression or complicate it in some way (many of these crises involve illness or death and suggest that ill health may have been an unrecognized factor in the disorganization that characterized the family before the depression) [p. 117].

Mirra Komarovsky's study of fifty-nine unemployed relief families during the depression focused on the impact of unemployment on the husband's authority position within the family. The findings indicate that one-fifth of the men experienced loss of authority within the family. The variables involved in the adjustment of the fifty-nine families included the prior pattern of relationship between husband and wife, the personalities of the marital pair, and social relations outside the family. Komarovsky points to three changes in the husband's role resulting from unemployment and welfare dependency: (1) Loss of the provider role; (2) economic failure with its negative prestige implication; and (3) loss of daily work routine. Concerning the first point, the author states:

The general impression that the interviews make is that in addition to sheer economic anxiety the man suffers from deep humiliation. He experiences a sense of deep frustration because in his own estimation he fails to fulfill what is the central duty of his life, the very touchstone of his manhood—the role of family provider [p. 74].

The conclusion of these authors may be summarized by the following points: (1) The crisis of unemployment and welfare dependency interacts with a family's previous equilibrium and methods of coping with crisis in determining the family's pattern of response. (2) Unemployment and welfare dependency tend to erode away the position and authority of the husband within the family. (3) The shifts in husband-wife interpersonal relations usually do not involve shifts in the division of labor, but rather create shifts in terms of respect, authority, and power. (4) Shifts within the family system are interrelated to changes in social life of the members outside the family.

From these studies, it seems clear that long-term unemployment and welfare dependency produce a variety of orientations on the part of the husband, and all of these would seem to function in one way or another to weaken the husband's potential to respond to opportunities for employment. If the husband's self-definition as a male breadwinner is maintained in significant degree by participation in a local social world that is linked with the male sociability arising from work situations, it also seems to be true that his role as father and parent operates to maintain the same self-image. These studies indicate that changes in interpersonal relations within the family resulting from unemployment and welfare dependency operate to weaken the husband's self-definition as a man who heads his own household.

With the background furnished by these three longitudinal studies, the data on 300 families from our larger sample of 1200 households can be examined to determine what shifts may take place in the division of labor between husband and wife, as such shifts may affect the husband's self-definition. The same method has been used as in previous chapters, except that no geographic classification has been given since the cases were drawn only from the San Francisco and San Jose areas.

Similarities in Husband-Wife Roles for the 300 Families

The picture of lower-class family life depicted in previous studies and in summaries of the research literature emphasizes the separation of husband and wife roles in the family division of labor in contrast with middle-class families.[1] The descriptions of black and Spanish-speaking lower-class families depart in certain ways from this social class model. The black lower-class family has been extensively studied and has been characterized as matriarchal or egalitarian in character.[2] The traditional Spanish-speaking family has been depicted as involving total separation in husband-wife roles with male authority being supreme. Thus, previous research provides a set of models against which our data can be evaluated.

Table 9-1 is organized to indicate those household tasks performed by the wife only, by the husband only, or jointly by both husband and wife. Household tasks of laundry, cooking, dishes and cleaning are clearly defined as women's tasks, as more than a majority of the 300 women say that they uniformly do this task without any participation by their husbands.[3] The number of men who take over such tasks as their exclusive responsibility is very small, not higher than 2.4% of the cases at most. Shopping does not follow this pattern, but is done in a majority of the cases by both husbands and wives rather than being exclusive to either.

---

[1] Mirra Komarovsky's recent study (1964) of blue-collar families and *Blue-Collar World* edited by Shostak and Gomberg (1964) contain summaries of the relevant research literature.

[2] See, for example, the Summary in Billingsley and Billingsley (1965).

[3] Komarovsky's data (*Marriage*, Table B, p. 50) show much the same result, except that a higher percentage of the wives took sole responsibility for these tasks. Her 58 sample families were of higher socioeconomic status, on the average, than the 300 families reported on in Table 9-1.

Table 9-1
Percentage Distribution of Husband-Wife Roles within the Family—Household Chores

Husband-Wife Roles by Task	Cases Classified by Dependency				Cases Classified by Ethnicity				
	NOA	STA	LTA	Total	Black	Span.	White	Other	Total
Laundry									
All roles	100.0	100.0	100.0	100.0[1]	100.0	100.0	100.0	100.0	100.0[1]
Wife only	65.9	69.9	76.5	70.1	59.8	73.0	75.8	76.9	70.1
Husband only	0.0	2.9	4.7	2.4	3.4	2.0	2.1	0.0	2.4
Husband & wife jointly	17.6	12.9	9.4	13.6	18.4	11.0	11.6	15.4	13.6
Others in addition to husband and wife	16.5	14.3	9.4	13.9	18.4	14.0	10.5	7.7	13.9
Cooking									
All roles	100.0	100.0	100.0	100.0[2]	100.0	100.0	100.0	100.0	100.0[2]
Wife only	73.0	64.0	69.8	67.9	59.5	75.0	68.8	57.1	67.9
Husband only	0.0	0.0	0.0	0.0	0.0	0.0	0.0	0.0	0.0
Husband & wife jointly	14.6	18.0	15.9	16.7	22.6	11.0	16.1	28.6	16.7
Others in addition to husband and wife	12.4	18.0	14.3	15.4	17.9	14.0	15.1	14.3	15.4
Dishes									
All roles	100.0	100.0	100.0	100.0[3]	100.0	100.0	100.0	100.0	100.0[3]
Wife only	50.6	54.3	48.4	51.9	38.6	53.5	62.3	42.8	51.9
Husband only	0.0	0.7	0.0	0.3	1.2	0.0	0.0	0.0	0.3
Husband & wife jointly	11.2	7.9	14.5	10.3	14.5	5.9	9.7	28.6	10.3
Others in addition to husband and wife	38.2	37.1	37.1	37.5	45.7	40.6	28.0	28.6	37.5
Cleaning									
All roles	100.0	100.0	100.0	100.0[4]	100.0	100.0	100.0	100.0	100.0[4]
Wife only	51.6	48.9	40.3	48.0	33.7	55.0	55.8	32.2	48.0
Husband only	0.0	1.5	0.0	0.7	2.4	0.0	0.0	0.0	0.7
Husband & wife jointly	16.5	17.7	21.0	18.0	20.9	12.0	18.9	35.7	18.0
Others in addition to husband and wife	31.9	31.9	38.7	33.3	43.0	33.0	25.3	32.1	33.3
Shopping									
All roles	100.0	100.0	100.0	100.0[5]	100.0	100.0	100.0	100.0	100.0[5]
Wife only	26.7	28.3	31.7	28.5	27.7	28.3	32.7	7.2	28.5
Husband only	7.7	8.7	11.2	8.9	7.3	9.1	8.4	21.4	8.9
Husband & wife jointly	57.8	56.5	47.6	55.0	57.8	57.5	50.5	50.0	55.0
Others in addition to husband and wife	7.8	6.5	9.5	7.6	7.2	5.1	8.4	21.4	7.6

[1] N = 295 answers from wives.
[2] N = 291 answers from wives.
[3] N = 291 answers from wives.
[4] N = 294 answers from wives.
[5] N = 291 answers from wives.

Child-care tasks present a quite different picture. Table 9-2 indicates that a majority of men are involved much more strongly, either as occasional or frequent helpers, or in a joint role. Some husbands take exclusive responsibility for such tasks as child discipline (11.8%), outings with children (5.8%), and help with school work (16.5%).

An item of particular interest is the control exerted within the family over the spending of money. Some 37.5% of the wives specify that they control the spending of money, 39.2% said that control over money was joint, and 21.7% stated that money control was in the hands of their husbands (Table 9-3).

Some explanation is needed of other persons who were involved in the family division of labor. This catch-all category included children, relatives or nonrelatives living in the household, and persons (relatives or nonrelatives) who came into the household for the purpose of performing a given task. The stereotyped image of lower-class families is that characteristically there are other members in the household over and above the nuclear family. Unless the reports from the respondents were gross distortions of reality, this picture is quite erroneous. For the 1200 families, there were only 94 relatives in all, only 29 nonrelatives, and 81 unrelated children living within these households. Counting those households where there was more than one resident relative, it can be concluded that over 90% of the 1200 households contained only members of the nuclear family. Thus the vast percentage of the routine participation by family members, other than the husband and wife, in tasks such as dishwashing, cooking, laundry and cleaning was by children who were members of the nuclear family.

It should be pointed out that the definition of a task as carried out jointly by husband and wife is not as clear and unequivocal in meaning as might appear at first reading, and this point is rather important for the interpretation of the data. In the questionnaire, the question was asked if a task such as grocery shopping was done "usually by the wife," "usually by the husband," "by both husband and wife," "usually by others," (such as a relative or child) or "by others as well as by husband and/or wife." These headings were reduced to those given in Tables 9-1 and 9-2. The "wife only" column in the tables represents the column in the questionnaire labeled "usually by the wife," and is reasonably clear-cut in meaning—namely, that the wife defines this task as part of her role to be performed without help from her husband. The same interpretation is given to the answers labeled "husband only." The label "husband and wife jointly" refers to all sharing, helping, demanding, wheedling, or threatening that results in some joint action in performing tasks. We cannot say that what is *joint* is *equal*. Consequently, the most that can be stated is that certain areas of role performance are characterized as involving both husband and wife.

A somewhat similar difficulty arises in the meaning of the question "controlling spending of money." Control can refer to major decisions about how money will be spent, or it may refer to the routine expenditure of money on a daily basis where the major policy decisions have already been determined. There was not time in the women's interview for the type of conversation that

Table 9-2
Percentage Distribution of Husband-Wife Roles within the Family—Dealing with Children

Husband-Wife Roles by Task	Cases Classified by Dependency				Cases Classified by Ethnicity				
	NOA	STA	LTA	Total	Black	Span.	White	Other	Total
Child care									
All roles	100.0	100.0	100.0	100.0[1]	100.0	100.0	100.0	100.0	100.0[1]
Wife only	45.8	42.3	31.1	40.9	37.0	36.2	48.9	42.8	40.9
Husband only	1.2	0.0	0.0	0.4	0.0	0.0	1.1	0.0	0.4
Husband & wife jointly	32.5	40.9	41.0	38.4	40.7	38.3	38.0	28.6	38.4
Others in addition to husband and wife	20.5	16.8	27.9	20.3	22.3	25.5	12.0	28.6	20.3
Child discipline									
All roles	100.0	100.0	100.0	100.0[2]	100	100.0	100.0	100.0	100.0[2]
Wife only	16.1	18.7	23.8	19.0	22.6	17.3	19.1	15.4	19.0
Husband only	6.9	14.4	12.7	11.8	3.6	13.3	13.8	38.5	11.8
Husband & wife jointly	73.6	61.1	61.9	65.0	67.8	64.3	64.9	46.1	65.0
Others in addition to husband and wife	3.4	5.8	1.6	4.2	6.0	5.1	2.2	0.0	4.2
Child outings									
All roles	100.0	100.0	100.0	100.0[3]	100.0	100.0	100.0	100.0	100.0[3]
Wife only	8.4	18.3	6.6	13.1	18.8	10.5	11.5	7.7	13.1
Husband only	7.2	3.8	8.2	5.8	2.5	9.5	3.5	15.4	5.8
Husband & wife jointly	77.1	69.5	80.3	73.8	68.7	73.7	79.3	69.2	73.8
Others in addition to husband and wife	7.3	8.4	4.9	7.3	10.0	6.3	5.7	7.7	7.3
Help with schoolwork									
All roles	100.0	100.0	100.0	100.0[4]	100.0	100	100.0	100.0	100.0[4]
Wife only	39.6	34.4	35.6	36.2	34.9	37.3	33.3	50.0	36.2
Husband only	15.1	18.9	13.3	16.5	12.7	19.4	17.6	16.7	16.5
Husband & wife jointly	35.8	36.7	42.2	37.7	39.7	32.8	43.1	33.3	37.7
Others in addition to husband and wife	9.5	10.0	8.9	9.6	12.7	10.5	6.0	0.0	9.6

[1] N = 281 answers from wives.
[2] N = 289 answers from wives.
[3] N = 275 answers from wives.
[4] N = 188 answers from wives.

Table 9-3
Percentage Distribution of Husband-Wife Roles within the Family—Control Over Spending of Money

Husband-Wife Roles	Cases Classified by Dependency				Cases Classified by Ethnicity				
	NOA	STA	LTA	Total[1]	Black	Span.	White	Other	Total[1]
All roles	100.0	100.0	100.0	100.0	100.0	100.0	100.0	100.0	100.0
Wife only	30.0	37.6	48.4	37.5	36.9	42.6	34.0	21.4	37.5
Husband only	28.9	20.6	14.5	21.7	14.3	24.8	23.4	35.7	21.7
Husband & wife jointly	40.0	40.4	33.9	39.2	47.6	29.6	41.5	42.9	39.2
Others besides husband and/or wife	1.1	1.4	3.2	1.6	1.2	3.0	1.1	0.0	1.6

[1]N = 293 wives; NR = 7 (2.4%).

would have led to a more accurate interpretation of these issues. With these qualifications in mind, the data are still quite useful in describing certain patterned aspects of husband-wife roles within the family.

Two questions were asked about issues of leadership or dominance in family affairs. A majority of the wives stated that they did take the lead in family affairs, and almost two-thirds specified that a family is better if the wife does settle most of the problems (Table 9-4).

Employment for wives is a possible critical issue in terms of the conflicting demands of child care versus low-family income. Table 9-5 indicates the wives' answers to two questions on this subject.

It will be remembered that only 11% of the wives are currently working (either full or part time). A majority of these women agreed that it is a good thing for a wife to work, and agreement with this view of a woman's role rose to an astonishing 89.4% under the hypothetical conditions where no children would be present in the family. The discrepancy between the husbands' and wives' attitudes is not surprising, with only 28.8% of 1200 husbands[4] indicating approval of the wife in the role of the breadwinner. The nature of the husbands' objection is clearly revealed by their answers to the question about wives working if there are no children in the home. Sixty-five percent of the husbands agreed that under these conditions it was acceptable for wives to work. It appears that husbands are not arguing that the wife's place is in the home *per se*, but rather that her role as a *mother* should be transcendent over other interests or responsibilities.

[4]In Table 9-5, the answers of the 300 wives are compared to the answers of all 1200 husbands. A better procedure would have been to compare the answers of the 300 wives with the answers given by *their* husbands. Despite this lack of matching in comparing husbands' and wives' responses, the size of the differences in their answers indicates that direct matching of husbands' and wives' answers would have produced the same results.

Table 9-4
Woman's Attitude toward Her Role as Housewife and Mother[1]

	Cases Classified by Dependency				Cases Classified by Ethnicity				
Attitude	NOA	STA	LTA	Total	Black	Span.	White	Other	Total
A wife knows she will have to take the lead in family affairs									
Those agreeing	60.9	59.2	57.1	59.6	58.1	61.8	63.2	28.6	59.6
Median score	1.6	1.6	1.8	1.6[2]	1.6	1.4	1.6	3.4	1.6[2]
Family is better if wife settles most of the problems									
Those agreeing	66.7	62.4	61.3	63.9	73.3	62.7	56.8	61.5	63.9
Median score	1.1	1.2	1.5	1.2[3]	0.8	1.3	1.7	1.6	1.2[3]
A young mother feels held down by children									
Those agreeing	59.1	57.7	47.6	56.4	54.7	58.3	54.7	64.3	56.4
Median score	1.6	1.7	2.2	1.8[4]	1.8	1.7	1.9	1.5	1.8[4]

[1] Scale: 0　1　2　3　4
　　　Strongly　　　　Strongly
　　　agree　　　　　disagree

[2] N = 297 wives; NR = 3 (1.0%).
[3] N = 296 wives; NR = 4 (1.3%).
[4] N = 298 wives; NR = 2 (0.7%).

Differences in Husband-Wife Roles

With reference to household tasks and child care (Tables 9-1 and 9-2), there is no clear-cut difference in husband-wife roles when the cases are classified by dependency status. The fact that LTA husbands have more time available for participation in household routines does not produce a shift in this aspect of the husband's role. This finding is not unexpected as the three studies summarized at the beginning of the chapter indicate that few long-time unemployed husbands tend to take over household tasks that are defined as the wife's exclusive responsibility. We can conclude that the ongoing division of labor between husband and wife lies at the very basis of what it means to be a man or a woman, and is probably that element in family life most resistant to the stresses resulting from the husband's unemployment and welfare dependency.

The major exception to this finding is with reference to control over money. Table 9-3 shows that there is a clear gradient of increasing control over money on the part of the wife with a concomitant decline in joint control and in

Table 9-5
Percent of Husbands and Wives with Favorable Attitude toward Wife Working

Attitude Toward Wife Working	Cases Classified by Dependency				Cases Classified by Ethnicity				
	NOA	STA	LTA	Total	Black	Span.	White	Other	Total
Attitude toward wife working (no qualifying conditions)									
Wives with favorable response	57.6	49.6	59.7	54.2[1]	58.6	59.4	46.2	50.0	54.2[1]
Husbands with favorable response	31.4	27.7	27.2	28.8[2]	50.4	21.2	19.5	32.5	28.8[2]
Wives predicting favorable response of spouse	31.5	30.2	31.7	31.3[3]	33.3	28.4	31.9	35.7	31.3[3]
Husbands predicting favorable response of spouse	50.4	47.9	46.5	48.4[4]	67.4	46.7	36.0	43.5	48.4[4]
Attitude toward wife working (if there were no children)									
Wives with favorable response	91.0	87.9	90.5	89.4[5]	89.4	87.9	90.4	92.9	89.4[5]
Husbands with favorable response	63.9	67.1	61.2	65.0[6]	75.1	64.0	58.2	62.5	65.0[6]

[1] N = 295 wives; NR = 5 (1.7%).
[2] N = 1173 husbands; NR = 27 (2.3%).
[3] N = 294 wives; NR = 6 (2.0%).
[4] N = 1156 husbands; NR = 44 (3.6%).
[5] N = 292 wives; NR = 8 (2.7%).
[6] N = 1149 husbands; NR = 51 (4.3%).

exclusive control by the husband. This finding is again consistent with the conclusions drawn from the research studies of unemployed and relief families during the depression.

The two questions in Table 9-4 focusing on the relative power and authority between husband and wife show a small but consistent decrease in the wife's authority as welfare dependency increases. These results are the exact opposite of what the depression research studies had led us to expect and are inconsistent with the data on control over money. While it is tempting to give these answers another interpretation than that provided by the manifest meaning of the questions, this would be inconsistent with the procedure used on the other attitude items. No obvious explanation could be found for these seemingly inconsistent findings.

In contrast to the lack of differences in husband-wife role performance when the cases are classified by dependency, significant differences between groups are manifested when the cases are classified by ethnicity. If the figures for the ethnic groups are ranked in terms of the low and high group for each household and child-care task, a pattern for each group emerges. The Spanish-speaking and white families look much the same in terms of the duties that are performed solely by the wife. In contrast, the black families show a much higher percentage of men who "share" or participate in the tasks performed by their wives. On three out of four items related to child rearing, there was a higher percentage of Spanish-speaking males who performed these tasks without the participation of their wives, though the proportion of these men never exceeded 20% of the total Spanish-speaking cases.

Generally speaking, the Spanish-speaking males tend to show the greatest role separation, though they are not markedly different from the white males. If the Spanish-speaking male does engage in a given task, he is more likely to perform this task without any participation by his wife. The greater participation of black males in tasks defined as part of the wife's role cannot be taken to imply equality or joint responsibility. It is equally likely that such sharing represents the inability of the black male to assert his autonomy from his wife *within* the household.

It was expected that Spanish-speaking males would show the strongest objection to having their wives work, but Table 9-5 shows that it is the white subgroup which has the smallest percentage who agree with this view. Almost twice as many black men approved of having a working wife as either of the other two ethnic groups.

Interpretation of Findings and Comparisons with Earlier Studies

Comparing our data to the findings of three studies of unemployment and family life during the depression, no clear evidence was found of a general decrease in the authority of the husband with increasing unemployment and welfare dependency. The one clear indication of such a change was the trend for increasing control by wives over money as welfare dependency status increased. In contrast to this finding, two attitude questions about the wife's authority position produced the opposite findings—namely, for a decrease in the wife's authority as welfare dependency increased.

Several other conclusions were derivable, however, from the analysis of husband-wife role performance. The major differences in the structuring of the husband's and wife's roles centered around ethnic status. Spanish-speaking families showed the highest degree of role separation, yet the role pattern for these families was only slightly different from that of the white families.

It is clear that husband and wife roles, insofar as the household division of labor is concerned, are highly resistant to change from the pressure of outside forces. It seems highly plausible that social-psychological changes in the position of the husband within the family do take place as a function of unemployment and welfare dependency, but the data that were reported in this chapter related to aspects of the husband's role that did not reflect such changes.

In Chapter 9, it was found that ethnicity was as important as dependency in structuring the orientation of the 1200 husbands. The data derived from interviewing 300 wives about the family division of labor reflect this same fact—that ethnic factors are of equal importance to dependency factors. Thus, we find that insofar as the husband's participation in the labor force is concerned, and insofar as the family's participation in a local social world is concerned, dependency is the most powerful factor shaping the family's life style. Where matters of subjective orientation and family interpersonal relations are concerned, ethnic status is equal to or of greater significance than dependency status.

10 Life Style Themes

James Hirabayashi, Anita Spring and
Gerardo Rosal

This chapter consists of an analysis of 16 open-ended questions on a selected sample of 137 wives of low-income families residing in San Francisco. These open-ended questions were designed by members of the primary study and were included in the questionnaires administered to 300 wives in San Francisco and San Jose. The analysis of the responses of the San Francisco sample was conducted by us after the data were gathered by members of the primary study and independently of the primary study in order to maximize the validity of the results. In addition to this, case studies of eight of these families were conducted over a period of three months. The following analysis of these data, therefore, adds a qualitative complement to the statistical generalizations made by the parent study.

*Rationale for the Analysis of the
Open-Ended Questions*

Appendix D lists the open-ended questions included in the women's questionnaire by the parent project (Questions Number 27 through 42 in Section III, Family History). These questions were not designed to elicit answers to be interpreted within a given framework of analysis, but merely to see what sorts of qualitative statements these women respondents would give to some broad questions dealing with some aspects of their life conditions. Thus, the open-ended questions were designed to elicit a range of answers with no particular focus except to tap some general attitudes on the part of these women to some questions concerning life in general. This analysis is not, therefore, a systematic attempt to characterize given values, attitudes and behaviors of the women in the sample. It is rather an attempt to use a nondirective method to tease out some factors which may be relevant to the life-ways of these people and the assessments are to be viewed in conjunction with, and as being complementary to, the statistical evaluations of the parent project.

Since these questions were not designed to elicit specific responses, the question of the criterion for analysis needed to be resolved initially. Necessarily, the analysis had to be one in which these responses could be judged according to some criterion which would either discriminate or show similarities in the responses by the subjects. A specific item analysis did not permit any kind of comparison, for the answers to any given question ranged considerably, i.e., the responses simply were not on the same subjects. Another factor which added to the variability of the responses to these open-ended questions was the range of experience among the interviewers. For some, it was their first experience resulting in rather terse responses, while other more experienced interviewers elicited full answers. In order to improve the comparability of the responses, and since some themes were not confined to one or two questions, we decided that these interviews should be taken as a whole and the responses would then be categorized in terms of a limited number of broad variables. The main guiding principle was to extract from these responses general themes which would permit some comparison, but not to the extent that they would lose their qualitative content.

Within this setting, then, we decided to examine value orientations as our framework for analysis. Value orientations, following Clyde Kluckhohn, may be defined as: "... a generalized and organized conception, influencing behavior, of nature, of man's place in it, of man's relation to man, and of the desirable and nondesirable as they may be related to man-environment and interhuman relations." (1962) Since there have been prior studies in terms of the framework, principally Florence Kluckhohn and Fred Strodtbeck (1961), it means that we were not only able to gain methodological insights, but insofar as the mode of analysis derives from a similar framework, some of our results may be comparable. Since Kluckhohn had designed her questionnaire to elicit responses along given continua, i.e., the respondents were given three choices in specific problem areas, she was able not only to categorize people, in terms of their responses, as having a given value orientation but also to rank order their preferences within the value orientation. Due to the nature of the data, we could not explicitly use her framework, her categories, and/or her method of analysis, an advantage which would have increased the comparability of the results of our analysis. However, her study did give us leads as to how we might examine our data and insofar as we were able to take advantage of her framework, some aspects of our analysis may become generally comparable.

In terms of the data available to us, we have isolated five general areas of orientations which we shall henceforth refer to as "themes." Themes here merely refer to areas of concentration of beliefs and behavior which give some characterizations of the life-ways of these people. These are labeled situational control, time, activity, relational, and family themes. It must be pointed out here that we were not concerned with problems of the logical completeness of our analytical framework but merely wished to devise a method of analyzing our data which would be meaningful to the parent study. The *situational* control theme deals with the respondent's attitudes towards situational factors and whether she believes she can do something about it or whether she feels unable to change the situation. The *time* theme deals with attitudes towards time, i.e., whether past, present or future time considerations enter into the attitudes and behavior of the respondents. The *activity* theme focuses on whether the respondent is doing anything or is not doing anything to resolve the life situation she is in. This category is somewhat of a behavioral corollary to the *situational control* theme, which focuses more on general attitudes. The *relational* theme centers on the strength of dependence upon kin ties. The *family* theme relates to whether the father or the mother is the central figure in the activities of the family.

Two methodological points must be made explicit. First, we had originally begun our analysis by assigning the answers elicited by given questions to a thematic area. We expected, for example, that question 35 (Chances for improving yourself and your family in different ways?) would give us some data on the situational control theme, i.e., it would elicit answers from which we would be able to determine attitudes concerning their ability to control their life situation. Each question and the answers were assigned to a thematic area and a partial analysis was accomplished. We found, however, that answers to a particular question would often contain relevant data for one or more themes other than the one to which it was initially assigned. In order to achieve maximal returns from the data, we decided to treat each interview as a whole and examined each statement for its relevance to one or the other thematic areas regardless of the question that elicited the response. Thus, for example, one entire interview may contain twelve statements concerning the situational control theme. In eight of these statements, the respondent may feel subjugated to the situation. (The judgment of these statements will be discussed below.) Eight would then be divided by twelve and the subject would then be given a percentage rating of .67 in this category. The ratios for all the members of a subgroup within the sample were then averaged, and this procedure provided a single index for that subgroup. By using this method of assessment, we can then abstract statements relating to an orientation regardless of where they may appear in the interview, and derive maximal usage of the data. Also, it will permit us to make comparative statements not only between individuals but also between categories of people.

Table 10-1 shows the number of respondents in each of the nine subgroups in the sample. The lack of equal numbers in each cell of the table and the small number of cases for three of the subgroups renders any argument about statistical signficance difficult. Therefore, the overall pattern of responses has been the base for evaluating differences between the subgroups.

Table 10-2 gives the number of responses that were classified by theme and

Table 10-1
Number of Respondents[1]

	Black			Spanish			White		
	NOA	STA	LTA	NOA	STA	LTA	NOA	STA	LTA
Respondents	39	25	15	15	5	6	13	9	10

[1] n = 137 wives

Table 10-2
Number of Respondents' Statements Classified by Theme and Dimension

Theme	Dimension	Black			Spanish			White		
		NOA	STA	LTA	NOA	STA	LTA	NOA	STA	LTA
Situational Control	Mastery	265	150	84	101	36	39	76	69	68
	Subjugation	297	171	123	105	45	46	86	71	76
Time	Present	200	139	75	70	26,	33	44	46	51
	Past	85	54	34	36	9	14	29	26	18
	Future	183	117	57	72	27	33	62	51	46
Activity	Doing	214	129	83	75	32	21	60	55	61
	Not Doing	213	143	84	86	27	44	58	63	56
Relational	Strong	150	104	60	86	26	21	49	35	33
	Weak	115	80	42	53	26	17	31	36	42
Family	Father	177	102	78	71	18	26	48	38	40
	Mother	137	113	52	39	18	16	35	34	42

dimension. For example, the interviews of the 39 black, NOA wives provided 265 statements that were classified as mastery over situations. Table 10-3 shows the average score for each subgroup classified by theme and dimension. It should be made clear that the scores in Table 10-3 were *not* computed from the frequencies given in Table 10-2. Rather, a ratio was computed for each respondent's statements for each thematic area. The ratios of all those respondents falling in a given subgroup were then averaged to provide a single score for the entire subgroup.

Secondly, these percentages must not be taken to be on an absolute scale for any given dimension. These percentages merely give us the relative relationship of responses within a thematic area, i.e., the percentage numbers in Table 10-3 indicate the average emphasis placed by the respondents within a given theme. Therefore, the analysis of each theme will begin with an overall qualitative assessment of the dimension of that area of focus.

The Analysis of the Open-Ended Questions

All the themes with the exception of time have dichotomous subdivisions. In these dichotomous thematic areas, the total number of statements abstracted from the entire interview of each respondent relating to this area is divided into number of responses of each of the subcategories of the same theme, as in the example above. This procedure needed to be modified for the time dimension since this particular theme has a trichotomous subdivision. Therefore, the sum of

Table 10-3
Respondents' Average Scores on Five Themes Classified by Ethnicity and Dependency[1]

Theme	Dimension	Black			Spanish			White		
		NOA	STA	LTA	NOA	STA	LTA	NOA	STA	LTA
Situational Control	Mastery	47	47	41	49	44	46	47	49	47
	Subjugation	53	53	59	51	56	54	53	51	53
Time	Present	43	45	45	40	42	41	33	37	44
	Past	18	17	21	20	15	18	21	21	16
	Future	39	38	34	40	43	44	46	42	40
Activity	Doing	50	47	50	53	54	32	50	46	52
	Not Doing	50	53	50	47	46	68	50	54	48
Relational	Strong	56	57	59	62	50	55	61	49	44
	Weak	44	43	41	38	50	45	39	51	56
Family	Father	56	47	60	65	50	62	58	53	48
	Mother	44	53	40	35	50	38	42	47	52

[1] The values in a given cell represent an average of ratios and equal 100; e.g., the values 47 and 53 for the white NOA cases for the situational control theme represent an average of the ratios of all cases in the cell and equal 100%.

all statements in this thematic area was divided into the totals for each of the three subcategories. Although this deivates from the general procedure, it allows us to make comparative assessments within the theme.

After each interview was assessed, the resulting ratios were grouped in terms of three ethnic categories, black, Spanish-speaking, and white, and each of these categories had three subdivisions: Long-Time Aid recipients (LTA), Short-Time Aid recipients (STA), and those Never on Aid (NOA), resulting in nine separate categories. Henceforth, in the text, these categories and subdivisions will be abbreviated as black, Spanish-speaking, white and LTA, STA, and NOA.

Situational Control Theme

The situational control theme, as stated above, deals with the respondent's attitudes towards situational factors and whether she believes she can do something about it or whether she feels unable to change the situation. The following statements are a sample of the ones which to us indicated a lack of control over situational factors.

"I cannot control my children."

"Nowadays children no longer obey their parents."

"I am not working because jobs are hard to find, and besides I don't have an education, and nowadays only people with an education can find jobs."

"This neighborhood is awful, but I don't think we could find a place anywhere else."

"I didn't want my sister-in-law to come and live with us but there was nothing I could do to stop her."

"I am always pregnant—I don't want any more children but I don't like to do things that go against God's will."

In contrast to these statements, the following statements indicated a certain amount of control over situational factors.

"We could use some more money and that is why I have begun to go to night school."

"I plan to get a job as soon as my younger son is old enough."

"I went to Planned Parenthood because I don't feel that it will be fair either to us or to the children to have more babies."

"My husband doesn't want me to work too much but I have a part-time job to help with some bills."

"I don't think this neighborhood is good for the children so we plan to move as soon as we can."

"When I first got married and I left my parents' house, I felt that the whole world had collapsed, but afterwards with some advice from other people, and my husband's help, we began to make out alright."

These statements contrast sharply with those given above and although the respondent may find some difficulties in coping with the situations, she feels some confidence in her ability to overcome these difficulties and to show mastery over the situation.

An impressionistic evaluation of the situational control theme is that, in general, these respondents feel an inability to change the outcome of situational factors in their daily existence. This impression is upheld by the fact that the subjugation percentage for all of the nine groups is above .50, indicating that on the average, the majority of the statements of the individual respondents were statements categorized as showing subjugation to the life situations.

Looking at the ethnic breakdown, cross-classified by dependency, we note first for the black group that the LTA subgroup has the highest subjugation percentage, followed by the other two subgroupings. A look at the figures shows that the real discrepancy is between the LTA group on the one hand and the STA and the NOA groups on the other. This indicates, insofar as these respondents are concerned, that there is a correlation between economic independence and more confidence in their ability to control situational factors.

The Spanish group shows a similar trend; its Never On Aid group has the lowest subjugation percentage. However, the Short-Time group ranked higher than the Long-Time group. This may be a function of the small number of respondents in these categories, but it is interesting to note that the large discrepancy is between those who receive welfare aid and those who never do. The white respondents, however, present a different configuration in their percentages. The STA group had the lowest subjugation percentage, while the LTA and NOA groups had the same percentages. However, the overall discrepancies were not great, either between the subgroupings for any group or between groups. When we take all of the subgroupings together, the black LTA group seemed to be the most distinctively subjugated to situational factors. The general conclusion remains, however, that these low-income people are similar in their "acceptance of fate."

Time Theme

The time theme deals with the respondents' attitudes towards time and has a trichotomous subdivision of present-time orientation, past-time orientation and future-time orientation. The following are some statements representing present-time orientation.

"We can plan things all we want but they never come out the way that we plan them—that's why I don't plan anymore."

"My children are too young to plan for their education—when they grow up it will be up to them whether they want an education or not."

"We don't have a bank account because we have too many bills and when we have some money extra we like to go out."

"I don't know what will happen to us in the future, that's why we try to enjoy ourselves whenever we can."

"My father was always saving money and he never enjoyed himself—I don't like to do that."

Following are some statements which we categorized as past-time orientation.

"My husband is a carpenter like his father—that's why he wants his son to be a carpenter too."

"I come from a large family and my mother says that women in our family have always had large families. That's why I have so many children."

"We are not very different from our parents and our children won't be very different from us."

"Things are not like they used to be when we were living in our home town, we were much better off then than we are now."

"We don't like to move around very much—if we move out of here we will go back to our old neighborhood—we were more happy there."

Statements dealing with future-time orientation can be illustrated by the following samples.

"I don't want my children to suffer as much as we have—I want them to go to college so that they won't have such a rough time."

"As soon as I can find myself a part-time job—we will be able to put some money in the bank. Right now we don't have enough but we'll soon be much better."

"We are planning to move out of this neighborhood as soon as we can and if my husband gets the job that they have promised him, we'll move out."

The general impressionistic view is that of a strong present orientation among all respondents. The percentage figures in the present-time category remain uniformly high. All respondents likewise are similar in that the past-time orientation is weak. However, in the comparison of the percentages for the future-time orientation, we note some differences between groups and the subgroupings therein. Whereas in the black sample, the future-time orientation is uniformly weaker than the present-time orientation in all three subgroups, the same cannot be said for the other ethnic peoples, with the exception of the white LTA group. The other subgroupings of the Spanish and white samples showed percentages in the future-time orientation as either the same or greater than the present-time orientation. For both the black and the white groups, there is a consistent increase in the percentage of the future-time orientation from the LTA to the STA and to the NOA categories. This indicates that there may be a relationship between economic independence and future-time orientation in these two ethnic categories.

Activity Theme

The activity theme focuses on statements indicating that the respondents are actually doing something to change their present status or statements they are not doing anything consciously to change their life situations. The following statements represent an orientation towards not actually doing anything concrete to change the situation in which they find themselves.

"I wish my children wouldn't get into so much trouble but I don't know what to do about it."

"My husband wants me to get a part-time job to help with the bills and I would like to but I don't have any training."

"If it wasn't so much trouble to look for another place, I would like to move out of this neighborhood because it is awful."

"If we could get a little more money, things wouldn't be so difficult but it is hard to make money."

"My husband likes to drink and he has gotten into trouble with the police because of that. They say you can do something about that but it probably costs some money."

Those statements which indicate that the respondents are doing some thing to change their life situations are represented by the following remarks.

"I was working full-time but my children began to get into too much trouble so I am only working a few hours now so that I can pay more attention to them."

"I had too many bills so I looked for a part-time job until my husband got a job that paid more."

"We haven't got anything to do with the police because I am always warning my children to stay out of trouble."

"We don't have enough money for the children's education yet but we have started to put some money aside for that. Also, I watch their school work so that they won't get bad grades. Maybe that way they can get some scholarships."

"I have to be very strict with the children and I sometimes wonder if I'm not being too hard on them but this neighborhood is rough and I don't want them to mess around with all these other children."

The overall conclusion that emerges from the results is that all of the respondents are not doing much to change their lives. Since there is a close relationship between the situational control theme and the activity theme, the results are in conformity. While there is this general conformity, and while there is a danger in making relative comparisons between themes (since the figures do not represent positions on an absolute scale), we might note here that there is a discrepancy in the percentages under comparison. One reason for this difference in averages may be due to the differences between ideal values and actual behavior. Looking at the figures more closely, we find that there is only one that is widely divergent from the rest. This is the extremely high percentage of the "not doing" orientation for the Spanish Long Time Aid recipients. This may be due to a cultural variable, i.e., the "being" position on the activity orientation of the traditional Latin-American culture in "... which there is a spontaneous expression of what is conceived to be 'given' in the human personality." (F. Kluckhohn, pp. 16 and 144.)

Relational Theme

The relational theme focuses on the strength of the relationships between the respondents and their kin. This theme refers specifically to the relationship between the respondent's nuclear family and those kinsmen who are not part of this immediate family group. The relationships center upon emotional, social and economic ties which exist in an extrafamilial context. The following are examples of statements featuring strong relational ties.

"I don't have much trouble with my children because every time I have to go out my mother-in-law or my sister takes care of them."

"As soon as we can we will send for my mother, she is now living in New Orleans but I can't get used to living without her."

"We are very short of money now because my sister-in-law is very ill and her husband does not have a job so we had to take care of some of their children."

"If my husband didn't have to help his family with some of their bills, we probably wouldn't be so bad off."

"My husband wants to move to another neighborhood and so would I but we don't want to move too far away from my family because they help us a lot with the children."

The following statements are samples showing weak relational ties with kinsmen.

"I was glad to move to California so we wouldn't have to do anything with our families."

"My husband was once in an automobile accident and I was very much in need of help but his family wouldn't have anything to do with us—since then I stopped visiting them."

"I miss my family once in awhile but when I think of all the trouble that they could be, I am glad I am miles away from them."

"It's been years since I have last seen my relatives."

"We used to live with my sister-in-law and her husband but it was so much trouble that we decided to move and we haven't seen them since."

An impressionistic view from reading the responses is that the respondents do not rely heavily on their kinsmen for mutual aid or for social relationships as compared with peasant societies. Nevertheless, the ratios for the relational theme given in Table 10-3 show that in general the respondents emphasize strong kinship relations more than 50% of the time. There are some differences which may be noted in the comparisons between the subgroups. The most obvious qualification to be put on this general pattern is the high percentage of responses for weak relationships in the aid subgroups of the white respondents.

Also, an ordering of the dependency categories within the white and Spanish ethnic group underscores an increasing dependence upon kin ties with increasing economic independence. In other words, for these two ethnic groups, there appears to be a correlation between the lessening of extended kin relationships and dependence upon welfare aid. Within the black group, however, there was very little subgroup differentiation. We might speculate here that this may be due to value differences concerning being on a dependency status when these groups are compared with the black respondents. We are suggesting that the Spanish and white groups may have stronger negative attitudes towards being on welfare and that this may account for the reduction of kin relationships as the dependence upon welfare aid increases.

Family Theme

The family theme focuses on those statements which indicated the involvement or the lack of involvement of the father or mother in matters of central importance to the family. Many statements were made of intense satisfaction or dissatisfaction in the performance by the husbands of their roles. The following statements are indicative of the strong role of the father in family affairs.

"I don't have much to do with the children's education—that is something he decides upon."

"I was working but my husband didn't like it, so I quit."

"I don't know much about the money situation because he never talks to me about things like that."

"I wish I could go out some more but my husband doesn't like me to go out alone and he seldom takes me anywhere."

"I don't ever do the big shopping—only the groceries."

The following statements, on the other hand, point to the central role of the mother in the family affairs.

"I have practically had to raise the children myself. I had two with the first one and one with this one."

"My husband is often without work—he spends little time here in the house."

"I am trying to get the divorce because my husband is of little help to us."

In general, there was a tendency to regard the role of the husbands as central to the solution of all of their life problems and to seldom regard their own roles as being more important for the proper functioning of the family. It must be remembered that the families which were sampled for the study were complete families, i.e., those with both parents and children. The Spanish show a stronger emphasis upon the male role in the family—reflecting the traditionally stronger role of the males in family affairs. There are no consistent trends in either direction in the groups, with the exception of the white sample, in which the male role increases with the increasing economic independence of the family from welfare aid.

Some Comparisons between Themes

We have already indicated that these ratios must not be taken to be on an absolute scale for any given dimension. The ratio figures merely give us the relative emphasis of answers within a thematic area. However, if we note the intuitive assessments made on each dimension, we may make some speculative generalizations concerning the relationship between thematic areas for given ethnic groups. We should expect to find some relationships, for the assumption is that people do have life styles which are characteristic of them and that these life styles have some internal consistency.

There appears to be some relationship between subjugation to situations, not doing anything to resolve life situations, and present-time orientation among the respondents in the black Long-Time Aid group. The Spanish LTA group showed a similar configuration except for the time orientation area. However, it must be noted here that the not doing orientation was the strongest among the Spanish LTA group when compared to all of the other subgroups. The white LTA group did not show obvious differences in any of these categories when compared with the white STA and NOA groups. The white LTA group, however, did distinguish from all of the rest in being by far the weakest in their relationship with kin.

The NOA categories for all ethnic groups were uniformly higher in the situational control (mastery) and the activity (doing) thematic areas. In addition, present-time orientation and future-time orientations were given equal weightings by these subgroups.

There is one final generalization that we may draw from the analysis of the data. We find that for all ethnic groups, the distinctions that arise between the subcategories either combine the LTA subgroup with the STA subgroup as being distinctive from the NOA subgroup, or that the LTA subgroup distinguishes from the other two groupings. Rarely did we find the LTA subgroup combined with the NOA subgroup to be distinguished from the Short-Time Aid subgroup in any of the thematic areas. We may tentatively conclude, then, that the life styles of Long-Time Aid people are different from those who never receive aid.

Summary and Conclusions

In this section, we have made a comparative analysis of responses given to open-ended questions by a sampling of wives of low-income families residing in San Francisco. We have attempted to improve the comparability and the reliability of the assessment by analyzing the data in terms of a conceptual framework of themes. These results, however, were combined with intuitive generalizations in the total assessments.

The following tentative conclusions resulted from the analysis of the data:

1. All low-income respondents generally feel an inability to change the outcome of situational factors in their daily existence.
2. Among the black respondents, there is a correlation between economic independence and more confidence in their ability to master situational factors.
3. The black LTA subgroup feels the most distinctively subjugated to situational factors.
4. All groups show a strong present-time orientation.
5. The Spanish and white NOA subgroups give equal weightings to present- and future-time orientations.
6. All groups show a preference for a not-doing orientation, i.e., spontaneous activity.
7. The Spanish LTA group is the most distinctive in the not-doing orientation.
8. All groups rely on kin ties, but probably considerably less so than is true in peasant societies.
9. There is a correlation between economic independence and heavier reliance upon kin among the white and Spanish respondents.
10. The role of the father and the husband is central to the activities of the family for all groups.
11. Male dominance is the most obvious among the Spanish.
12. There are internal consistencies in the life style patterns as seen through the analysis between these thematic areas for any given subgroup.
13. The life style pattern of the Long-Time Aid group is distinctive from the Never On Aid group for all three ethnic peoples.
14. The Long-Time Aid group is distinguished by fatalism, present-time orientation, and spontaneous activities.
15. The Never On Aid group shows more mastery over life situations, gives equal weighting to present- and future-time orientation and plans activities more often.

11 Case Histories

James Hirabayashi, Anita Spring and
Arthur Rotman

From the sample of 137 families reported in Chapter 10, eight families were chosen for more detailed study. An evaluation of these cases is given in this chapter along with two of the case histories. The eight cases are presented in outline form in Appendix C.[1] Interviews, casual conversations, observations, and participant observations constituted the methods for gathering data. A case history interview schedule was designed which made the reports comparable on some of the major issues but also was flexible enough to allow the unique life styles of the individual case histories to be manifested.

The central concerns in the development of the interview design were (1) to allow a description of the life styles of the families on factors which might have a relationship with their low-income status; and (2) to permit general comparisons with the analysis of the open-ended questions (and ultimately with the parent study). The criteria used for the comparative analysis listed in the introductory section include basic background data (demographic characteristics of the family, housing, neighborhood, employment and/or welfare status). The next section includes some general attitudes toward welfare, employment and education.

The third section is on selected themes. Themes were worked out in conjunction with the analysis of the open-ended questions. (See the discussion on the rationale for the analysis of the open-ended questions, Chapter 10.) The following thematic areas were isolated as relevant in the assessment of the case history data on these families: (a) general outlook (general outlook on life and on people); (b) control of life circumstances (whether or not they feel in control of the life circumstance in which they find themselves); (c) time (past-, present- or future-time orientation); (d) activity (deals with the style of treatment of their activities, i.e., whether orderly, planned, goal-oriented-"doing"; or haphazard, "spur of the moment" decisions, situational-"being"); (e) relational (deals with the foci of social relationships, the nuclear family, kin relations or friends).

---

[1] These case histories were the result of research conducted by the members of a seminar in Method and Theory in Anthropology during the fall semester, 1964. We express appreciation to the members of the seminar for their contributions of data upon which this report is based. The members of the seminar were: Lawrence Axtell, Ronald Campbell, Harlo Hansen, Wilhelm Higgenbotham, Richard Reeves, Arthur Rotman, Anita Spring, and Tod Wallace.

The final section includes some miscellaneous and general features of the family, e.g., authority patterns, the central figure in family activities and the relationship of the family to the world around them.

Generalizations from this sample to the population in question are not attempted here due to the size of the sample. The purpose is to present stylistic descriptions of the selected families in our sample. Therefore, proper evaluation of our generalizations requires that they be considered in conjunction with findings from other parts of the overall study. It must also be pointed out that the validity of generalizations drawn from case history data comes primarily from an analysis of the internal consistency of the life style patterns. With this in mind, we have included two brief case histories to give qualitative illustrations of the life style patterns of these low-income families.

Some General Attitudes

A general impression gained from an overall view of the case histories is a characterization which has been described in the literature as a "culture of poverty" representative of families of the lower economic stratum. In their general outlook, the welfare group tends to be pessimistic and resigned to the world around them, while the NOA group is more optimistic about relating to life and to the dominant society. As far as ethnicity is concerned, the black and Spanish-speaking respondents have lower self-esteem and see less chance of bettering themselves when compared with the white respondents. However, the NOA minority groups are "hard workers" for the most part and this raises their self-concept. Nevertheless, there is a decided "felt" subjugation to the white dominant society which is attributed to actual experiences and incidences of prejudice.

Welfare. There are a variety of attitudes about being a recipient of welfare aid. Most of those on welfare ascribe their status to external circumstances such as the lack of employment opportunity or some accidental or circumstantial events which necessitated being on aid. Others cite the lack of educational background and/or vocational training. A few felt that they were so poor when they came to the city that they did not have a chance to get started. Two felt that welfare was due them from society for being subjected to racial prejudice. In general, those on welfare related their status to external factors over which they felt they had little control.

There is some tendency to desire to get off welfare; some consider it a temporary measure used to get over a crisis situation. However, for some, welfare has become a way of life since it provides security and creates a situation in which the husband does not need to work. The NOA families, on the other hand, are hard workers and take much pride in this fact. They say they would do "anything" to keep off welfare.

Work and Employment. Most of the income of the low-income families goes for living expenses—any extra income is not generally for the parents but for the children. Parents acquire things for the children, try to give them security and a chance for them to improve their life chances. The black and white NOA families espouse the "Protestant work ethic" (work is good in and of itself), while the Spanish-speaking NOA families stated they were just working for the money.

Some of the men of the welfare families seemed to express little desire for a job. They do, however, pick up odd jobs to supplement the income received from the welfare department but indicated that they keep this fact from the welfare workers. The Spanish-speaking welfare recipients, in addition, have what one field worker termed the "gringo" concept. This is characterized by a belief that they are scapegoats of the dominant white society, that the whites are against them and restrict their getting and keeping jobs, and thus keep them in a low-income bracket. Therefore, when they do work they claim that they slack off sometimes in order to get back at their white employers.

Education. The case history data show a general lack of education and a lack of motivation to learn which is often attributed to the overwhelming pressures (as perceived by these families) of the dominant society. Any educational goals are not for the individual himself but for his children. Education is seen as a means of mobility through job training eventuating in security. The black families appeared to be the most concerned over their children's education and helped with the children's schoolwork. The two Spanish-speaking families, however, did not associate the lack of education with low-income status. In several of the families there was a general reticence on the part of the husband to allow the wife to acquire further education and training regardless of her expressed desire to better herself, even if it would mean an increase in the family income.

Themes

Thematic trends have been abstracted from their attitudinal statements and observations on their behavior. There is a certain amount of conscious or unconscious idealization of middle-class values. This appears in the incongruities between ideal value statements and actual behavior. In passing, we may note here that one way this "idealization" expresses itself is in an overemphasis on material goods as a means of emulating middle-class values.

General Outlook. People in general are viewed as being inherently good or neutral (neither good nor bad). The NOA families view the world about them in more optimistic terms, whereas there is more pessimism voiced by the welfare recipients.

Control of Life Circumstances. Generally, there is a feeling of subjugation to situational circumstances. In the black and Spanish-speaking families, this is often attributed to the fact that the dominant society keeps them down through the practice of racial prejudice. White respondents also feel subjugated and feel that they can not do anything about the circumstances in which they find themselves. Since they do not have recourse to racial prejudice, they cite other external reasons. For some respondents, there is a tendency to use religion to rationalize or justify a situation. This may appear simply in the acceptance of a situation as "the will of God" or the viewing of a circumstance as "chance" or "luck."

Time Theme. These families fall predominantly into the category of present-time orientation in most aspects of their lives. There may be some looking to the future on the part of a few families, but this is largely in terms of their children's future. Generally, however, there is a lack of planning and utilization of time as a commodity—"they just do what they are doing."

Activity Theme. These low-income families were generally characterized by a being orientation. There was little evidence of motivation or attempts to improve themselves, little planning of specific activities, and little time spent in constructive (in terms of dominant society standards) pursuits. Three families tended toward a "doing" orientation and these were NOA families.

Relational Theme. There was a decided tendency for a nuclear family orientation. Only one of the Spanish-speaking families had extended kin relationships. Four of the welfare families had almost no social relationships outside of their own nuclear family members, either with other relatives or with friends. In two families, the wives had very strong relationships with the children, while their husbands were peripheral to the activities of the families. These families have characteristics which have recently been summarized in the literature as matrifocal or matricentered families (Smith, 1962).

In the black and white families, there is either a strong nuclear family orientation or the wife is dominant and tends to be the motivating force. In the Spanish-speaking families, the men are dominant. Families appear fairly isolated in their contacts with others, especially those on aid. This isolation is from both their extended kin and from families in the same economic stratum. If the families are arranged from low to high interaction with relatives, friends, and the community, the white and black families are at the low end of the scale, while the Spanish-speaking families have relatively high interaction.

In the Spanish-speaking families, the case histories are characterized by the "gringo" concept in which they believe that the white dominant society is trying to exploit them. There is a correspondingly strong in-group feeling among the Spanish-speaking community. The male peer group is an important focus for associational, recreational and mutual aid relationships.

The white families appear for the most part to have traditional American ideal values. These values may be colored by some fatalism, but there is a tendency to perceive themselves as different and somewhat better than the members of the surrounding community which is racially mixed. There is a tendency for the black families to be individualistic and also to be religiously oriented.

Two other generalizations may be made of these low-income families. Most of the houses were reported to be dirty and messy in appearance (by comparison with middle-class standards). There were two exceptions to this: both of them were black and Baptist. Secondly, there was a relatively high intake of alcohol noted among these people, but there was no discernable pattern—there were chronic drinkers, social drinkers and some who drank only at home.

Summary

This study suggests that the low-income families in our sample share some common characteristics which are internally consistent and distinctive from the dominant middle-class pattern of life. They were generally resigned to the life situation around them with a pessimistic attitude towards improving their life chances. By and large, their situations were attributed to external circumstances over which they felt they had little control. Thus, they were inclined to be subjugated to the world about them and to accept it as given. They tended to behave spontaneously on an *ad hoc* basis in conformity with their predominantly present time orientation. These families were also inclined toward a nuclear family orientation with limited relationships with kinsmen and/or friends. The NOA low-income families, however, tended to diverge from these patterns toward the dominant middle-class patterns on most of these dimensions.

There were, however, some differences between the ideals held and the behavior exhibited. Often middle-class values were espoused without appropriate behavioral correlates. The main area in which these people approached middle-class values was to voice hope for betterment in their children mainly through education.

Two Brief Case Histories

These presentations will briefly describe some characteristics of two low-income families, a black welfare family and a black NOA family, the former living in the Bayview District and the latter living in the Hunter's Point district in San Francisco. The case histories will focus on a limited number of central features and their internal relationships. The emphasis will be on the qualitative aspects of those patterns which will allow the isolation of idiosyncratic value and behavior patterns.

Case History One: A Long-Time Welfare Family

The black family described here lives in the San Francisco Bayview district. They have been receiving public welfare for approximately two-and-one-half years.

The family consists of a father, age 54, a mother, age 47, and three children, T., age 15, M., age 10, and K., age 7, and a dog, Rex. Mrs. S. is a semiinvalid, being blind and diabetic, and has recently had an operation for removal of a cancerous growth. She confines herself to the home and spends most of her time in an easy chair in the kitchen. Mr. S. is unemployed, although he occasionally does odd jobs. He spends about half his time during the day in the home and the remainder on the street within the six-block neighborhood. The children attend school; the oldest is in the tenth grade at Mission High, and the younger two are in the third and fifth grades, respectively.

The S.s are originally from Georgia and came to California in 1943, when Mr. S. was in the Navy. Previously, he resided in Atlanta, where he completed the eighth grade. Mr. S. has worked at many occupations during his lifetime, e.g., painter, burner, truck driver. His work history was moderately continuous until 1962 when he stopped working due to a leg injury.

Mrs. S. comes from a small town in Georgia. She was one of the few blacks in her town to finish high school. She often helped teach in the black school. She continued her education in Atlanta where she attended a nursing school and graduated with an R.N. degree. She met her husband at this time and married. Mrs. S. worked mostly as a private duty nurse while she was in the South. When they moved to San Francisco, she worked at San Francisco City and County Hospital for seven years and also as a private duty nurse. She stopped working in 1951 due to an injury.

The training and job experience of this family accounts for: the emphasis on education, the feeling of being different from others in the neighborhood who have little education and work experience, the use of medical facilities, the speech and vocabulary of Mrs. S., etc. However, some aspects of their life style are particularly incongruous, e.g., Mrs. S.s lack of health care, and lack of cleanliness habits. These life patterns are discussed below.

The S.s live in a low-rent area. Although the neighborhood is predominantly black, there are a few white and Spanish-American families. The dwellings are thirty or forty years old and consist of two or three flats in each house. Each family occupies one floor or flat. Although three houses have been recently painted and two have new false fronts, the rest of the homes on the street are in disrepair. Many of the families on the block own late model automobiles. The S.s have an old truck which Mr. uses to haul junk. It is not considered as the family car nor as transportation for the family.

The S.s moved during the time they were being interviewed. First, the family lived in the lower flat in a very run-down building. The apartment consisted of a kitchen, three bedrooms, a bathroom, and a porch which was used as a sleeping area. The walls were extremely dirty. The hardwood floors were cracked and there was a visible layer of debris, dust, papers, and food littered on the floor. Cockroaches were visible on the floors and walls. Even though there was electric lighting, the house was extremely dark. In the bedrooms, clothing and furniture were scattered around. There seemed to be little room to put things away.

The S. family did not appear to be particularly pleased with this house or its condition; but, they liked the fact that there were more bedrooms and space than they had in their previous house. Mrs. said, "It's nice here, but it needs paint. There's plenty of room, plenty of storage and large closets."

The second flat which the family moved into during the Christmas season was located two houses down the street from the earlier one. It is an upper flat consisting of three bedrooms, a kitchen, a bathroom and a back porch. The number of rooms is similar to the other flat, but the layout is different. The outside of the house has been recently painted, and it is the nicest looking house on the block. On the inside, the walls have been painted within the last few years; the floors have linoleum on them, and there are no insects. This place is generally brighter and cleaner than the other flat. When the family first moved in, the flat was filled with debris. Mr. said, "I'm not going to clean it up," but on Christmas day, everything was clean and in order. There has been a tendency to keep it this way.

It is interesting to note that the S.s had not anticipated moving until two weeks before they actually did. So the condition of the old flat prior to moving was in its usual state. However, in the new flat, although things are in some disarray, there has been a greater effort to maintain order, neatness, and cleanliness. For example, the stove in the old house was black from soot and grease, whereas, when the stove was moved to the new flat, it was cleaned and has been kept this way in subsequent months.

It also appears that since the family has moved to this new flat, more people have visited them. The kitchen is in the middle of the flat and all rooms face it, whereas in the old place it was located in the rear. It provides a place to sit and chat since the living room area is used as a bedroom. Consequently, the mother, who always remains in the kitchen, now has more people around her. In sum, it appears that the new residence has been more livable for the family.

The S.s could have moved out of the neighborhood and into a small house several miles away in the same district, but Mrs. chose to remain in the neighborhood because of the availability of schools and her relations with a few neighbors. She says, "Here it's convenient to everything. I don't have to worry about anything. There's a store and a laundry. There's no meat market, so my husband does the shopping at the big market." She describes the neighborhood in general: "This isn't a bad neighborhood, it's just run-down. If they would build it up, people would think more of it."

Although shopping and services are convenient, Mrs. does not feel she has the same kind of neighborhood relations in San Francisco that she had in the South.

"I like a small place. They are more neighborly. When you need help, they are apt to help you and come around and do things. In my home town, we knew everyone on the street and in the neighborhood. Neighbors all helped. You didn't expect things. They gave us vegetables and we gave them milk. That was neighborly. You didn't have to have money. If parents or children got sick, they would be taken care of by the neighbors. They make you feel you're wanted. They are like that in small places. Not in Atlanta or San Francisco. It's probably like that in small towns in California. It's like that in the church, but you expect them to."

The S.s perceive themselves as being different from their neighbors. They consider themselves as atypical in terms of other people on welfare, as well as those of low income in the surrounding area. For example, the oldest son said if people did not know him personally, they would think that he had been in jail, and did poorly in school, since most of the young people his age in the area had these characteristics. He said, "Your friends judge you from the neighborhood," but implied that he was different since he had never been in jail (Juvenile Hall) and did moderately well in school and liked to read.

Mr. S. said that he was not like the other men who "hung out" on the corner drinking with their buddies or stayed many hours in the local bars. "In this neighborhood, I don't do what they do. They drink too much. That's my complaint. When I drink, I drink in the house and then go to bed."

Mrs. S. indicated that she was very protective of her children and saw to it that they did not get into trouble and were brought up correctly. She says that in her neighborhood, "It's easy to get out of being caught or out of Juvenile [Hall] if you have someone good to stand up for you." Both she and her husband defend their children from outsiders.

Mrs. S. talked about her children's friends, some of whom have been in jail. "He can associate with these boys, but only one is allowed to visit T. Mr. S won't let them out of the house together." On the other hand, she believes that the children of her pastor, who live in the Fillmore District, exert a good influence on her children and help to keep them out of trouble. One of T.s neighborhood friends is constantly at the S.s house. "His parents think a lot of us," Mrs. S. said.

Aside from the children's friends, the family seems to have few relationships with others in the neighborhood or whole Bay Area. Mrs. S. has two or three people in the area whom she considers friends. The woman next door is particularly helpful in child care. Mrs. S. says, "I have a friend on 22nd Street . . . they visit . . . and one on 10th Street. There are some people who moved to Mississippi Street. I don't visit them. I used to visit the people next door before I lost my sight." She said her friends were people that she knew when she worked as a nurse, but she rarely saw them since they were still working and she was not. It appears that since she has been ill and lost her sight, she rarely associates with others.

On the other hand, Mr. says, "I don't have no friends. One of the worst things you can do is have friends. They are always wanting things for free." He does not seem to have any friends in the neighborhood. He says, "I don't have any Negro friends; they are all Italians, Puerto Ricans or Mexicans." These appear to be casual friendships. The reason he does not have black friends is "it's their character." He seemed to change his position on friends; "I don't visit too much. They come here every once in a while. The last time was about a month ago. Both of my good friends have been sick. They're not young people. They're older than I." In sum, he dislikes the neighborhood and the black people in it. The family does not visit others, although a few people visit them.

The family seems to be very individualistic. They keep to themselves and have few dealings with others, including their relatives. Mrs. says, "I have a sister in the city. I haven't seen her in two years. She don't visit me and I don't visit her. Our husbands don't get along. He [Mr.] and my sister never got along, but we did visit. He got along with her first husband."

The rest of their families are in the South. Mrs. went to visit her relatives in Georgia in 1951 and her mother and sister came to California once. She has one sister in Georgia who buys most of her daughter's clothes. "She sends clothes without me asking, especially at Christmas and Easter time. She sends some for the little boy too. Sometimes she tells us to call her, but we haven't seen each other for years." None of Mr. S.s family has visited him, nor has he returned to the South to see them. He says he likes living far away from his relatives.

The S.s main associations are, therefore, inside the home with each other. Outside the home, the mother and children's activities center around the church. (This is discussed below.) The only time Mrs. leaves the home is to attend church meetings. She does, however, prepare her children for outside activities, especially those related to church functions. She gives them a Bible lesson every week before Wednesday night church meeting.

Some of the children are involved in activities connected with school; the oldest boy is on the football team, the youngest boy belongs to the school Cub Scout group. Occasionally, the father takes the children to sports events such as baseball games or the roller derby. For everyone except Mrs. S., the major form of recreation is television and radio. The family owns one television and about three radios. The radio is constantly playing. Mrs. listens to religious, soap operas, and music programs during most of her waking hours, the children listen to rock and roll, and the father listens to baseball games and the fights. No family activities are planned, although Mrs. said that before her illnesses, the family sometimes went on picnics.

Due to Mrs. S.s confinement, Mr. has to do many of the household chores. Mrs. says, "I can't cook or wash, but I can do many things. My husband does lots of things for me." She explained that Mr. did the shopping, cooking, washing, ironing, and cleaning. On any typical day, Mr. spends most of the day doing these things, while Mrs. spends most of the day next to the radio. At the same time, she directs and disciplines the children.

She also apportions money for groceries, children's treats and clothing, and Mr.s spending money for cigarettes and beer. (She first puts money aside to cover rent and bills. There is none left over for savings.) Before most meals, usually the evening meal, Mr. asks Mrs. for some money to buy a few items for that meal. She usually gives it to him and he purchases the items directly. The children ask her for money for school each day to buy lunches or snacks. T. said he preferred to receive money every day instead of a periodic allowance because he could have more this way. "Allowances cut you down," he says.

Mr. said, "Kids today are different. My parents didn't give me fifty or seventy-five cents to spend. Kids today have to have a dollar or they are going to get it someplace. These kids spend twenty-five to a dollar a day . . . we give these kids every day. Not a day passes when they don't get something going and coming from school."

The family is almost constantly buying in small amounts. Food is rapidly consumed and the children always want money for more. They buy candy on the average of four or five times daily.

The house is cluttered with objects many of which are in disrepair. Possessions seem to have little values; often they are broken a day or two after they are purchased. For example, K. received a toy piano for Christmas and the next day the legs and stool were broken. Similarly with T.s record player and M.s transistor radio; and one time, Mr. said that K. had "seventy dresses,' but most were dirty and he bought new ones instead of washing the old ones.

Mrs. has always handled the family's finances. At present, she apportions the welfare allotment. (The check is addressed to her.) Mrs. said that before the family was on welfare, they received some aid from his former employer's disability insurance. The family also received money from the Aid to Needy Children fund. Concerning welfare she said, "It's better. I don't have to worry about the children. They give $50 per child and pay the rent. Other than that we look out for ourselves. As long as my children are taken care of. For my oldest boy we get things that are good and durable so they will last. The little boy doesn't take care of his things. They [Welfare Department] check up. They don't stay on your back, they see how the children are."

Mr. was asked how he felt about being on welfare. He said, "Don't like it, but I can't do any better. I couldn't get a painter's job." And, "It worries me to be on welfare. I never had to have anyone help me do anything. I've always been in the okay. You're looking at a strictly independent man. I'll pay it back if I ever get the money. They have that on record. You don't meet many of my type. A lot of people on this [welfare] is for it, not me. I'm suing someone, and if that comes through, the welfare will be paid back."

The parents take an active part in their children's schooling. Every afternoon when the two youngest return from school, they must read their lessons aloud to their mother before going out to play. Although this "homework" is a must from the family's point of view, they are concerned with few other assignments or other times for studying. The emphasis is on reading skills, which the mother and father consider as the mark of an educated person. Mrs. says:

"With the two boys I taught them the alphabet. But with K., I said, 'I'm going to let them teach her.' This was very wrong. I made a big mistake. Now I can't see. I can't help her. She does awful. She's not interested in reading. It's the system, not the teacher. When M. was in school, I asked him to bring the book home to teach him to spell. They taught sight reading. I'm old-fashioned; they should learn to spell."

"I taught school at home for four months. I don't have the patience for sight reading. I didn't promote but two who could read. The principal promoted all of them. I think a child should know something. My girl doesn't try hard. I don't have to help her with arithmetic. In my family we were all good in arithmetic. It's just reading. Every evening when she comes home from school, before she goes out to play, I make her read her lesson. Then she can play. Then she has to read again."

The mother does her best to help the children with their homework. However, being blind, she cannot see the books or lessons. The children try to trick her and make up words which will fit the story, if they cannot read a word. Also, her conceptions of what each should know for the level or grade they are in is dependent upon what she remembers from her schooling in the South, which she herself describes as inadequate.

The father, on the other hand, believes that education for his children, is the key to their mobility. He himself, having only an eighth-grade education, is often ineffectual in helping the children do their work. Mrs. said, "M.s not doing so good and neither is K. Her daddy's not interested in her work. He tells her to get on out. He's impatient with her more than the others, 'cause she's only a girl." But Mr. says about educating his children: "As long as they are under this roof, they have to go to school." But he has little interest in aiding their daily progress, and often hinders it by ordering them out of the house if he wants peace and quiet.

Education to him is important as a job qualification. He said, "Suppose I put in an application at *PG&E* and I had to read a rule and I couldn't. I would need some education. Or in the work I was doing suppose a person wanted a iron so many inches. You got to be able to measure in inches. You got to have an education to dig a ditch today. Used to be you didn't. They go by the rules now." In regard to his lack of education and its hindrance, he says, "In one way yes and in one way no; there's no job I couldn't do. The way I was brought up was by 'mother-wit.' Kids today are different though."

The S.s take a very lenient attitude in disciplining their children. Little physical punishment is employed, and many verbal admonishments are given, but not taken too seriously. Mrs. says about her husband, "He always tell them how he's going to punish them, but they know he won't. He's like that with all of them. But they know he's not telling the truth." Mrs. says, "With my children, I try to instill the right way. You can make them do something, but you can't decide for them. All parents can do is try. I make them go to church. If you instill some things they will have these things in them." Both parents believe that religious training provides the guidelines for right conduct and discipline.

Many times during the interviews, each parent expressed how they tried to give their children as much as they could, even to the point of depriving themselves. Mrs. said:

"I didn't take care of myself—just general rules. I didn't dress for the weather. I neglected myself. I was busy with the children. I would get things for the children rather than for myself. Things they didn't need, just wanted, when I really needed for myself. But I gave it to them."

Mrs. realizes that she hurt herself by having this attitude. She says, "This is uncalled-for negligence ... I know it's wrong, but God gave me the decision. If He were guiding me, He wouldn't let me. But I do it anyway." For example, she says, "I wanted K. to have a doll and she didn't even ask for it. K. was satisfied but I wasn't." Each parent often remarked that when they were working, they were able to give their children more things. The oldest received many more things than the others because the parents could afford them when he was younger. Hence, there is a feeling with the other two that perhaps they missed out and that they should be compensated.

There seems to be no martyrdom on the part of the parents, even though they indulge their children and take a lenient attitude with them. They simply believe that children are to be loved and given as much as possible. The above statement about neglecting herself was admitted in reference to Mrs. S.s illnesses.

Ideally, Mrs. realizes and says, "It's bad to let the children get their way all the time," but on the other hand, she says of her children, "They are very strong-minded. They pick out what they want to do." And Mr. says that he cannot direct what his children will do or be, "Whatever they want to do, that's left up to them."

Part of this lenient and self-sufficient attitude stems from the family's religious beliefs. Mrs. is an extremely religious person. She believes that her faith in God helps her make decisions, be they right or wrong, helps her discipline her children and helps cure her illnesses. She says:

"God is a superior being—all-knowing and wise . . . He gives us the will to decide our destiny. You know something is right or wrong, and the decision is up to you. People have the ability to know, not a child though. M. should know better sometimes. Christ started at 12 to make his own destiny. Up to 12—God and parents. From 12 to 21 parents are responsible for guidance. After 21, you yourself are responsible all the time. Destiny is your own decision. If He made decisions, all would be good."

"If you choose on your own, you can choose Satan. The world today, they choose Satan. They try to persuade you, it's up to you, if you want to go. People can't make or force you, if you want to be like them better. It's your decision and God has nothing to do with it. There are always two choices: right and wrong. It's up to the individual."

"I make them go to church. If you instill something, they will have these things in them. T. has the Bible school deep down in him; it's instilled in him. M. is devilish and mean, but he says the right things in church. K., we have to help her. It hasn't been instilled in her too good. I try to instill the Golden Rule. K. is sometimes very good, sometimes not."

"Your faith in God helps in sickness. I had faith to get well from cancer. By being blind, my symptoms, I was not able to detect. But through faith, He let someone else see it. I never had any pain. Faith helped me. As far as my blindness, God works in mysterious ways. Sometimes we don't take care of the body, which I didn't. My blindness—not exactly a punishment. We must obey nature's rules. I just accept it. I will see someday, in time.'

Mrs. uses faith to accept her fate on earth. She justifies anything that happens and her unwillingness to change the situation as God's will. Her religion makes her accepting of situations. She says, "There's no hell. If anything's worse than here on earth with all the suffering, sickness, pain, and hunger, that's hell within itself." But, she believes that, "Suffering is relieved by the wisdom of man, for example, man's cures for some sicknesses, but not all."

Mrs. believes that one should trust people and treat his fellow man right. "Go out of your way to be nice. You can't do too much for others. Even if they have more, there's something you can do. I believe in Christian fellowship."

Mrs. especially likes the church she belongs to presently. She thinks that the people are nice and she knows many of them. The family has a close relationship with the pastor, who gives them a ride to the church meetings every week and who prays for them when anyone is sick. People in the church have been helpful to the family when they were in need. Mrs. said:

"We needed a little help. They took up boxes and food. One Christmas, they sent money, so did the missionary aid. When Mr. was out of work, they first helped us. Now they ask, but we don't need particularly, so I don't accept. They gave us a lot of things."

Mr. said he never attended church because he "had no time." But he said, "Do you have to have a church? My father didn't have a church and I believe he went to heaven. I was born and I'll die a Methodist." Mrs. feels badly that he does not attend church. She is a regular churchgoer. In fact, the only time she leaves the house, since her illness, is to attend church on Sunday morning, prayer meetings on Wednesday night, and Missionary meetings once a month on Monday nights.

Although Mr. subscribes to many of the religious beliefs of the church, he is not as bound to it as his wife is, nor does he use faith to justify his life situation. He says, "I don't suffer. I can get anything I want. All I have to do is ask the right people." And whereas he does not do anything to change their current way of life, he says in reference to his children, "I'm not raising them to do this."

In summary, the S.s justify their present welfare status as a result of life misfortunes and circumstances and accept their situation as God's direction. The family as a whole accept their present position, but look to their children for change; they do not expect their children to have the same kind of life. Consequently, education and job training are stressed ideally, but within the home, the children are indulged and treated leniently. The family is self-sufficient and individualistic, having few outside associations with friends or relatives. The primary activities for the woman and children are sought in church participation.

Case History Two: A Nonwelfare Family

On the initial contact with the family, Mr. W. told the investigator that other students had been there before and he had declined to let them come back because "their presence would do his family no good and only add to the confusion of the house." He could understand why we wanted to do the study on his family, but he felt that his family would "derive no benefit out of it." He also thought that he saw life differently from the way others did, because he "lived from day to day, taking things and accepting things as they came." He learned a long time ago that "nobody gives you anything and you have to work hard for everything you get," and that you can't trust anyone. So he had to learn the hard way that "the best thing to do is to mind my own business and leave others alone, as it's hard to get along with all people."

He also contended that he came from a different background, and that his education was spotty, although he did get some high school. He said that things were pretty bad now, "I'm raising thirteen children and working at several jobs. There are eight kids in this house and five elsewhere." Continuing, he said, "I'm fifty-seven years old, work hard, never been on welfare and don't ever intend to be on it. I had a tough life growing up –had to fight to get my schooling, and then had to fight the other kids in order to get home from school—you just have to work hard and make the most of everything you have." Mr. does not drink now and never has, although he has observed others drinking: "As soon as you get two drinks in you, you start acting crazy, lose your senses and fall down on your responsibilities."

It can be seen from this first interview that certain features are already observable. From the outset, Mr. shows us that he is not the kind of person who goes looking for the pot of gold at the end of the rainbow. When his oldest boy, R., (age 15), walked through the room, he said, "I want a better life for my son, and for him to get a good education." His strong position about receiving welfare aid clearly points to the fact that he is a person firmly grounded in the principles of the Protestant work ethic and espouses the view that one must work hard because "nobody gives you anything." He also indicated that he and his family usually have little or nothing to do with either relatives or outsiders. The family as a whole tends to be very individualistic—almost loners.

During this conversation, Mr. began to see the investigator's point of view and reluctantly agreed to let him come a couple of times to observe his family in their daily routine. Mr. also introduced his wife, and an appointment was made with her for the following week.

On subsequent visits, it was learned that Mr. was a general laborer, usually working on building construction projects. However, he was usually unemployed for several months out of the year, so he had to find outside part-time employment at various other jobs which would supplement his unemployment compensation insurance check. On weekends, he often worked as a pool-table attendant in the Fillmore district. He would also get periodic jobs laying wall and floor tile or rebuilding a room or two in someone's home or office. Mr. states that his annual income is about $4720 per year—$3840 in salary, and $880 in unemployment. On this income, he supports his wife and eight children.

The W.s live in the Hunter's Point Housing Project in a seven-room bungalow apartment. There are five bedrooms, a kitchen, living room, and bathroom. They pay $87.00 per month in rent. They have worn furniture, but in good serviceable repair. There are few items, but enough for comfort. The apartment is always clean and neat, even though there is evidence of it being lived in and there is continuous mending of clothes on the open sewing machine. They have lived in the project for almost nine years, and came to San Francisco in 1945 from a rural farm complex in Arkansas (Mrs.) and Louisiana (Mr.).

When the children are at home, there is a constant hum of voices and persons going in or out of either the front or back doors. One is also struck by the lack of quarreling and antagonistic behavior between the children. There isn't much friction between them, nor is there evidence of sibling rivalry. The eldest son, R., usually supervises when he is around the house and does some disciplining. When the younger children need discipline, a stern voice from either Mr. or Mrs. is sufficient. In this respect, the parents are cooperative and consistent, and it is quite apparent in the children's behavior.

Child discipline, however, was not designed to intimidate nor subdue the child's developing personality. Mrs. was strongly concerned about the fact that after her children were old enough for school, she noticed a change in the way they acted. They had become quiet in school and around strangers. She observed that, "They seem to be very talkative at home, but when they get outside they are shy and nonverbal." She says that the older children are very quiet in school, and R.s teacher remarked that he is so quiet, at times she doesn't even know he is there. Another thing that the investigator found peculiar was the fact that none of the children had any close friends or playmates in the neighborhood. They would all come home from school and either play in the house or out in the back yard by themselves. Mrs. still has hope for the youngest child, C. (age 4), who has not started school yet. He still has a good deal of social spontaneity and gregariousness in social situations. But she is fearful that he too will lose this as the others did.

Mrs. is a pleasant-looking woman of medium height and figure for her forty-five years. She has had an eighth grade education, and when asked if she desired more, her reply was:

"It's vital for an individual, I see that from my own experience. Without an education you miss out on a lot of things—like jobs, speech, and you can't understand things. I thought about going to adult evening classes this year to get some more schooling, but Mr. was working so I had to take care of the children. Before I had so many children, I wanted to continue on in school but he talked me out of it. I always listen to him. Mr. feels that one should get his education when he is young. A person just can't get an education when he is older and has many responsibilities on his shoulders."

"We want the children to at least finish high school and maybe go to college. We tell them, if you don't finish high school, you won't know what you've missed until it's too late. I tell the older children that if they don't complete their education now—at least high school—it will be very hard on them later on in life when they get older and want to get married and have children of their own. It will be worse on their children than it is on them right now. An education can give them a better life, they will be happier, and they will have to work less."

Mrs. does not believe in birth control or family planning, "That's God's will." After her sixth child, the doctor asked her if she wanted her "tubes tied," she said, "No, I'm too old for that." She subsequently had two more children.

She felt somewhat discouraged about their financial situation, but had a note of optimism in her daily outlook, "We get along as best we can." (She shrugged her shoulders and turned away.) "It's hard on us when my husband is not working steady. His being out of work gets worse as we go along, push button stuff and tractors get more, I guess there'll always be laborin' though. There's never enough money but we make out on what we have." Mrs. does not worry too much about the future or what lies ahead because her biggest immediate problem is just taking care of the children, seeing them off to school.

When questioned about her views on receiving welfare aid, Mrs. answered this way:

"I don't like it. They make too many demands on you. I know people on it, and in order to get on it, they had to get rid of their car. If you own a car, TV, washing machine, etc., you have to get rid of them—and that's too much of a hardship. It's very difficult, that's why we don't like welfare. Some people get it and throw it away on foolishness, which makes it hard for other people to get it. One good thing about it, you get more per month on it, than on unemployment, but you have to sacrifice more on welfare."

Mr. feels very much the same way as his wife. When asked what he thought of welfare and the people on it, he replied, "It's fine for some people, but not for me. The idea of welfare for those who need it, is good. It does apply to the people that can most use it. Then again, there are those who abuse it, because some people just don't know what they are doing. I know several people on it, but I'm not saying whether they should be on it or off it. But if that's what they want and they can get it, I say let them have it."

Mr., as mentioned earlier, seems to have a very pragmatic approach to life. He says, "I look straight up and down, and don't have any illusions about how things are going to be tomorrow. I don't live in a make-believe world, like most people that go to church. These people (like my wife) are only fooling themselves. They can pray all they want, but nothing is going to help them. I don't worry about what others have, I take what comes and make the most of what I have. I don't buy anything I can't pay for right away. I don't want someone coming around here in the middle of the night knocking on my door, getting me out of bed. The only thing I want to worry about when I go to bed is whether I'll wake up the next morning. Because nobody knows when he's going to die. Besides, I'm getting on in years and that's the reason I don't have a lot of bills outstanding. My wife and children would have to go out and work to pay them off. I never know when I might kick-off and die—only God knows that."

The statements expressed here suggest that this family is bound very tightly by the "press" of their social milieu, the pressures of unemployment, the very meager family income, and deficient education. To a large degree, however, these deficiencies are compensated by personal integrity, strength of character, and existential wisdom. They seem to be a congenial and happy family—even though they have few material possessions. They realize that the future well-being of their children lies mainly in their education. Hence, all energies of the parents are directed toward this goal. Even though Mr. does not have a steady source of income, he does not want his wife to get a job outside the home. He feels that only one person in the family should work, and that one is himself, "otherwise it creates friction between the two of us." He feels that it is his job to bring home the money, and her job to raise the children.

To the inquiry: What's the most important thing to keep in mind about your family?, Mr. answered —

"First is to love the Lord thy God with all thy heart, soul and strength. Second is to love my family and do everything in my power for them. Next is to think about myself. I've worked at many jobs doing hard labor work, and I only have one thing on my mind, and that is to clothe, feed, and have a place for my family to live. If I were single, I wouldn't have to work at all. I could get along by playing pool or billiards (I'm as good as any professional), cards, or dice; and have a good life that way. But I'm not by myself, and I got to think about my family and go to work. I'm a construction worker, and I don't always have steady work, so I do other jobs like floor tiling. I used to be a driver and helper for two years, and I wanted to join the union, but they wouldn't let me because my skin was dark. I also work in a pool hall in the 'Fillmore' for more cash."

Mr. also told his sons about what he has always done no matter what kind of job he has. If he sees a job across the street where he can make "a few dollars more," he'll get that job and do it well—even if he has to give up one that's nice and easy, or secure, and he's making steady money, or if it is clean or dirty work. He says, "I put my faith in my God and myself, and with that combination, I have to succeed in whatever I'm doing."

It is fairly obvious that this family places much importance on individual initiative and self-reliance for "getting their way in the world." Here, family themes such as industriousness and hard work go hand-in-hand with a considerable stress on individual and family isolation. In this latter area, the W.s are very explicit in their feelings about "staying clear" of neighbors, and less frequent contact with their relatives. Mr. has said many times that it's very hard to get along with all people, he learned that a long time ago. So now he just keeps to himself and minds his own business, and leaves others alone. He says that he has some relatives in Oakland—an aunt and uncle—but seldom goes over to see them. He does not get along with them and has not seen them in many years. He does not believe in mutual aid with his neighbors, in fact, he hardly ever talks to them. He says, "I've never borrowed any money from neighbors, about the only thing I've done with them is help someone move heavy furniture when they can't find anyone else to help them. I only have one real friend, Elias,

I see him once or twice a month at work. If I have any problems, I try to work them out myself. If I can't, I just back away from them." Mr. feels that:

"The reason I have little trouble with my children is because they feel secure. They see that my wife and I are happy with each other. And when they see we never argue and don't mess around having fights or drinking, then they get a good impression and they feel secure, and their outlook is better than most."

Mrs. actions are quite similar to those of her husband's in dealing with the outside world. She has several brothers and sisters but has not seen them in many years, and does not write to them very often. She has only one close friend, Mrs. B., who is godmother to all her children. They met when she came to San Francisco in 1945.

Mrs. spends most of her time around the house. She says that her present neighbors are not too friendly. All the old ones have moved out and she does not see them any more. "Now I keep pretty much to myself, as do the children and Mr." She and the family watch TV mostly, and there is little they do in the way of outside entertainment. She occasionally goes to a movie by herself or with the older children, while Mr. watches the other children, but it has been a year now since she has seen a movie. She does, however, attend P.T.A. meetings at the school and sometimes bakes cakes and cookies for their sales. She also goes to adult programs at the school when they are given at night. To the question: How do you get along with your husband?, she replied –

"We get angry once in awhile, then we let it drop at that. We don't let it go on and on. Only once did we ever have a big argument, and that was before we got married. We just don't believe in arguing. Sure we have some differences of opinion, but we usually work it out."

Mrs. does not like city life as well as she liked her rural farm life. She says, "There are lots of open spaces on the farm, like the one I came from. I put up with city life because there is nothing I can do about it. I stay by myself. I've always been one to stay home by myself—I never went to parties or dances or the like. I teach my children to be this way too, because it's too hard to get along in the world and with other people." "Actually," she says, "I don't have much to do with my neighbors. I stay here by myself. Once you get too friendly, they come over early in the morning and they're around all day until late at night. I'd rather not talk to them and keep my distance from them, and be by myself." Mrs. attends the El Bethel Baptist Church twice a month in the Fillmore, but is not friendly with any of the women. She says, "I don't like crowds." She talks over her personal problems with her husband and her friend, Mrs. B.

According to Mrs., people are born with the capacity for doing both good and evil. It is all a matter of learning and training. Her accounts from her childhood and the story about her son, F., suggest that people are usually good to others, but them sometimes think they can "get away with something" (like lying or stealing) and they try it. Eventually they get caught, and then have to "learn the hard way." Many times people do wrong acts toward others unintentionally, which result in hurting someone. She would class this as unnecessary actions. Mrs. feels that in order to avoid problems with people, e.g., unfriendly neighbors, she just does not talk to or associate with them. She also keeps her children from playing with the hostile children at the top of the hill behind their house—so that "there won't be any chances for antagonisms or fights." She has consistently referred to avoidance patterns with the outside world. She functions well as an individual moving in and out of different social situations, but makes little attempt to be friendly to people. Even as a girl (mentioned before), she never went to parties or dances. She has never referred to man's nature or his actions as being derived from God or that man was created out of original sin or that he fell from grace. To her, man's nature is simply a matter of learning by experience and using the capacity he was born with. A person accumulates, in the growing-up process, all kinds of experiences—good and bad—and regulates his behavior to minimize troublesome situations.

On the other hand, Mr. feels that all humans are made in God's image, but that he is mortal and is subject to doing evil as well as doing good. Man is governed by his conscience and must answer to it for all of his behavior. A man's actions are determined by his faith in God. "As for me, I put my faith in myself and in my God, and with that combination, I have to succeed in whatever I'm doing." Mr. feels that, "The essence of man is in his spiritual feelings. God is in your heart. A man is supposed to feel God. If he feels Him and know He is there and has His spirit inside him, then he can do anything. There is nothing more than that to religion." He thinks that those people who go to church and observe all kinds of rituals are observing nothing more than tradition, and he asks: "How can that help their belief in God?" He thinks that it does not do them any good to go to church on Sunday, and then go out the next day and hurt their neighbor. He contends that the secret to a good life is in remembering the Second Commandment, "Love thy neighbor as thyself, that's all that is necessary to be a good man. If a person observes the Ten Commandments, he will have a good life, and he will not do evil deeds." "Even ministers," Mr. states, "are rascals." "They don't always care about the people they are preaching to. They can be crooked too."

In summation, the family appears to be very happy and content within the security of their internal home surroundings. The major form of individual emotional expression is through a high concentration on religious conviction, which is expressed in their personal values and daily interpersonal behavior. They also tend to have as few dealings with the outside world as possible. This is due to the fact that both parents feel "It's hard to get along with all people, so we just leave others alone and mind our own business." As a result, the family places much importance on individual initiative and self-reliance for "getting their way in the world." Here, hard work and industriousness go hand-in-hand with a stress on individual and family isolation.

Section V: Overview

12 Summary of Findings

As stated in the Introduction, the purpose of this study has been to provide reliable information on the characteristics of welfare and nonwelfare families in order to determine those factors that might explain the welfare status of the one group and the nonwelfare status of the other. To achieve this goal, a sample of 600 current welfare families representative of three ethnic groups was selected from four geographic areas of California. An additional 600 nonwelfare families selected from the same four areas were matched with the welfare families for income, ethnicity, and family composition. The 1200 cases were then reclassified in terms of their welfare experience into three groups: (1) those who had never received welfare aid (NOA); (2) those with a short-time aid experience (STA); and (3) those with long-time aid experience (LTA). The 1200 cases were also classified separately by ethnic status and by geographic location. Social, economic, and psychological characteristics of the cases were reported first in terms of their dependency status; second, in terms of their ethnic status; and third, in terms of their geographic status.

Social Characteristics

The first topic to be analyzed was that of the social relations that take place outside the confines of family interpersonal relationships. This topic was divided into two categories, kinship and non-kin social relations, and the following conclusion was made: The frequency of interaction, intensity of relationship, and range of functions performed make kinship the most important social system in the lives of these low-income families. Characteristically, they see one or more of their relatives once a week. More often than not the person whom they choose as a confidant is a close relative. Relatives are the persons they turn to most frequently for help in times of crisis, and relatives are the persons who most often call on them for help. Relatives are the persons most often involved with family members in ritual activities. Relatives play a much lesser role with reference to the economic functions of lending money, providing employment, or helping kinsmen in finding jobs.

The physical proximity of relatives appears to be a significant factor affecting social participation with kin. Interrelated with this factor is a small but clearly patterned reduction in contacts and use of relatives as the welfare dependency of a family increases. This pattern involves a reduction in mutual aid, in frequency of visits, and in ritual activities. No such clear pattern of differences was found when the cases were classified by rural-urban status or ethnic status.

The non-kin social relations of these families tend to focus on the local neighborhoods where they live. Except for church membership, participation in voluntary associations is low by comparison with participation in an informal network of friends and acquaintances. Work is a significant source of friendships for husbands but is of minor significance for wives. The reduced participation of the Long-Time Aid families in a network of kin relations is not compensated for by a *proportionate* increase in relationships with friends, neighbors, and acquaintances. For these LTA families, several of the functions performed by relatives are successfully transferred to nonrelatives, but this is specifically not the case with ritual activities.

The overall social network of these families shows a concentration within a local social world linked to the larger society primarily through work and church membership. The LTA families show a pattern of social withdrawal from this world of relatives, neighbors and friends. Furthermore, the LTA husbands show a decrease in the number of their friends who were first met at work. Correlatively, friends of this type (first met at work) show less participation in the local social world of the LTA families than is true of the NOA families.

The social withdrawal of the LTA families from participation in a local social world, their weakened kinship ties, and reduction in systematic social linkage between work and the neighborhood world point to the relationship between welfare dependency and social life. A family's social withdrawal from this world may be both a cause and an effect of welfare dependency. It seems plausible that for some families weakened kin ties resulting from physical mobility may be a contributing factor to the onset of welfare dependency, and in turn, the continuation of the welfare dependency condition may contribute to continuation and/or intensification of social withdrawal and isolation. For other families, social withdrawal may start with the onset of the welfare dependency experience. In either case, the same conclusion holds, namely, that the social life of these very low-income workers tends to link work and nonwork worlds together and hence sustains the worker on his job. This linkage is weakened under conditions of protracted welfare dependency.

Economic Characteristics

The second topic to be studied was the economic characteristics of the cases. This topic was also divided into two categories, the first dealing with current income, level of living, and economic security; and the second dealing with employment, income history, and occupational status. An inventory of material household possessions showed that almost all the families had TV sets and radios, with a large number also owning old-model cars; but encyclopedias, Bibles, bookcases, and newspapers were utilized by only about a third of the families. When these facts are combined with the conclusions about the social life of the 1200 families, it is evident that TV and the radio constitute major avenues for their contacts with the larger society, possibly outweighing any other form or medium of symbolic communication.

Utilizing the number of material possessions as an index to level of living, the rural Valley cases and the LTA cases showed the lowest level of living, and the NOA and urban cases showed higher living levels.

Data were collected on twelve indexes involving the economic security and foresight practices of these families in past, present, and future. The indexes included Social Security coverage, use of unemployment compensation, union status, personal savings, life insurance, burial insurance, checking accounts, use of credit unions, debts, home ownership, and retirement and pension coverage.

On the average, these families have little or no cushion to take care of the economic crises of unemployment except for those covered by unemployment compensation. Taken as a group, these families have no savings at present, expect to have none in the future, are not covered by employer or union pension schemes, and cannot look to significant help from relatives. Economic insecurity is at the very center of their lives in the past, in the present, and in the future. Their only source for support in old age is the Social Security program of the federal government.

A comparison of the ratio of the 1200 families having savings with a sample of New Haven low-income workers in the 1930s showed that fewer families in the 1964 sample have savings. Comparisons of our sample cases to current national statistics on the debts of low-income workers indicate that our sample families have higher debts than this population. These two sets of facts indicate again that the population represented by our sample is at the bottom of today's low-income population, and suggests that this very low-income group may exhibit as much economic insecurity as was true of low-income workers in the 1930s.

Differences in economic security and foresight practices were found, with the rural cases and the LTA cases once again ranking low and the NOA cases and urban cases ranking high on these indexes. With certain exceptions, it was found that the current income of a given group correlated with level of living and with level of economic security. The NOA families with a median annual income (last twelve months) of $3682 and median family size of 6.8 persons showed greater economic security and level of living. The LTA families with a median annual income (last twelve months) of $3068 and a family size of 6.8 persons showed lower levels of living and economic security. The rural Valley cases with a median income of $3009 and a median size of 6.7 persons showed the same lower economic security and level of living as the LTA cases.[1]

The work and wage histories of the 1200 husbands show their occupational status to be predominantly that of unskilled and semiskilled workers. These men have manifested little occupational mobility and can be characterized as fixed in occupational status. Their low wages coupled with lack of continuity in

---

[1] The median annual income (last twelve months) and median family size of the other subgroups were as follows: STA—$3190, 6.9; San Francisco—$3586, 6.9; San Jose—$3364, 6.9; Los Angeles—$3330, 6.7; black—$3489, 6.9; Spanish speaking—$3351, 7.4; and white—$3162, 6.2.

employment pinpoint the cause of their economic insecurity. Unemployment of varying duration is endemic to the entire group. Job changes are frequent, and a high proportion of these workers have been involved in seasonal work.

When the various indexes derived from analysis of the husband's work histories are combined, differences between the dependency and rural-urban cases were found. When compared to urban areas, the rural Valley cases showed the lowest wages in the past, the least occupational mobility, the highest percentage of husbands in unskilled jobs, and the least continuity in employment. As expected, seasonality of employment was high for this group. The LTA cases showed a quite similar pattern except with reference to wages. If the LTA and STA cases are combined and compared to those workers who have never received public assistance, those with welfare experience show greater oscillation in earning power. Their wage rates have been both lower and higher than the wages earned by the NOA workers.

If the various indexes of the economic condition of these families are combined, it is clear that the rural Valley cases and the LTA cases manifest the greatest handicaps in income, level of living, occupational status, and economic security. The lowered level of living and higher economic insecurity of the Valley families is clearly a product of their entire work histories. In the case of the LTA families, it is difficult to determine whether their greater economic insecurity is confined to the protracted period of their welfare dependency or extends throughout their job histories. When the cases are classified by ethnic status, no such pattern of handicaps is clearly manifested for any one ethnic group.

To understand more fully the present economic situation of the 1200 respondents, we obtained information about their evaluation of aids and barriers in the job-finding process, and about their likes and dislikes on the job. Ill health, lack of skill and training, and age were seen as the chief barriers to employment. Self-help, friends, and the state employment service were listed as the three most important aids in job finding. Money was mentioned most frequently with reference to work itself. The second most important aspect of work concerned the quality of interpersonal relations on the job.

The LTA cases showed the highest percentage listing ill health and lack of skill as barriers to work. They also indicated the least use of friends and relatives as aids in the job-finding process. The white cases also perceived more barriers to finding work than did the other two ethnic groups. In terms of perceived handicaps in the search for work, dependency status is again the most important—though not the only—factor structuring the relationship of these men to work.

Orientations of the 1200 Families

The orientation, i.e., the personal or subjective outlook of these 1200 respondents, can be thought of as both a cause of their life circumstances and as a product of these circumstances. The factors determining their orientation may derive from early experience, from past adult experience, and from the current circumstances under which they are living.

Attitude scales designed to measure psychological dependency, feelings about responsibility between parents and children, and anomie (feelings of hopelessness and alienation) were administered to the 1200 respondents. The results showed the LTA cases to be high in psychological dependency, and high in anomie. The high degree of psychological dependency referred not only to the respondent, but also to his orientation toward his own parents and his own children. The NOA cases showed low scores on these attitude scales.

Equally large differences on these two scales were found for the cases when classified by ethnic status. The Spanish-speaking subgroup showed the highest dependency and anomie scores and the whites the lowest. As these attitude scales predict *both* dependency and ethnic status, the meaning of the anomie and the psychological dependency scores must be interpreted in terms of the ethnic cultures with which the respondents are identified. Our interpretation is that the psychological dependency of the Spanish-speaking respondents is translated behaviorally into interdependence of nuclear family members across three generations. The high anomie scores are quite possibly due to strong solidarity of the nuclear family coupled with a high degree of suspicion and mistrust of outsiders and of the larger community.

At the same time, the differences in orientation of the dependency groups can be interpreted as true differences. It would be expected, then, that the Spanish-speaking Long-Time Aid cases should show the highest anomie and psychological dependency scores within the Spanish-speaking subgroup. A preliminary check of this hypothesis indicates its validity.

The data from the attitude tests suggest that personality factors and present conditions of life probably interact in producing the orientation of the LTA case. His outlook is characterized by a strong inner feeling of dependency and a high degree of hopelessness and alienation. His orientation toward his children is to demand dependency and autonomy at the same time.

Three longitudinal studies of unemployment and welfare dependency during the depression of the 1930s all point to shifts in family relationships resulting from the crisis of unemployment. It was found that the husband's orientation shifted as his authority tended to decline. Attitudes of dependency, denial, rationalization, etc., were some of the reactions of husbands to shifts in their role. To check on this aspect of the worker's orientation, 300 wives from the sample of 1200 families were interviewed concerning the division of labor within the household and their attitudes toward taking the lead in making family decisions.

The separation of husband and wife roles in the family division of labor was found to be similar in pattern to that described in other research studies of blue-collar families. A majority of wives felt that they were dominant in making family decisions and slightly more than one-third said that they controlled the spending of money. When the dependency subgroups of the sample of 300 families were compared, the only major shift in responsibilities that appeared was an increasing control by the wife over the spending of money as welfare dependency increased. In sharp contradiction to this finding, on two attitude questions concerning the distribution of decision-making between husband and wife, there was a reverse pattern with the LTA wives indicating a decrease in their authority.

The major differences in husband-wife roles were in terms of ethnic status. The Spanish-speaking families showed the greatest separation between husband and wife in the family division of labor, though they were not markedly different from the white families. Black families showed the highest degree of husband-wife sharing in the family division of labor.

As with the attitude test data, the ethnic status of the sample families appears to be of equal or greater importance than dependency status in structuring husband-wife roles within the family. The wives' reports did not indicate significant shifts in their orientations toward their husband's role as an authority figure within the household.

An independent check on the orientations of the sample families was carried out by Dr. Hirabayashi, utilizing the answers to open-ended questions on the women's interview schedule. The analysis focused on themes or basic value orientations that express an individual's outlook on the world. The five themes that were analyzed included: mastery or subjugation over life situations; present-, past-, or future-time orientation; orientation toward "doing" or "not doing" in terms of changing life circumstances; orientation toward strong or weak kinship ties; and orientation toward the strength of the father's or mother's role within the family. Unlike the data presented in the other chapters, the respondents' answers were cross-classified by dependency and ethnicity; this made it possible to ascertain if patterned differences between dependency groups are found in each ethnic group.

The sample cases showed a majority emphasis on subjugation to life situation, on present-time orientation, on a 'not doing" orientation, on strong kinship ties, and on dominance of the father. For the white and Spanish-speaking respondents, increasing welfare dependency was associated with decreased relationships with kin. The NOA cases showed more mastery over life situations, gave equal weighting to present- and future-time orientations, and planned activities more often. The Spanish-speaking cases showed the highest degree of male dominance, and were distinctive in their emphasis upon the "not doing' orientation. Almost without exception, these findings support the conclusions drawn in the other chapters of this report.

The eight case studies of families selected from the sample cases in San Francisco point to the same patterns that were revealed in the analysis of life style themes. Additional factors that were stressed included the tendency of respondents to see their *minority* status as a handicapping factor accounting for their depressed socioeconomic position. The case histories emphasize the need of these respondents to rationalize their position. While the white respondents used a different set of explanations than the black and Spanish-speaking cases, they felt equally impelled to explain why they are at the bottom of the socioeconomic ladder.

Two Major Conclusions

When the findings of each chapter are combined, two major conclusions emerge. The first of these is that a coalescence of handicapping factors can be seen in the life history and present circumstances of the LTA families when compared with the other two dependency groups. These handicaps include a pattern of social withdrawal; economic handicaps in level of living, occupational status, income, and economic security; ill health; and attitudes of hopelessness, defeat, and despair. No such combinations of handicaps occurs for any other subgroup of the sample. The rural Valley cases suffer from economic handicaps as severe as the LTA cases, but do not show concomitant social, psychological, or health handicaps. The white cases show as high a percentage of husbands who suffer from health handicaps as the LTA cases, but do not manifest a correspondingly high level of handicaps in other areas.

The very reverse condition obtains in the case of the NOA families. Given the disadvantaged economic status and the economic insecurity of the entire sample of 1200 families, the NOA cases show the least handicaps in terms of social relations, economic condition, and social-psychological orientation. There is a gradient, then, of an increasing range of handicaps that correlates with an increasing degree of welfare dependency.

The second conclusion concerns the relative importance of dependency status, rural-urban status and ethnic status as factors shaping the life styles of the 1200 families. If the central factor differentiating the life styles of these families was ethnicity, then differences in social relations, in economic behavior, and in social-psychological orientation would have been uniformly patterned by membership in an ethnic group. The strength of this ethnic factor would have blurred or obliterated the patterning of family life style that might be associated with dependency or rural-urban status. If the most powerful factor determining life style was rural-urban status, differences in family social, economic, and psychological characteristics would have clustered around this dimension.

In actuality, we found that dependency status was the most powerful factor patterning the life style of these families in terms of their participation in a local social world. Dependency status and rural-urban status were of equal weight as factors in patterning the husband's participation in the labor force, and in major aspects of family level of living and foresight practices. Dependency status and ethnic status were of equal importance in patterning the respondents' outlook except for matters of interpersonal relations within the family. Ethnic status functioned as a patterning factor in family life style primarily with reference to the orientation or subjective outlook of family members, and in certain limited respects with reference to consumption behavior and foresight practices.

Thus, dependency status appeared to be a factor patterning family life styles in all areas of life except within the nuclear family framework. Rural-urban status operated as a factor primarily with reference to economic matters, and ethnic status functioned as a patterning force with reference to subjective outlook and internal family relations.

13 Comparing the Poor and the Affluent

It has become common practice to think of a statistical poverty line as separating one group of families who are uniformly poor from another group who comprise the nonpoor class. Such a poverty line also suggests that variations within the poor and nonpoor groups are insignificant by contrast with the differences between them. In addition, the notion that there is a culture of poverty reinforces this view that the poor are homogeneous in certain key characteristics when compared with the nonpoor. To be more specific the term *culture of poverty* posits the existence of certain socially inherited, common conditions of living and associated, shared outlook. William Wellisch (1968), in his summary of varying usage, states:

Thus, we find from the multitude of statements issuing forth, that a poverty culture as defined includes groups and individuals (1) whose incomes are inadequate to meet their needs as defined by current standards, and (2) who have a particular and consequent outlook on life, characterized by hopelessness, futility, pessimism and fatalism [p. 36].

While there has been considerable discussion about the concept of subcultures and poverty within the lower class,[1] to date few if any statistical studies have been done of variation in lower-class culture judged against the *base line* of middle-class cultural characteristics. Consequently, we do not know with any accuracy at all about how variations in poverty may compare in magnitude or significance with the differences between poor and nonpoor. Neither do we know whether the differences between poor and nonpoor exclude the possibility of the two groups sharing certain cultural elements.

The results of our study, summarized in Chapter 12, have already pointed to important differences within the sample of low-income families, even though taken as a group these families fall below the poverty line. A pattern of differences has been described in life chances and in resultant modes of adjustment, associated with increasing welfare experience, that constitutes a gradient or scale of increasing impoverishment. Utilizing these results, we wish to compare the 1200 low-income families to a sample of middle-class families to see how these intraclass differences compare with the differences that exist between

---

[1] For a discussion of the generic problem of defining subcultures, see *The Sociology of Sub-Cultures*, edited by David Arnold, Berkeley, Calif.: The Glendessary Press, 1969. For a detailed critique of the culture of poverty concept, see Charles Valentine, *Culture and Poverty*, Chicago: The University of Chicago Press, 1968.

lower and middle class. As we just indicated, in making such comparisons we can also look simultaneously for characteristics that the two classes may have in common.

The comparison group consisted of 43 families selected from the San Francisco Bay Area who could easily be classified as upper middle class on the basis of education, occupation and income. The cases, collected in the Fall of 1965, constituted a quota sample, just as did the 1200 low-income cases. When the average annual per capita income of $486 for the poverty families is matched with $3,191 per person for the upper-middle-class (UM) households, the poverty gap takes on the characteristics of a gulf.[2]

Given this large income difference, the comparison of other economic, social, and psychological elements in the life style and life chances of these families allows assessment of whether or not the same gulf separates them at all points. The alternative possibility is that for a significant number of characteristics, there may be only small differences or no differences at all between the two groups.

Socioeconomic and Demographic Comparisons

The 43 families[3] selected for comparison had a median annual income of $15,000 (last 12 months ending in the summer of 1964), a median education of 16 years' schooling, and all the husbands but one are involved in either skilled, professional, clerical, or managerial occupations. Compared with the low-income households, their families are only two-thirds as large and show longer residence in one place (Table 13-1). The husbands are slightly older (age 40 as compared with age 37). These high-income couples have been married, on the average, for 14 years, compared with 11 years for the low-income sample. Husbands in the high-income group report no welfare experience, compared with an average of 23.6 months for the low income breadwinners.

The picture of the two groups, then, reveals a gulf between them in socioeconomic status and, by comparison, much smaller differences in such demographic indices as husband's age, family size and family stability. The couples appear as middle-aged, stable parents, each family having one or more children.

The ethnic composition of the 43 UM class families is 81.4% Anglo-white, 11.6% black, and 2.3% Spanish-speaking, a radically different distribution from

---

[2] Reducing the $3,191 upper-middle-class income figure by 5% ($160) to adjust for one year's inflation changes the ratio of high to low incomes from 6.6 to 1, to 6.3 to 1.

[3] In certain ways, it appears incongruous to compare 43 cases (a rather small sample) to 1200 cases (a rather large sample). If reasonable caution is used in interpreting the meaning of differences between the two samples, there is no statistical reason negating the procedure. No tests of significance were computed. Rather, patterns of difference between the two groups, when compared on a number of items, were considered to be better than chance differences.

Table 13-1
Background Characteristics of High-[1] and Low-[2] Income Families

Indexes	Related Tables	High-Income Families	Low-Income Families
Socioeconomic			
1. Median annual income (last 12 months).	(3-10)	$15,000	$3,306
2. Median education (years of schooling)	(3-10)	16+	9.4
3. Usual occupation (per cent unskilled and semiskilled)	(3-10)	2.3%	85.4%
Demographic			
4. Family size	(3-10)	4.7	6.8
5. Husband's median age	(3-10)	40	36.9
6. Years married	(3-6)	14	11.2
7. Median months residence in same neighborhood	(3-10)	46	25.4
8. Those with a history of some rural residence (husband)	(3-10)	58%	70%
Welfare			
9. Median months on welfare (entire job history)	(3-10)	0	3.6
10. Median dependency index	(3-10)	0	50.6

[1] n = 43
[2] n = 1200
[3] To avoid needless duplication of results already presented, for each characteristic listed, additional table numbers are shown (in parentheses) where appropriate statistics are given for subgroups of the Low-Income sample.

the roughly tripartite division of the low-income cases. For purposes of comparing differences *within* the lower class to differences *between* lower and middle class, it was concluded that the ethnic distribution in the high-income sample did not have to be similar to that of the low-income group.[4]

Neither was any attempt made to collect cases of middle-class families from a rural environment, as was done with the low-income sample. Thus, the comparison across class levels was of a large, variegated lower-class sample with a small, homogeneous, upper-middle-class set of families representing an ideal type or blue-ribbon sample of urban, middle-aged, middle-class people.

It is not surprising, then, to find that the range of variation in attitude and act

---

[4] The term *low-income families* will be used interchangeably with lower-class, working-class, proletariat, and poverty families. Correspondingly, *high-income families* will be used interchangeably with middle-class, upper-middle-class, bourgeois, and nonpoor families.

is less for the middle-class cases than for the more diversified lower-class sample. Whether or not there is as large a range of life styles or as great a melange of subcultures within the middle class is not known. We are assuming that the inclusion of more middle-class cases in our sample would not change our basic conclusions.[5]

Our comparisons of the middle- and lower-class cases will be presented under headings corresponding to the topics taken up in each chapter of the report, with the exception that no thematic analysis was made (as in Chapter 10) of the open-ended questions for the upper-middle class questionnaires. A summary and interpretation of the results provide a synthesis of the detailed comparisons made in the body of the chapter.

Kinship Bonds

The differences between lower- and middle-class use of kin shows up most clearly in the stronger economic relations that middle-class families have with their relatives. It was noted in Chapter 4 that economic aid of all types among kinsmen is the function most conspicuous by its absence among low-income families. This function *is* performed by kinsmen among upper-middle-class families (Table 13-2). A second difference is found in the greater concentration of intimacy within the nuclear family (Item No. 11, Table 13-2) for the UM class households.

Not having held constant the confounding factor of geographic propinquity as a determinant of interaction, we can not say categorically that high-income families visit their relatives less often than low-income families, but various items suggest that different patterns are involved. One clue is given in the differential participation in ritual, with low-income families showing more of such activity with kinsmen than the UM sample. It appears that lower-class people *rely* more on kin, even though at the same time they do not, and apparently can not, provide the mutual economic aid that is forthcoming between kinsmen of the high-income group.

Each of the differences that has been described is clearly class structured as the difference is found when the high-income sample is compared with each of the 10 subgroups of the low-income sample. Furthermore, the interclass differences for these indexes are larger than any differences between ethnic groups in the low-income sample.

Non-Kin Relations

The comparison of high- and low-income groups in Table 13-1 indicated that the former group has higher residential stability. Such stability may well explain the larger number of neighbors known to high-income families (Table 13-3).

---

[5] Recent research challenges the long-standing conclusion that the values of middle-class life, both in the United States and in Europe, restrict the range of life styles more narrowly than is true for either lower- or upper-class cultures. See, for example: *The Sociology of Sub-Cultures* (Arnold, 1969).

Table 13-2
Indexes of Interaction with Kin; for High-[1] and Low-[2] Income Families

Kinship Indexes	Related Tables	High-Income Sample[1]	Low-Income Sample[2]
1. Median no. of relatives in local area	(4-1)	3.1	3.5
2. Percent of cases with relatives in local area	(4-1)	74.4	85.5
3. Percent of local relatives living in same neighborhood	(4-3)	6.5	24.0
4. Median no. of visits per yr. with 1st local relative	(4-4)	32.4	51.4
5. Median no. of visits per yr. with 2nd local relative	(4-4)	10.0	41.2
6. Median no. of visits per yr. with 3rd local relative	(4-4)	6.0	33.9
7. Percent participating with relatives in ritual activities	(4-6)	12.2	18.4
8. Crisis mutual-aid with relatives (expressed as % of total aid)	(4-7)	23.3	45.2
9. Relatives used as confidants (expressed as % of all confidants)	(4-8)	40.5	43.4
10. Percent of husbands having no confidants	(4-8)	21.4	33.5
11. Of those using relatives, percent of husbands using wife as confidant	(4-9)	88.2	50.8
12. Percent paying money to relatives in last year	(4-10)	25.6	10.8
13. Percent receiving gifts from relatives in last year	(4-11)	57.1	31.4
14. Percent of husbands receiving help from relatives in getting a job	(4-12)	48.8	29.8
15. Percent of husbands having worked for relatives	(4-13)	25.6	14.2

[1] n = 43
[2] n = 1200

The indexes of non-kin interaction given in Table 13-3 show only one clear difference between our two samples, and this is in the use of voluntary associations. Not only do UM class persons make much more extensive use of churches, rotary clubs, alumni clubs, etc., to mention only a few of the various types of associations peopled by the middle class, but both secondary schools

Table 13-3
Indexes of Interaction with Nonkin for High-[1] and Low-[2] Income Families

Indexes	Related Tables	High-Income Families	Low-Income Families
1. Percent knowing one or more neighbors	(5-1)	100.0	85.2
2. Median no. of neighbors known	(5-1)	8.0	5.2
3. Percent of husbands listing one or more friends	(5-3)	100.0	92.7
4. Percent of husbands belonging to one or more organizations	(5-5)	81.4	58.6
5. Median no. of organizational memberships of husband	(5-5) (5-6)	2.5	1.2
6. Percent of families participating in crisis mutual aid (last 12 months)	(5-2)	69.8	74.4
7. Median no. of family's crisis mutual aid relationships (last 12 months)	(5-2)	.41	2.3

[1] n = 43
[2] n = 1200

and colleges are significant sources for the development of long-time friends. This does not appear to be the case for the husbands of our lower-class sample.

The outstanding exception to this pattern was found in the attachment of lower-class Spanish-speaking families to the Catholic Church and to its various subsidiary organizations. Some 90% of these families' organizational affiliations were with the Catholic Church and its associations (Table 5-6).

Except for this clear difference, patterned differences in the lower- and middle-class social networks did not show up in indexes such as frequency of interaction with friends or number of neighbors known. Some patterns *do* emerge when both kin and non-kin participants in the family's overall social network are classified by where such participants first met.

Modal Patterns in Overall Social Networks

The data in Table 13-4 show patterns differentiating lower and middle class that are similar to the results of other studies. That is social networks of lower-class persons focus on a local social world that includes first kin and neighbors and, second, friends met at work. Middle class persons' interaction networks are more broadly based, focusing first on people met at work, second on kin, and third on friendships made through voluntary associations and through neighbors.

Table 13-4
Three Indexes of Interaction of High-[1] and Low-[2] Income Families Classified by Source of Participants

Indexes by Source of Participants	Related Tables	High-Income Families	Low-Income Families
1. Percent of participants in family crisis mutual aid	(5-9)		
(a) First met at work		11.8	7.9
(b) First met in neighborhood		29.4	35.6
(c) First met at home or through relatives		38.2	49.0
(d) First met other (school, etc.)		20.6	7.5
Total		100.0	100.0
2. Percent of participants in men's routine mutual aid	(5-11)		
(a) First met at work		19.5	21.7
(b) First met in neighborhood		43.5	45.0
(c) First met at home or through relatives		29.3	27.3
(d) First met other (school, etc.)		7.7	6.0
Total		100.0	100.0
3. Percent of husband's friends	(5-12)		
(a) First met at work		40.2	27.0
(b) First met in neighborhood		19.7	50.2
(c) First met at home or through relatives		14.2	15.1
(d) First met other (school, etc.)		25.9	7.7
		100.0	100.0

[1] $n = 43$
[2] $n = 1200$

What other research has not focused on adequately is the fact that there is as much variation between subgroups within the lower class in the use of kin, for example, as there is between lower and middle class. Thus *two* findings emerge. Lower- and middle-class families' social networks are distinguishable by the bases or sources on which mutual aid and friendship interaction are developed. This base is essentially *provincial* for the lower-class families, and by contrast, more *cosmopolitan* for the middle-class families.[6] At the same time, large variations in

---

[6]The terms *provincial* and *cosmopolitan*, as used here, are slightly changed, but still basically similar, to Merton's terms, *locals* and *cosmopolitans*.

the use of any *one* base of social relations, such as the neighborhood or kinship, are found when ethnic or geographic groups within the lower class are compared (Tables 5-9, 5-11, and 13-4).

Health and Economic Security

The poverty gap is also a health gap, as none of the high-income families is hampered by illness, whereas almost one-third of the low-income families had members whose school or work was limited by illness or injury (Table 13-5). In similar fashion, when the two groups are compared for indexes of economic security, there is a gulf separating them that seems to dwarf any differences that appear within the lower-class sample. The only exception to this rule is in federal Social Security coverage, where the two groups are almost equal.

Whereas 98% of the high-income husbands are covered by pensions or other retirement plans, only 18% of the poverty breadwinners have any provisions for economic security in old age other than the federal government's social security system. The figures for percent of families having savings, life insurance coverage, and home ownership are much the same. As stated earlier in this study, while 56.6% of low-income husbands have held a union job at some point in their work careers, only 13% have had as many as three union jobs. Because these men have held many different jobs during their working lifetimes, in the main they do not enjoy the additional economic security that continuous union membership brings to the lower-class worker. As a final point, we note that the low-income families are lacking in even such routine middle-class practices as the use of a checking account.

Whether viewed in terms of kinship, mutual aid, personal saving, investments or ownership of real property, or in terms of company pensions or union retirement schemes, these low-income families are lacking in economic security, both in the short run (with reference to unemployment, sickness, or other financial crisis), and in the long run with reference to old age. The only *two* supports against economic insecurity that they do have are federal-state unemployment insurance and federal Social Security.

The facts about the employment history and present employment position of the low-income husbands (Table 13-6) present both similarities and differences to the UM-class husbands. All but a handful of the low-income group have been unemployed at some time, and this experience has not been just a one-time affair (Table 13-6). The combination of frequent job changes and seasonal employment means that unemployment and the search for work is a recurrent and never permanently solved problem. The high-income group presents almost the exactly opposite picture. While the high-income husbands show no current unemployment, we note that the differences in current employment for lower-class males are larger than the differences between lower- and middle-class breadwinners.

Table 13-5
Indexes of Health and Economic Security for High-[1] and Low-[2] Income Groups

Indexes	Related Tables	High-Income Sample	Low-Income Sample
Health			
1. Percent of families with ill health	(7-12)	2.3	31.0
(a) Husband with ill health or injury		0	16.5
(b) Wife with ill health or injury		0	4.0
(c) Children with ill health or injury		2.3	7.8
(d) Others with ill health or injury		0	2.7
2. Percent of husbands having difficulty getting a job due to ill health	(7-13)	0	16.4
Economic Security			
3. Percent of husbands covered by Social Security	(6-4)	88.4	83.0
4. Percent of wives covered by Social Security	(6-4)	53.8	30.2
5. Percent of husbands having utilized unemployment compensation	(6-5)	0	41.8
6. Percent of husbands expecting pensions or other monies on retirement	(6-6)	98.0	18.7
7. Percent of husbands having held one or more union jobs	(6-7)	16.3	56.6
8. Percent of families with savings	(6-8)	83.8	9.0
9. Median amount of savings (for families with savings accounts)	(6-8)	$1,600	$217
10. Percent of families with life insurance policies	(6-9)	85.4	25.9
11. Median amount of life insurance (for those families having insurance)	(6-9)	$37,500	$5,000
12. Percent of families with checking accounts	(6-11)	97.7	11.3
13. Percent of families belonging to a credit union	(6-11)	34.9	7.1
14. Percent of families with debts	(6-12)	87.2	76.5
15. Family median debt (for families with debts)	(6-12)	$17,000	$649
16. Percent of families owning own home	(6-15)	76.7	12.9

[1] n = 43
[2] n = 1200

Table 13-6
Occupational History and Employment Continuity for Husbands of High-[1] and Low-[2] Income Groups

Indexes	Related Tables	High-Income Husbands	Low-Income Husbands
1. Percent of husbands in professional and managerial occupations	(7-1)	53.5	1.6
2. Percent of husbands in unskilled and semiskilled occupations (for entire job history)	(7-2)	2.3	85.4
3. Percent of husbands who have never been unemployed	(7-6)	83.7	12.0
4. For those with unemployment history, median no. of months unemployed	(7-6)	3.0	9.6
5. For those with unemployment history, median no. of times unemployed	(7-6)	1.6	2.1
6. Percent of husbands having same job for last three years	(7-7)	71.4	32.9
7. Percent of husbands having three or four jobs in last three years	(7-7)	16.7	40.9
8. Percent of husbands with one or more seasonal jobs in last three years	(7-8)	2.3	41.8
9. Percent of husbands currently employed full time	(7-4)	100.0	50.0

[1] n = 43
[2] n = 1200

Material Possessions

The large difference between the two sample groups is not as great when they are compared for ownership of such items as TV sets, radios, and refrigerators. We find that 95.3% of the high-income families have cars, while this figure is 70.4% of the low-income households (though, in the latter case, the cars are older models). However, the variation in car ownership within the lower class is quite large, ranging from 49 to 85% (Table 13-7).

The same picture does not obtain, though, where material possessions related to *reading* are concerned. Here upper-middle-class families are uniformly above low-income families. We can conclude that the provincial character of lower-class social networks is revealed yet again in the lack of cultural items that reflect reading habits. Interclass differences are much larger than intraclass variation for these items.

Table 13-7
Material Possessions, Including Indexes of Reading, for High-[1] and Low-[2] Income Families

Material Possessions	Related Tables	High-Income Families	Low-Income Families
Percent of Families Having:			
1. Radio	(6.2)	97.7	87.8
2. Telephone	(6.2)	100.0	48.8
3. Television	(6.2)	88.4	89.4
4. Vacuum cleaner	(6.2)	93.0	27.7
5. Washer	(6.2)	90.7	45.4
6. Washer and dryer	(6.2)	65.1	4.1
7. Sewing machine	(6.2)	86.0	42.7
8. Refrigerator	(6.2)	97.7	89.1
9. Automobile	(6.2)	95.3	70.4
10. Auto less than 4 yrs. old	(6.2)	60.5	5.9
Items Related to Reading:			
11. Bible	(6.2)	79.1	35.7
12. Bookcase	(6.2)	97.7	32.4
13. Newspaper subscriber	(6.2)	95.3	37.9
14. Encyclopedia	(6.2)	76.7	21.9

[1] n = 43
[2] n = 1200

Job Finding, Job Satisfaction, and Values of Work

The data collected on how husbands in the two groups engage in job finding show large and important differences. UM-class husbands mention reliance on self-help almost three times as often as lower-class husbands (Table 13-8). The table also shows that UM-class husbands are able to *personalize* the process of job finding much more than is true for lower-class males. Relatives, employers, and friends are all mentioned more often by high-income husbands as important aids in finding jobs (Table 13-8), whereas lower-class husbands resort more often to use of want ads and the California State Department of Employment, even though they list these sources as low in producing results (Tables 7-14 and 7-16).

When asked about the qualities of work itself, husbands in both groups agree that work provides a living and that it should pay more (Table 13-9). Beyond this similarity, the groups diverge sharply in satisfactions that work provides them. The high-income males see work as purposeful and interesting, bringing self-respect and friendships and not much more. Thus, work is supportive of positive self-conceptions for middle-aged, middle-class males. It is much less

Table 13-8
Most Important Sources of Aid in Job-Finding as Specified by High-[1] and Low-[2] Income Husbands

Sources of Aid in Job-Finding	Related Tables	High-Income Husbands	Low-Income Husbands
1. Percent of husbands listing self-help	(7-15)	69.8	24.5
2. Percent of husbands listing employers	(7-15)	23.3	5.7
3. Percent of husbands listing relatives	(7-15)	18.6	8.1
4. Percent of husbands listing friends	(7-15)	23.3	19.8

[1] n = 43
[2] n = 1200

Table 13-9
Positive Characteristics of Work Mentioned by High-[1] and Low-[2] Income Husbands

Positive Characteristics of Work	Related Tables	High-Income Husbands	Low-Income Husbands
Percent of Husbands Listing:			
1. "Provides a living"	(7-16)	51.2	40.5
2. "Friendship and Association with nice people"	(7-16)	46.5	22.8
3. "Brings self-respect"	(7-16)	37.2	9.0
4. "Interesting and purposeful experience"	(7-16)	62.8	18.3

[1] n = 43
[2] n = 1200

supportive for lower-class males but not, therefore, lacking in relevance, as additional indexes indicate.

Several other indicators are significant in ascertaining what meanings work has for the two groups of males. The data on employment already cited (Table 13-6) indicate clearly that the low-income husbands have much less continuity of employment, and therefore less job security than the high-income husbands. This difference should not, however, cover over the fact of very large differences in employment history of the low-income husbands when classified by welfare experience. While no UM-class husbands are currently unemployed, 19.8% of the NOA husbands in the low-income sample are currently out of work, compared with 48.1% for STA husbands, and 73.8% of the LTA male heads of households.

It appears, then, that while the NOA husbands have much less job security than the UM-class husbands, when compared with the LTA cases, they look more like high-income husbands in so far as having a job is concerned.

Still another measure of the significance that the job has for lower-class males is found in the fact that work is an important source of friendship and mutual interaction, even though subgroups of the low-income husbands show large variations on this factor. Taking all these indexes into account, we conclude that work carries common meanings for low- and high-income husbands at the same time that it also carries very different meanings.

Husband-Wife Roles

The differences between lower- and middle class families in intrafamily division of labor center primarily on greater husband-wife *role-sharing* or joint responsibility in the case of middle-class households. Middle-class parents engage in child-centered activities more often on a joint or shared basis than does the sample of lower-class parents. Father tends to help his daughter with homework as often as the mother, whereas in the lower-class families, the tendency is for either one or the other parent, but not both, to carry out this activity (Table 13-10).

Table 13-10
Husband-Wife Roles: Sharing of Household Tasks and Child Care by High-[1] and Low-[2] Income Couples

Activities and Tasks	Related Tables	High-Income Couples	Low-Income Couples
Percent of Couples Sharing a Given Task or Activity:			
Household Tasks			
1. Laundry	(9-1)	4.8	13.6
2. Cooking	(9-1)	7.1	16.7
3. Dishes	(9-1)	16.7	10.3
4. Housecleaning	(9-1)	14.6	18.0
5. Shopping	(9-1)	28.6	55.0
Child-Centered Activities			
6. Child care	(9-2)	52.6	38.4
7. Child discipline	(9-2)	73.7	65.0
8. Outings with children	(9-2)	83.8	73.8
9. Helping with schoolwork	(9-2)	78.6	37.7
Money			
10. Controlling money expenditure	(9-3)	63.4	39.2

[1] n = 43 wives
[2] n = 300 wives

The same finding holds for control over the spending of money. Almost two-thirds of the upper-middle-class families say that control over money is a joint responsibility, compared with one-third of the low-income families.

The second important finding is that for *household tasks*, no really clear pattern emerges separating lower- and middle-class households. Differences between ethnic groups within the lower class are as large as differences between lower and middle class (Tables 13-10, 9-1, and 9-2).

Anomie and Dependency

One element in the poverty pattern about which all writers seem to agree is that the poor manifest attitudes of apathy, hopelessness and alienation, as well as psychological dependency.

This conclusion is upheld insofar as the UM-class husbands showed much less anomie than lower-class males (Table 13-11), and this finding holds when they were compared separately with each of the subgroups within the lower-class sample (Tables B-1 and B-2).[7] The gradient of increasing anomie associated with increasing welfare experience for the low-income sample is smaller in range than the average difference between lower- and middle-class samples.

Slightly different results were found for the variable of psychological dependency. All the subgroups within the low-income sample showed higher unacceptable dependency than was true for the high-income sample (Tables 13-11, B-1, and B-2).[8] At the same time, differences in the dependency scores for ethnic groups within the lower-class sample are as large as the differences between lower and middle class.

Summary and Interpretation of Results

Starting from the large income difference that separates them, the data on poverty and nonpoverty families show *clear differences*[9] between the two groups in a whole range of vital characteristics. For these characteristics, poor and nonpoor appear as two homogeneous groups separated by different life chances and different subjective outlooks.

They are radically different in educational attainment. In economic security,

---

[7] The scale range for anomie scores is from -2 to $+2$. The higher the score, the higher the level of anomie. The average anomie score for the UM-class sample was $-.99$; the average for the low-income males was $+.01$.

[8] The scale range for dependency scores is also -2 to $+2$. The higher the scores, the higher the unacceptable dependency. The average score for UM-class cases was $-.97$; the average for low-income cases was $-.46$.

[9] By "clear differences," we mean that for a given characteristic, differences *within* the lower class are smaller than differences *between* lower and middle class, and the statistics for the middle class will be consistently different in the same direction (higher or lower) when compared with the statistics for subgroups of the lower-class sample.

Table 13-11
Attitudes of Anomie and Dependency for High-[1] and Low-[2] Income Husbands

Anomie and Dependency Scales: Mean Scores for 19 Items[3]	Related Tables	High-Income Husbands	Low-Income Husbands
Unacceptable Dependency Scale	(8-1) (8-2)		
1. Item no. 87		− .88	− .60
2. Item no. 89		−1.42	− .66
3. Item no. 95		− .30	− .53
4. Item no. 98		− .62	+ .02
5. Item no. 100		−1.28	− .43
6. Item no. 102		−1.30	− .57
Acceptable Dependency Scale	(8-1) (8-2)		
7. Item no. 86		+1.02	+1.14
8. Item no. 88		− .10	+ .14
9. Item no. 92		+1.2	+1.17
10. Item no. 93		+1.1	+1.55
11. Item no. 94		+1.2	+1.62
12. Item no. 99		+ .21	+1.06
Anomie Scale	(8-5)		
13. Item no. 70		−1.42	+ .06
14. Item no. 72		− .26	+ .29
15. Item no. 73		−1.17	+ .06
16. Item no. 75		−1.16	+ .30
17. Item no. 78		−1.35	+ .53
18. Item no. 82		−1.28	− .29
19. Item no. 83		− .31	− .92

```
                Scale Values
        −2    −1    0    +1    +2

        Low dependency    High dependency
        Low anomie        High anomie
```

[1] n = 43
[2] n = 1200
[3] For the list of items comprising each scale see Appendix Tables B-1 and B-2.

job security, occupational status, and occupational mobility, the lower-class cases are the *have nots* and the UM cases the *haves*. The same conclusions hold true for the health handicaps that plague a disproportionate number of lower-class families. They also *read* less than middle-class people.

In social relations, economic aid of various kinds from kinsmen is a significant practice in the middle class, but is lacking among the poor. With one major exception (the Catholic Church), the use of schools and voluntary associations as a base for personalized social interaction is concentrated within middle-class families. In two important aspects of family life, the controlling of money and in child-rearing activities, responsibilities in the middle class are joint (between husband and wife), but are much more nearly separate for lower-class marital pairs. In terms of subjective outlook, the proposition that the poor have attitudes of hopelessness and futility was found to be true when their average score on the anomie scale is compared to the sample of middle-class males. Table 13-12 summarizes these clear differences between poor and nonpoor.

Let us then summarize those characteristics that do *not* clearly differentiate lower and middle class or, what is even more important, those characteristics shared by the lower and middle classes. While there are large and imposing differences between the two groups in material possessions, there are also some near similarities which must be listed—ownership of radios, TV sets, refrigerators, and even of automobiles. In frequency of interaction, and in a *given base* for interaction, such as kinship or work, the two groups do not appear as dissimilar. It is only in *overall pattern* of interaction that they differ. From this, we conclude that the provincial base of lower-class interaction networks, when compared with middle-class cosmopolitanism, involves both similarities and differences, and does not constitute a *clear difference* between the two groups.

In the division of labor within the family, there is more variation among lower-class families than there is between classes. In somewhat similar fashion, it is not clear that psychological dependency characterizes the lower class by comparison with the middle. The variations in level and in the meaning of psychological dependency between ethnic groups in the lower class are so large as to warrant the view that there is not a clear difference between the two groups.[10]

Finally, and most importantly, we can point to the fact that differences in current employment within the lower-class sample are larger than the difference between lower and middle class. The 79% of the NOA husbands who are currently employed participate in the same breadwinner role that is shared by all the UM husbands in the sample. By the same token, we find that for these lower-class males, work is a source for generating mutual aid and friendship interaction almost as frequently as it is for UM males. The difference between the two social classes in the use made of work as a source for social interaction is a difference, then, that rests upon a common base—fulfilling of the breadwinner role.

Now, in evaluating these similarities and differences between poor and nonpoor as they refer to the term culture of poverty, we must necessarily consider the cultural elements that have been described as more than a list of items to be counted and summed. Each cultural element or set of elements has

---

[10]The same point is made by Oscar Lewis in the Introduction to *La Vida* (1965).

Table 13-12
Indexes that Do Clearly Differentiate[1] High-[2] and Low-[3] Income Families

Indexes	Related Tables
Socioeconomic	
1. Average number of years schooling	(6-1)
2. Occupational status	(7-1), (7-2)
Social Network	
3. Percent of families showing economic reliance on kin.	(4-10), (4-11) (4-12), (4-13)
4. Frequency of visits with 2nd and 3rd local relatives	(4-4)
5. Crisis mutual aid with relatives (expressed as percent of total aid)	(4-7)
6. Percent of families knowing one or more neighbors	(5-1)
7. Frequency of family crisis mutual aid	(4-7)
8. Number of husband's organizational memberships	(5-5)
9. Percent of husband's friends first met at work	(5-12)
Health	
10. Ill health of family members	(7-12), (7-13)
Economic Security	
11. Percent of husband's having utilized unemployment compensation	(6-5)
12. Percent of husbands expecting pensions	(6-6)
13. Percent of families with savings	(6-8)
14. Percent of families with life insurance	(6-9)
15. Percent of families with checking accounts	(6-11)
16. Percent of families belonging to a credit union	(6-11)
17. Family median debt (including mortgage)	(6-12)
18. Percent home ownership	(6-15)
Work	
19. Percent who have never been unemployed	(7-6)
20. Percent of husbands having same job for three years	(7-7)
21. Seasonality of jobs	(7-8)
22. Percent of husbands currently employed full time	(7-4)
23. Percent of husbands mentioning self-help, employers and relatives as important aids in job finding	(7-15)
24. Percent of husbands specifying that work "brings self-respect" and "is an interesting and purposeful experience"	(7-16)

Table 13-12 (cont.)

Indexes	Related Tables
Material Possessions	
25. Telephone in home	(6-2)
26. Vacuum cleaner in home	(6-2)
27. Washing machine in home	(6-2)
28. Washer-dryer in home	(6-2)
29. Sewing machine in home	(6-2)
30. Automobile owned (less than 4 yrs. old)	(6-2)
Material Possessions Related to Reading	
31. Bible in home	(6-2)
32. Bookcase in home	(6-2)
33. Newspaper subscriber	(6-2)
34. Encyclopedia in home	(6-2)
Husband-Wife Roles: Sharing of Household Tasks and Child Care	
35. Shopping	(9-1)
36. Child care	(9-2)
37. Help with schoolwork	(9-2)
38. Controlling spending of money	(9-3)
Dependency and Anomie Orientation	
39. Average anomie scores	(8-5)

[1] Where intraclass differences are smaller than interclass differences, and central tendency measures for high-income group are uniformly different from those for the low-income group.
[2] $n = 43$
[3] $n = 1200$

to be taken as a clue or indicator of function, that is, of the tendency for cultural differences to separate lower and middle class, and of similarities or shared elements to bind them together. Our concern, then, is not only with cultural traits but also with social bonds and with social distance, both within and between the two groups.

From the summary just made, it would appear that what is common between poor and nonpoor is less than what differentiates and also separates them.[11] Yet, this gives us no evaluation of near similarities and shared elements.

One way to accomplish this end is to compare the interclass differences and similarities that have been found to the differences *between* welfare groups within the lower-class sample. When this is done, a striking conclusion emerges.

---

[11] In summarizing his conceptualization of the concept, culture of poverty, Lewis describes a key consequence as: "Lack of effective participation and integration of the poor in the major institutions of the larger society...." (1965), p. xlv.

Table 13-13
Indexes That Do Not Clearly Differentiate[1] High-[2] and Low-[3] Income Families

Indexes	Related Tables
Social Networks	
1. Frequency of visits with 1st local relative	(4-4)
2. Percent of husbands using relatives as confidants	(4-8)
3. Percent of husbands having no confidants	(4-8)
4. Number of husband's friends	(5-3)
5. Percent of husbands belonging to one or more organizations	(5-5)
6. Percent of families participating in crisis mutual aid	(5-2)
7. Percent of families participating with relatives in ritual activities	(4-6)
8. Sources of participants in men's routine mutual aid	(5-9)
Economic Security	
9. Percent of husbands covered by Social Security	(6-4)
10. Percent of husbands having held one or more union jobs	(6-7)
11. Percent of families with debts	(6-12)
Work	
12. Median number months unemployed (for those having experienced unemployment)	(7-6)
13. Median number of times unemployed (for those having experienced unemployment)	(7-6)
14. Percent of husbands specifying that "work provides a living and creates friends"	(7-16)
15. Percent of husbands mentioning "use of friends" as an important aid in job finding	(7-15)
Material Possessions	
16. Radio in home	(6-2)
17. Television in home	(6-2)
18. Refrigerator in home	(6-2)
19. Automobile owned	(6-2)
Husband-Wife Roles: Sharing of Household Tasks and Child Care	
20. Laundry	(9-2)
21. Cooking	(9-2)
22. Dishes	(9-2)
23. Housecleaning	(9-2)
24. Child discipline	(9-2)
25. Outings with children	(9-2)

Table 13-13 (cont.)

Indexes	Related Tables
Anomie and Dependency Orientation	
26. Mean scores, attitudes of acceptable dependency	(8-1)
27. Mean scores, attitudes of unacceptable dependency	(8-1)

[1] Where intraclass differences are as large or larger than interclass differences
[2] n = 43
[3] n = 1200

The coalescence of handicapping factors that differentiates the NOA cases from the LTA families (with the one exception of social withdrawal from kin) turns out to be precisely the same set of cultural characteristics that differentiate lower from middle class (Table 13-12). For example, if lack of economic help from relatives is a handicap occurring more frequently among LTA than NOA families, lack of help from relatives also occurs, on the average, much more frequently among lower class- than middle-class families.

Now, the LTA cases are *furthest removed* and the NOA cases are *closest to* the middle class precisely for 33 of the 39 items that differentiate the two social classes. (See Table 13-12.) But we also know from the comparisons just made that the differences between NOA and LTA lower-class families are in every case smaller than the differences that differentiate lower- and middle-class life styles. So what is the function of these highly patterned, small differences within the lower class when judged against the large differences separating lower and middle ranks?

The condition of the LTA families represents not only a widening and deepening of the already existent differences between lower and middle class, but represents at the same time an erosion of near similarities and of the breadwinner role that employed workers share with their middle-class counterparts. Unemployment and subsequent welfare status are associated with an increase in provincialism, and a narrowing in the base of the family's social network. The social withdrawal of the LTA families seems to create a difference in type of interaction pattern when compared with the nonwelfare lower-class families that is not found when the NOA families are compared with the middle-class households. What is of equal or even greater importance, the protracted loss of the breadwinner role, resulting in subsequent welfare status, involves changes in self-definition and identification on the part of the lower-class male that constitutes a weakening or loss of a critical element in life style that is shared by the employed poor and the nonpoor alike.

This view leads us to a statement about the culture of poverty, taking into account both similarities and differences between poor and nonpoor viewed against the baseline of middle-class culture. The subculture of poverty consists of at least two major types. The first type of poverty involves families whose life chances and subjective outlook are quite different from the nonpoor, yet who still share certain common cultural elements with the nonpoor. While lacking in economic security, suffering from ill health, and apathetic and alienated by contrast with middle-class families, the husbands of these lower-class families are employed a large enough percentage of the time so that they retain their self-definition as breadwinners, and thus share a vital element of middle-class culture and values.

The second type of poverty represents an intensification of all those attributes that define poverty as contrasted with nonpoverty, while at the same time eroding or destroying those cultural elements shared with the middle class. The living condition of this second type of poverty, for both rural and urban groups in California, and for white, black, and Spanish-speaking alike, are those of near-pauperization, increased social isolation, threatened loss of respectability, and erosion of, or change in, the male breadwinners' self-definition.

We might expect these poor persons who are different from the middle class in major respects, but who share certain vital elements, to display values that *combine* elements of lower- and middle-class life.[12] This is the position taken by Hyman Rodman in his description of "The Lower-Class Value Stretch" (1965). This type of value pattern would appear to be consistent with the life style of the NOA families in our sample. The LTA families, suffering from an intensification of poverty conditions, and at the same time, losing common elements with the middle class, would be subject to a much more potent *stretch* of values—a stretch that may cause the fastenings, secured at one end by a middle-class anchor, to tear loose.

In Chapter 11, the conclusions drawn from the case histories, derived independently from the questionnaire data, and drawn up without prior consultation with the study director, are identical with the interpertation just given.

---

[12] Oscar Lewis (1965) suggests that among the poor he has studied, there is recognition of middle-class values and verbal use of them, but little tendency to put them into practice. While he is not discussing poverty in the United States, his point is that of the *value stretch*. See the identical conclusion drawn by Hirabayashi, et al., in Chapter 11 of this volume, concerning verbal idealization and actual behavior of lower-class (LTA) males.

14 Interpretation of Findings

This chapter will be devoted to an explanation of the ways in which handicapping factors in the lives of these 1200 families coalesce to produce differential adjustments for the male head of household. An outline will be presented of those factors in lower-class life tending to reinforce and those factors tending to weaken the worker's identification with the world of work. The response of male workers to these forces will be described in terms of four types of adjustment. Three of these types are covered by the NOA, STA, and LTA cases within our sample. Description of the fourth type will be based on other studies.

The dynamics of adjustment producing the first three types of family life style will be analyzed in terms of two feedback cycles, one that takes place during the predependency experience of a family, and a second that takes place during the welfare dependency experience itself. The implications of this model for policies and programs in the welfare field will then be discussed briefly.

Forces Affecting the Lower-Class Breadwinner Role

Perhaps the first point to be made is that any theory purporting to explain the causes of welfare dependency must also explain what it is that maintains people at work. E. Wight Bakke states this necessity succinctly:

The effects of and adjustments to unemployment among the working class are meaningless unless they are seen as the products of men's attempts to maintain what comfort and assurance can be had from participation in the ways of the folk. The study of unemployment becomes therefore a problem in searching for an accurate description of the normal course of working-class life which the lack of earning and work interrupts [1940, p. 305].

Studies of unemployed and retired blue-collar workers point uniformly to the conclusion that work signifies more to these men than just the wages received.[1] Perhaps first among the factors in the work situation that are significant to the blue-collar worker is his participation in the informal and social system and the

---

[1] See for example, Friedmann and Havighurst (1962), Morse and Weiss (1962), and Loether (1964).

225

microculture of work.² The answers of our respondents in evaluating their work experience are consistent with the findings of other studies that the human relations within the work setting are of importance to workers.

Still another significant factor is the quality or skill level of the work itself. There appears to be a gradient of decreasing significance attached to the qualities of the job as the skill level of work declines.³ As the bulk of our 1200 respondents have worked at low-skilled jobs, it was not surprising to find this factor to be of little significance in their statements about likes and dislikes on the job. For those workers with a lifetime expectation of unskilled and semiskilled jobs, sociability would appear to be the dominant value derived from the work experience, second only to the central importance of money.

The significance of work for white-collar employees, and particularly for professionals, is quite different. These middle-class workers tend to identify with the qualities of the job itself. The character of the work done and the self-definition of the worker are intertwined. Achievement, status, contribution, profit, and service are all symbols that have significance. Work and income, in and of themselves, are taken for granted. While they are the most important elements in the work situation, middle-class workers nevertheless take them as given. The investment of self in work tends to be maximized. Herbert Gans describes the middle-class worker's ideology in the following way:

Therefore, work is not simply a means for achieving the well-being of the nuclear family, but is also an opportunity for individual achievement and social service. Although the career, income, status, and job responsibility are important, job satisfaction is even more important although it is not always found. Indeed, professional work satisfaction is a focal concern not only for the breadwinner, but often for the woman as well [1965, p. 307].

In contradistinction to this orientation, for lower-class persons the character of the work done is secondary to the fact of working. Lower-class workers consider working and income as goals to be *achieved*.⁴ This emphasis upon the achievement of a working status becomes even more central for those workers at the bottom of the occupational ladder, where there is less continuity of employment, and where the unskilled nature of the work provides little basis for personal identification.

The lower-class worker's identification with working, with the money earned thereby, and with the sociability to be found on the job does not attach him to any particular work place or firm. He can shift from one job to another, but the elements in work that have significance for him are relatively constant.

---

²The body of literature starting with the famed Hawthorne Western Electric Studies of the 1930s has grown to include a large number of research studies and commentaries. Miller and Form's *Industrial Sociology* (second edition, 1964) provides a summary of the "human relations in industry" research.

³See, for example, Kornhauser (1965) and McKinley (1964).

⁴See Gans (1965), Bakke (1940), Morse and Weiss (1962).

Another characteristic arising from the continuous practice of work activity is the patterned set of habits and the routine that orders one's life on a daily basis. The studies of retirement among blue-collar workers indicate the force of this factor in maintaining people at work.

All these elements are tied together in the worker s conception of himself as a *breadwinner.*[5] The breadwinner role is significant first because of the necessity for cash income to maintain a livelihood within an industrial order.[6] Beyond this level of necessity, the breadwinner role functions in the life of the blue-collar worker to link him to the Protestant ethic of the dominant society, at the same time that it is significant for his self-definition as a man. His male ego—his conception of himself as a man—is both expressed and reinforced by working, by income, and by participation in the microculture and informal relationships on the job.

Occupational Status, Mobility, and Aspiration Level

For those workers at the bottom of the occupational ladder, this breadwinner role is status conferring with reference to his role as a man, but is *not* status conferring in terms of occupational prestige or social class position except in the negative sense, i.e., it defines him as at the bottom of the social order. Furthermore, there are no aspects of his job that allow any escape from the occupational status that identifies him as low man on the totem pole. Some types of jobs are low in occupational prestige but high in pay; others confer some occupational prestige but carry quite low salaries. By and large, neither of these occupational opportunities have been open to the 1200 respondents in the study sample.

Still another element of occupational life that tends to bind persons to work is the opportunity for advancement, either within the same occupational category or through occupational mobility. The 1200 workers we studied show a very low degree of occupational mobility and manifest little or no trend for increases in wage level with increasing years of work. While these facts do not prove, as such, that occupational advancement was unavailable to these men, it seems clear that their opportunities for occupational mobility have been very limited.

The other side of the opportunity for mobility is the desire for it. While we did not question the husbands about their occupational aspirations, their

---

[5] The central role of breadwinner for blue-collar workers is posited by a very large number of researchers, including Bakke (1940), Hurvitz (1964), Komarovsky (1940) and (1964), and others.

[6] The cases included in our sample are all families who have been caught up in the industrial system and do not have an alternative economic base outside the industrial wage system to which they can return. The importance of such alternatives is discussed in Hughes' (1962) analysis of the role of ethnic groups in industry.

comments on likes and dislikes at work indicated that occupational mobility was low in significance for them. Other studies have indicated that the aspiration levels of blue-collar workers are lower than those of white-collar workers.[7] At the same time, studies such as Komarovsky's *Blue-Collar Marriage* (1964) and Kornhauser's study of mental health among auto workers (1965) point to the blue-collar worker's frustration due both to fixed status and low job satisfaction.

In the main, the mobility aspirations of these men appear to have been transferred to their children, as a very high percentage of them *hoped* that their children would go to college. Komarovsky (1964) and Rainwater (1959) found this same displacement of occupational aspirations from parent to child among the blue-collar families they studied.

The relative absence of prestige, skill, and occupational mobility in the jobs of very low status blue-collar workers has led some writers to argue that such workers have little or no identification with the world of work. As has been indicated in our discussion, the absence of these elements in the blue-collar worker's job does not warrant the inference that the breadwinner role has no significance in linking him to the work world. It is true, nevertheless, that the bonds arising from the job itself that link the worker to his work are more limited for the very low status worker than for any other occupational group.

The factors that have been listed are not, of course, the only elements that affect the worker's relationship to the job world. The nonwork side of life—the worker's involvement in family, school, church, and in the ways of the "folk" all influence his conduct and orientation, and have potential significance in weakening or strengthening his ties with work.

Social Relations and Work Identification

Studies and commentaries on the values or central life interests of the very low status worker have produced somewhat conflicting viewpoints about the significance of work in his scheme of things. Davis (1946), Dubin (1956), and Gans (1965) have emphasized its limited significance; whereas Bakke (1940), Komarovsky (1940) (1964), Morse and Weiss (1962) and Hurvitz (1964), among others, emphasize the relative importance of work as a value. Despite differences in emphasis, all these writers recognize that the significance attached to work may vary for the various levels and types of groups contained within the lower or working class.

An alternative way of casting light on this issue is to look at those kinds of relationships that may act as *reflectors* of the value that the worker attaches to

---

[7]See, for example, the summary discussion in Chapters 5 and 13 of *Work and Society* by Edward Gross (1958). Miller and Riessman (1964) suggest that stability and security are of preponderant importance to blue-collar workers by comparison with occupational mobility.

his job. Writers on lower-class culture seem in general agreement that informal social relationships carried on in the worker's local social world are of central value to him.[8]

If the local social world (including friends, family and kin) is a dominant focus for lower-class male identification, the crucial question to be answered is whether or not this world interconnects at any point with the world of work. Are these two spheres of life totally separate for lower-class persons or are they interconnected? If they are interconnected, does this linkage strengthen or weaken the identification of the worker with the job world?

The interconnection between the work and nonwork worlds of lower-class men occurs primarily through friendships and informal social relationships. The sources of a man's friendships, the use made of these friends, and the interconnections between circles of friendship are a valuable index to the relative importance of the various sectors in a man's life. For the 1200 husbands in our sample, we found the first source of friends to be from the neighborhood, the second source from work, and the third source from family and kin.[9] Some 27% of the husband's friends were first met at work. Some 7.9% of persons involved in family crisis mutual aid relationships were friends first met by the husband in a work setting. This figure increased to 21.7% for friends from this source involved in routine mutual aid relationships with the 1200 husbands. Both of these types of mutual aid tend to be centered in the husband's local social world rather than around the job context.

The number of a man's friends first met at work and the participation of these friends in his local social world show a decline with increasing welfare dependency. This reduction in the use of friends first met at work is correlated with a pattern of social withdrawal by the LTA cases.

If it were true that lower-class workers have no identification with work, and that their central identification is within a local social world, then there should be little or no interconnection between friends derived from these two sources, and there should be little or no disturbance in the worker's local social world due to prolonged unemployment. The very opposite results are indicated by our data. Consequently we conclude that the significance of the worker's social relations on the job are reinforced by systemic linkage between the job circle of friendships and participation in peer groups within a local social world. His self-definition as a man is supported by an interlocking of work and nonwork social worlds. Work is secondary in importance for the blue-collar worker, but his social relations outside the job tend to support his attachment to the work world.

---

[8] The value of men's peer groups is emphasized by most of the writers on lower-class culture such as Davis (1946), Miller and Riessman (1964), Blum (1964), Rainwater (1959), and Gordon and Anderson (1964).

[9] Blum's discussion (1964) of studies on the sources of workers' friendships points to the conclusion that work is less important to blue-collar workers as a source of friends than is the case with white-collar workers.

Family Stability, Illness, and
Employment Continuity

Another element in the low-status worker's social world that holds him at work is the stability of the family unit. Allison Davis, in his classic article, "The Motivation of the Underprivileged Worker" (1946), posits lack of family stability as a central factor in the low work motivation of the men that he studied. S.M. Miller (1964), Riessman (1964), and Gans (1962) consider the same factor as central in defining the characteristics of these stable workers who are at the bottom of the occupational ladder. The studies of unemployment during the depression all lead to the conclusion that the position of husband and father are key elements in the breadwinner role, and thus support the blue-collar man in his linkage to the labor market.

Still another factor whose effect on the worker is obvious is that of illness. Davis has suggested malnutrition and lack of sleep as additional factors weakening the motivation of the low status worker.

Elements in the orientations or attitudes of the 1200 husbands that seemed to reduce employability were a high degree of psychological dependency and anomie. Another value of lower-class culture that may also interact with the above-mentioned factors in weakening the motivation of blue-collar workers is that of the "con-man" orientation. Walter B. Miller (1965) and Sidney Bernard (1964) suggest that this may be a focal concern of lower-class persons.

The last to be listed and undoubtedly the most important factor affecting the low-status worker's tie to the work world is the lack of continuity of his employment resulting from the demand for labor. Lack of continuity in employment appears to weaken the worker's motivation for work, while simultaneously weakening the social matrix that maintains his identification with work.

The Coalescence of Forces

While each of the above factors has been described in terms of its presence or absence, it is obvious that each is a variable and operates in terms of degree. It is also clear that the strength of each factor is related to the presence of the other factors. Taken in the aggregate, then, this set of factors when operating at full strength functions to maximize the low-status worker's attachment to the labor force. At the opposite pole, the absence of these factors produces a weakening effect.

The coalescence of all those factors tending to weaken the worker's capacity to fulfill the breadwinner role (with the one exception of family stability) can be seen in the lives of the Long-Time Aid families, and something of the opposite conditions can be seen in the lives of the Never On Aid families.

What is suggested then is a set of forces creating a gradient of worker attachment to the labor force, though, as will be explained, this gradient is undoubtedly not a straight-line function. As worker attachment to the work world is weakened by a coalescence of forces, a redefinition of the self takes place and the individual becomes less and less able to respond to employment opportunities or to participate in activities such as training programs that may eventuate in employment. A variation of this same pattern can be seen in the man who works only intermittently and briefly and does not define himself as a "regular" worker in the labor force.[10] Though considerably less than ideal, the index of worker attachment or of unemployability that we have used is the length of the husband's welfare dependency experience.

The coalescence of social, economic, psychological, and health factors that have been listed serve first to differentiate the 808 families with one or more months of welfare experience from the 392 families who have never received public assistance. Secondly, within the welfare group, the same set of factors functions to differentiate the 571 Short-Time Aid cases from the 237 families with Long-Time Aid experience. These groups may thus be roughly ranked from high to low along a gradient of unemployability. But the gradient of unemployability extends beyond these types to a fourth class of workers whose high degree of unemployability is associated with family instability. Though this type of case was not included within our sample, a brief description of these workers is valuable in explaining the life style of the families we studied.

The Alienated Nonworker—One of the Subcultures of Poverty. This group of workers has been described by Allison Davis, David Matza, Herbert Gans and S.M. Miller. The key factors affecting their lack of attachment to the labor force are family instability and low continuity of employment. This type of worker suffers from a high rate of unemployment, is chronically ill, may suffer from malnutrition and sleeplessness, is not part of a stable family unit, has experienced a low level of employment continuity, and manifests a very low level of living. He may also manifest high psychological dependency and anomie, though there is no direct evidence from research studies to substantiate this hypothesis. Allison Davis' description of such workers emphasizes the system of adaptation that emerges from the characteristics that have been listed. Widespread mutual aid and sharing are used as mechanisms to cope with fluctuating levels and sources of income. These workers do not, then, show the same type of social withdrawal pattern that has been identified in the intact family LTA cases. The values of these workers, according to Davis, emphasize living in the present and direct impulse gratification.

This pattern constitutes a subcultural system of mutual expectations that negate the breadwinner role and support the participant in a role of nonworker.

---

[10] Lack of geographic mobility is one of the standard elements listed by economists as a factor associated with unemployment. This factor did not show up as significant in any of the various types of data that were collected. However, the data were not organized to identify this factor—hence, it may have been operative in the occupational histories of the 1200 sample families.

The fulfilling of this role is built around almost total insecurity, and undoubtedly involves a strong emphasis on the "con-man" orientation. Participation in the labor force is intermittent and for brief periods. Considerable effort and energy may be directed toward obtaining money, but the definition of such activity makes it qualitatively different from legitimate work.

While the participants in this subcultural pattern may constitute a changing population, and at the periphery may include families in various stages of disintegration, it is plausible to assume that stable families with a male breadwinner would have a low rate of participation within this system.

The carriers of this subculture may manifest varying degrees of rebellion, defeat, and despair in their orientations to life, but one common characteristic is the tendency for alienation from key values of *both* the stable lower-class and middle-class worlds. The reference group of these people must necessarily be themselves. Perhaps the chief remaining social link between these people and the outside world would be through kinship linkages.

The routes by which the alienated very low status worker reaches the position that has been outlined probably vary, ranging from the young adult who has never had much work experience or stable family of his own, to the individual who has had stable work periods, but over a period of time has been subjected to all the forces that have resulted in family breakup and loss of capacity to fulfill the breadwinner role.

Stable Family Low-Status Workers. The characteristics of the other three worker types can be illustrated by the NOA, STA and LTA cases from our study sample. While the employability of the husbands varies, all three types look quite similar by contrast with the alienated nonworker type. In a variety of ways, these families look much alike in their life chances and life style. In educational level, and in their occupational and income histories, they manifest only small differences; all of them share the common quality of functioning as *intact* families. It is the coalescence of handicapping factors in social relations, health, and psychological dimensions *coupled* with economic handicaps that leads to variations in degree of employability.

The NOA Worker. The image of the very low status worker who successfully fulfills the breadwinner role is a man with an intact family whose work provides some modicum of job stability. His linkage with kin and his participation in a local social world are extensive. Judged in terms of the statistical characteristics of lower-class persons, he tends to be healthy, shows relatively low psychological dependency and does not have strong feelings of hopelessness and despair. His orientation to life and his family relations may be as strongly patterned by his ethnic background as by his low socioeconomic status, but this does not affect his participation in the labor force. While his family suffers from a high degree of economic insecurity, he does engage in those limited foresight practices that his meager income level allows. His frustration due to lack of status achievement may be high, but the other elements in his adult life offset the debilitating effects of such frustration insofar as his work orientation is concerned.

This qualitative description of the very low status worker who successfully fulfills the breadwinner role is quite similar to the picture of the blue-collar husbands in the families described by Mirra Komarovsky in her volume *Blue-Collar Marriage*. Although a large percentage of these husbands held jobs that were higher in occupational status than the occupations of our respondents, the family life style is similar in major outline to the 392 NOA cases of our sample.

The STA Worker. The 571 families in our sample who were classified as Short-Time Aid cases show a higher incidence of all those factors that operate to weaken the worker's attachment to the labor force. Their employment continuity has been lower, they show some weakening of kinship ties, and some loss of social linkage between work and nonwork worlds, and manifest the most marked withdrawal from non-kin social relationships. A higher percentage mentioned illness as a barrier to work, and the husbands showed a higher degree of psychological dependency and anomie than the NOA husbands. They did not show significant shifts in family relations except an increase in control by the wife over the spending of money.

Despite the presence of these factors, the STA husbands show strong capacity for fulfilling the breadwinner role, as the period of their welfare dependency has been short. Their strong attachment to the labor force is signified by their rapid return to work.

Among this group of families are an unknown number who will become Long-Time Aid cases. As will be explained later in the chapter it is our hypothesis that the welfare dependency experience itself interacts with family handicaps to determine the LTA case. Consequently, at the outset of the welfare experience, it may be difficult to identify those particular families who will eventually show a low degree of employability.

In the responses to attitude questions, and in their reports of their conduct, there were hints that these husbands react strongly to the onset of welfare dependency. These men may be making efforts to cling more strongly to those patterns that maintain the breadwinner role, even though various forces threaten to erode the bases that maintain these elements in their life style. The studies of families who experienced unemployment and welfare dependency during the depression indicated the operation of such processes during a family's initial adjustment.

Because the employability of these men remains high, we can conclude that their major difficulty is related to the availability of employment. While their background shows a coalescence of handicapping factors, the precipitating crises that have resulted in a resort to public assistance do not weaken their ability to recover and to reenter the labor force.

The Long-Time Aid Cases:
Near Pauperization

The LTA cases in our sample show the highest incidence of illness, have experienced the lowest level of employment continuity, manifest a high level of psychological dependency and anomie, show the weakest links with kinsmen, and display the strongest withdrawal from participation in a local social world. The data that were collected indicate that the husbands of these families do not show any major shift in fulfilling their accustomed role within the family unit. The one shift that does occur is for increased control by the wife over the spending of money.

The Long-Time Aid status of these families is an index to their relatively low employability. While all of the factors that have been mentioned produce an erosion of capacity to fulfill the breadwinner role, they have not resulted in the disintegration of the worker's family or of his position within it.

These two characteristics of the LTA families in our sample—the maintenance of an intact family unit and the maintenance of the husband's role within this unit—indicate important differences between the LTA husband and the alienated workers who participate in a nonworker subcultural system. At first glance, these findings appear to be contradictory to the conclusions drawn from the depression studies of family response to unemployment and welfare dependency. The depression studies emphasized the loss of the husband's authority within the family and the tendency for family breakup under long-time unemployment and welfare dependency.[11]

One possible explanation for this discrepancy arises from the AFDC-U welfare program itself. It operates as a selective agent in providing support for those families that show a high survivor value in withstanding loss of the husband's breadwinner role. If the family does break up and public assistance is required for the mother and children, they are then transferred to the AFDC public assistance program and disappear from the AFDC-U rolls.

Other possible explanations can also be suggested. Closer examination of the cases might reveal differences in adjustment between ethnic groups, and there are some hints of such differential adjustments in the data presented in Chapter 10. It may also be the case that the questionnaire used in this study was not adequately designed to identify changes in authority patterns within the family.[12]

---

[11] Ferman (1964) suggests that the type of family studied during the depression period was patriarchal and that many present-day low-income families are matriarchal. Hence, the loss of the breadwinner role in matriarchal low-income families would not be paralleled by loss of the husband's authority. While this argument sounds plausible, it does not hold up when applied to the Spanish-speaking families in our sample. These families are patriarchal and do not appear to manifest loss of the husband's authority with extended welfare dependency.

[12] S.M. Miller (1964) has epitomized families of this type as "copers" and suggests they may have manifested downward mobility. In actuality, there had been little opportunity to identify the characteristics of the LTA family type until a higher degree of social visibility was given to them by the inception of the AFDC-U public assistance program. Our data do not indicate any pattern of downward *occupational* mobility for the LTA families on a large scale, but the case studies suggest that they may have *feelings* of downward mobility, and that they are coping to resist this trend.

Our hypothesis is that the LTA cases described in this study represent a set of families who have, for various reasons, been able to withstand the stress involved in the husband's loss of the breadwinner role. Maintenance of family stability operates to keep the loss of the breadwinner role from eroding away the man's role as husband and father. We have interpreted the husband's withdrawal from participation in a local social world as due, in part, to fear of sliding down into the subculture of the alienated worker. Maintenance of family life would appear to be a last bastion against loss of public respect and self-respect.

Unlike the STA cases, the Long-Time Aid husbands manifest a considerable degree of unemployability. The coalescence of forces weakening their capacity for reemployment has undoubtedly resulted in some redefinition of the self. The case studies indicate that these men talk in contradictory terms. They have been on public assistance at least a year and yet they *talk* in terms of identification with the breadwinner role. The data in Chapter 10 indicate that these families show less planning for the future, tend to live in the present, and are more resigned to the circumstances of their lives than either the NOA or the STA cases. The attitude test data indicate that they show a greater sense of hopelessness and defeat.

The contradictory elements in the conduct of the LTA husbands when considered in conjunction with their tendencies for withdrawal suggest that these LTA families represent an adjustment pattern that is not adequately supported by a subcultural system. The adjustment of each family is made individually, and represents a response to life chances that are parallel to rather than interactive with that of other LTA families.[13] We would predict then that there is little or no tendency for LTA families to seek out others in similar circumstances and to thus form the social basis for development of a subcultural system.

The Predependency Feedback Cycle

The four modes of adjustment among low-status blue-collar workers result from combinations of social, economic, medical, and psychological forces in the worker's world. The analysis posits the central significance of the breadwinner role in the lives of these families, but does not describe the dynamics whereby a given adjustment is reached. Our explanation of the processes that bring about differential adjustments will be made by positing two feedback cycles. The analysis will be restricted to the 1200 intact families that were studied and will not cover workers with broken families. The first of these feedback cycles occurs during a family's predependency period before any welfare experience has occurred, and the second refers to the welfare dependency experience itself.

While it has been mentioned before, we wish to reemphasize the fact that the differences in the predependency experience of the NOA, STA, and LTA families are very small. It is only when various handicapping factors coalesce in a

---

[13] Ferman (1964) points to the need for differentiation between parallel responses to similar life changes and subcultural systems that provide supports for the participants.

family's prewelfare dependency experience that differences in family adjustment take place.

Of the various handicaps that have been listed, it is difficult to know how many are present in the prewelfare conditions of the worker's life and how many are present only as a result of the welfare dependency experience itself. Consequently, the reconstruction of how these handicaps operate through time, and at given points in time, will necessarily be largely hypothetical.

In the predependency experience of the sample families, the factors that serve to differentiate the 392 nonwelfare from the 808 welfare cases can be classified as elements in the worker's environment or elements in his personal orientation. In environmental factors, the 808 welfare cases show slightly more economic insecurity, more medical problems and more social isolation than the nonwelfare families. In their personal orientation, they also show more anomie, more psychological dependency, and more tendency to live in the present without planning.

A first factor probably appearing in the predependency experience of some families is illness. Whether viewed as organic or functional in character, illness turns the individual back on himself and produces regressive tendencies. Thus, it might seem plausible that illness tends to increase psychological dependency. On the other hand, it is equally plausible to suppose that a high degree of psychological dependency may produce psychosomatic illness.

Another factor probably appearing in the predependency environment of the welfare families is a weakening of kinship ties. One factor creating this handicap is a family's geographic mobility. In all the various mobility patterns that take place, some significant number of workers become physically isolated from their kin. The resultant weakening of kinship ties may be associated with the worker's sense of loss of social support. This loss of social ties may then produce feelings of anomie. However, the opposite sequence is equally plausible. Families whose personal orientation includes a strong sense of isolation and/or alienation from others, and from the norms and goals of the larger society, are precisely those persons we would expect to have weak kinship ties. It may even be the case that an individual's personal orientation dictates, in some degree, his geographic mobility. Those who move most frequently may be the most ambitious and resourceful, but they may also be drifters who have no social roots and who manifest little sense of attachment to other persons or groups. Thus, the mobility that produces lowered kinship participation may be due, in part, to the personal orientation of the individual.

We know that the third factor of economic insecurity operates more strongly in the predependency experience of the 808 families with welfare experience than it does for the 392 nonwelfare families. Such economic insecurity may tend to create attitudes emphasizing living in the present, acceptance of fate, and lack of planning. Where the future seems always uncertain, the worker's attitude may be to accept these conditions in his life. Just as with the other factors, we can argue with equal force that workers whose values emphasize living in the present, who seem unable to plan, and who accept their environment as fixed and determined would also tend to occupy those jobs that provide the least economic security and the fewest material rewards.

Following this reasoning, we can not assign a priority either to environmental factors or to elements in the worker's personal orientation as predictors of subsequent welfare experience. It is equally plausible to consider the worker's environment or his subjective orientation as cause or effect of each other depending upon how the two variables are arranged in temporal sequence. The concept of feedback offers a model to explain this reciprocal cause and effect relationship between environmental conditions and the worker's personal orientation to his life circumstances. Our first conclusion is, then, that environmental elements in the worker's predependency experience and elements in his personal orientation are linked by a feedback cycle.

Our second conclusion is that a single environmental factor, such as increased economic insecurity in a family's predependency experience, is not necessarily predictive of a particular aspect of his personal orientation, nor is such a single environmental factor predictive of subsequent welfare status.

For example, when the cases were classified by ethnic status, the white families show as high a level of medical problems as the Long-Time Aid cases, but did not show the same high level of psychological dependency as the LTA families. The Spanish-speaking families showed as high a level of anomie as the LTA families, but did not show a parallel level of economic insecurity and lowered level of living.

We can state, then, that a factor such as psychological dependency by itself is predictive neither of a high degree of illness nor of welfare status. But, a high incidence of illness, of economic insecurity, and of social isolation, when coupled with psychological dependency, anomie, and a tendency to live in the present without planning, represent the coalescence of factors predictive of welfare experience. The feedback cycle that operates between an individual's environment and his personal orientation rests upon the interaction of a cluster of elements in each of these two major aspects of his predependency experience.

If this feedback cycle between the worker's personal orientation and his environment were complete, we could state that the individual and his social life were merely aspects of the same thing. For example, if all the forces that have been listed as differentiating the predependency experience of welfare and nonwelfare cases operate to erode a worker's self-definition as a breadwinner, then the resort to welfare status would serve as an external index of a worker's changed self-definition. However, certain facts argue strongly against this type of conclusion. Of the 808 cases in our sample having some welfare experience, 571 families may have been in a welfare status more than once, but the limited length of these experiences points to their ability to reenter the labor market in response to employment opportunity. Thus, it would seem that their self-definition as breadwinners remains unchanged, despite their unemployment status and welfare experience.

Our conclusion is that the feedback cycle in the predependency experience of these 571 families produces a lowering of their capacity to cope with crisis, but does not produce significant change in their self-definition as breadwinners. The precipitating crisis resulting in a resort to welfare dependency may be a combination of illness, family disturbances, difficulties with the law, or lengthened unemployment. Whatever the particular combination may be, the lowered capacity of the worker and his family to cope with a precipitating crisis results from the feedback cycle between the combined handicaps in his environment and the handicaps in his personal orientation.

A reduction in the worker's coping behavior implies a reduction in the flexibility of his response to the conditions of his life. While his self-definition as a breadwinner remains strong, his capacity to alter his environment or to respond to changes in his environment is probably narrow. His coping ability thus operates effectively only within a limited range of environmental circumstances.

The particular combination of elements in the predependency experience of very low status families that lowers their capacity to cope with crisis and results in welfare dependency may vary from one family to another and from one ethnic group to another. The data in this report suggest the range of factors involved and the interactive effect of a combination of factors.[14] These factors

---

[14] Chinese and Japanese ethnic groups are represented in California's low-income population, but interestingly enough are not represented in our sample. In 1960, 10% of San Francisco's population was black. The second largest minority racial group was the Chinese, who constituted 4.9% of the population. When classified by family size and income level, there was a lower proportion of Chinese than black families who could be characterized as potential AFDC-U recipients. Assuming that Chinese families in San Francisco would be represented on the AFDC welfare rolls in proportion to their numbers in the very low-income population, we might expect this ethnic group to constitute a small but identifiable segment of the welfare population. In actuality, in San Francisco during the late spring of 1964, the number of AFDC-U families with oriental names was not more than a *dozen*!

Leaving aside the factors of illegal immigration, two characteristics of the Chinese ethnic group probably account for their conspicuous absence from the welfare rolls. First, the strength of the family system is maintained in part by seeking out those types of employment that allow the family to function as an economic unit. Secondly, a complex culturally based system of kinship aid and mutual aid associations functions to support those who become financially dependent.

The tendency to seek out types of employment that create a unity between family and work relationships maintains the integration of the husband-father and wage-earner elements of the breadwinner role. When unemployment and financial dependency do occur, public respect is maintained by the provision of mutual aid from kinship or other social groupings, and thus the nonrespectable status of the public welfare client is avoided.

In effect, the operation of cultural patterns distinctive to the Chinese community act to offset the combinations of factors in the lives of these very low status families that would otherwise result in welfare dependency.

The black, Spanish-speaking and white families represented in our sample are not participants in a system of cultural traditions that maintains such a powerful linkage between family roles and the role of breadwinner in the occupational sphere. Nor do they reflect cultural patterns of mutual aid that are strong enough to absorb financial dependency within the confines of nongovernmental groups. The group where such extensive mutual aid *does* occur, according to Allison Davis, is among those alienated workers who live outside a system of stable families.

include social and psychological as well as economic dimensions and reach back into the worker's early experiences (as well as covering the conditions of the recent past).

The Welfare Dependency Feedback Cycle: Route to Near Pauperization

The model of a predependency feedback cycle offers an explanation of the differences between the 392 NOA cases and the 571 STA cases. It remains to be explained how the STA and the LTA cases differ from each other.

The LTA families show 26.7 months as the median length of their welfare experience in contrast to 4.5 months for the STA families. However, the index of dependency that combines length of welfare experience with the time of its occurrence is 62.5 for the LTA cases and 51.4 for the STA cases (and the difference between the two groups becomes less dramatic).

In Chapter 3, it was pointed out that the grouping of the cases with welfare experience into two groups was essentially an arbitrary one. Recognizing the limitations imposed by this procedure, the comparison of the two groups is valuable in uncovering the processes that lead to different lengths of welfare dependency.

As previously indicated, the data on a family's welfare experience did not include the number of *times* a family has received public assistance. Hence, we could not differentiate the chronic case, i.e., the person with several such experiences, from the person whose public assistance experience was one continuous period. From the job history data, it appears obvious that a large percentage of welfare families in the two rural valley counties are chronic public assistance cases. They work during late spring, through the summer, and into early fall in the agricultural sector of the labor force, and are unemployed, underemployed, or on public assistance during the winter months. Depending on the accuracy of the report given to an interviewer, some of these families would be classified as STA families and some as LTA cases.[15] The welfare dependency

---

[15] The data obtained from the male respondents as to their welfare experience was a record of total months of welfare aid, and the date when the most recent aid terminated. We did not determine for each person how many welfare periods had been experienced or the duration of each period. Consequently, the LTA cases consist of some persons whose welfare experience was one continuous period, and others who could be defined as *chronic* welfare cases. The designations of predependency period and welfare dependency represent oversimplifications of the actual experiences of the respondents.

Published reports on the welfare histories of low-income families seem to be completely lacking. The excellent volume, *Blue-Collar World*, (1964) covers a wide range of topics, but not one single statistic is presented concerning the welfare experience of low-income families. As county and state welfare departments exchange information about only a very small percentage of their clients, their data do not allow any valid inference about the chronic welfare recipient. In fact, there appears to be no valid estimates about how many low-income persons have had welfare experience during their working lives. Everyone seems to agree that such experience is widespread among blue-collar workers, but this hardly constitutes a statistical estimate.

feedback cycle to be described may apply to both the chronic and continuous LTA case, but our hypothesis is that it applies primarily to the continuous LTA family.

The LTA group shows the highest percentage of persons manifesting social withdrawal, illness, lowered level of living, occupational handicaps, lowered economic security, and feelings of hopelessness and psychological dependency. These differences in the characteristics of the LTA and STA families do not, however, allow any direct inference about differences in the predependency experiences of the two groups.

Because the welfare dependency experience of the STA families was brief, their personal and environmental handicaps could be identified as having taken place in their predependency experience. We can reasonably assume that LTA families have been caught up in the same predependency feedback cycle as the STA families. Thus, they must have shown, at the very least, the same lowered capacity for coping with crisis that resulted in a resort to public assistance. What is not clear is whether their predependency experience was characterized by a *higher* level of handicap than the STA cases and therefore resulted in a feedback cycle that created *greater* loss of coping ability and a change in self-definition.

The job history data show that the LTA families manifested a slightly higher level of economic insecurity in their predependency period than the NOA or STA families. It is also probably true that the high level of psychological dependency manifested by the LTA husbands reaches back into their predependency experience. It is more difficult to conclude, however, that the higher incidence of illness and higher level of anomie exhibited by the LTA husbands were also present at the same level in their predependency experience.

The longer period of welfare dependency that characterizes the LTA families may be due entirely to an acceleration of the feedback cycle that occurs during their predependency experiences. On the other hand, this difference may be due solely to differential experiences that occur during the welfare dependency period itself. Still a third possibility exists that there is an interaction between the experience of a family in the predependency period and its experience during the welfare period that results in the Long-Time Aid family.

This same knotty, empirical and theoretical problem confronted Bakke, Cavan and Ranck, and Komarovsky in their longitudinal studies of unemployment and family life during the depression of the 1930s. Their analysis posits the interaction of a family's prewelfare experiences with the circumstances of their welfare dependency in producing a given type of adjustment.

Following this analytic framework, a description will be given of a second feedback cycle that occurs during the welfare dependency period in the lives of these families. The impact of this second cycle produces a change in the self-definition of the male welfare recipient, and reduces his capacity to fulfill a breadwinner role.

The welfare dependency feedback cycle rests upon the continuation of those elements found in the predependency cycle, but with an intensification of certain specific handicaps, and with the addition of two handicaps not present in the predependency period. While the handicap of illness may persist at much the same level during the welfare dependency period, social isolation and economic insecurity appear to be increased as welfare dependency lengthens. Two environmental elements, a nonrespectable income source, and a nonrespectable social status, are new handicaps arising from the circumstances of welfare dependency.

From the data on attitudes toward work and the job-finding process, as well as from the case histories, it seems plausible that feelings of dependency and anomie, of apathy and resignation to fate, increase as welfare dependency lengthens. Hence, the second feedback cycle consists of the same interaction between the worker's personal orientation and his environment as was true of the predependency cycle. The result of this second feedback cycle is a change in the self-definition of the LTA husbands, resulting in a marked inability to fulfill the role of breadwinner.

The Generic Meaning of Welfare Dependency

The generic meaning of welfare dependency arises from the position of indigent persons in the general society. As Simmel (1965) points out, welfare status has a unique quality in that the state accepts obligations for an individual only because of his inability to hold any other status from which he can claim rights. While each welfare family shares a common condition, this condition results from a lack of any other organic position within the society that gives the family a claim to recognition. Hence, the obligation that the state incurs for the welfare of indigent families creates a common status that is unconnected to any other status position within the society.

The quality of welfare status that emerges from this unique condition is the lack of reciprocity between the rights of welfare clients and the obligation of the state to care for them. In his article on poverty, translated and reprinted in *Social Problems* in 1965, Simmel summarizes the condition of the welfare client as follows:

To deprive those who receive alms of their political rights adequately expresses the fact that they are nothing but poor. As a result of this lack of positive qualification, as has already been noted, the stratum of the poor, notwithstanding their common situation, does not give rise to sociologically unifying forces [1965, p. 140].

The welfare person, by social definition, is an individual whose status is not defined by reciprocity. There is nothing that the welfare person does, by virtue of his status, that matches the responsibility assumed by the state. This lack of reciprocity, when mingled with an indigent condition, creates a status that carries no social respect. There is nothing that the welfare client can do within the context of his dependent condition that merits respect. His only solution to this lack of respect is to remove himself from it. If this is not possible, then some form of adaptation must take place leading either to redefinition of the self and the adoption of alternative values, or to some individual form of escape from his situation, or to the acceptance of defeat.

In order to see the importance of this underlying quality of welfare status, we can contrast it to the status of persons who accept vows of poverty. Historically, such vows always have to do with persons who are members of a group claiming status on grounds other than poverty. These grounds are usually religious. Their claim to public charity is both a voluntary choice and an avowal of intense attachment to *another* status that carries rights and duties. The recipients of public welfare are in exactly the opposite position. It is their lack of attachment to any other group that epitomizes their status and designates them as public welfare cases. Religious vows of poverty give rise to social respect, whereas poverty that designates only the individual's inability for self-maintenance evokes disrespect.

This pariah element in the life of the welfare client is counterbalanced by a second force in his life—the need to make out. The need to make out is a utilitarian need for money to maintain a livelihood, and a social-psychological need to preserve one's sense of self-worth. Bakke (1940) and Bernard (1964) have accurately described this side of the welfare family's dilemma. The operation of these contradictory forces, a pariah status and the need to make out, can be seen in the attitudes of welfare clients toward the acceptability of public welfare as an income source, and in their attempts to maintain self-respect.

Public Assistance: A Nonrespectable Income Source

The need to make out forces the welfare family to deemphasize the pariah quality of welfare income, and to treat it as yet another source of money in making ends meet. In his study of AFDC mothers in Boston, Bernard (1964) found that the acceptability of public assistance as an income source for oneself varied with the individual's welfare experience. Bernard summarizes his respondents' attitudes as follows: "The distribution of these views of AFDC function among the user-types was clearly as expected: the more the use, the more favorable the view." (1964, p. 81) Bernard also points out that kinsmen and friends of welfare users did not disapprove of the respondents' resort to public assistance. He concludes that, "The use of AFDC is a recognized and accepted aspect of lower-class life."

Our conclusion is that the attitudes of lower-class persons toward welfare arise from the play of opposite forces, the one force being the pariah quality of welfare income, the other being the necessity to make out and, therefore, the need to treat welfare as simply an alternative source of income. The interaction of these two forces produces a general tolerance or acceptance of public assistance as an income source. However, lower-class persons differentiate between the use of welfare as an income source by *others* and use for *themselves*. The further removed they are from direct public assistance experience, the less likely they are to look on this income source as acceptable for their *own* use.[16] Our case histories point to the same pattern of attitudes among the sample families concerning the use of public assistance.

This interpretation points to the conclusion that the respectability of one's income source is a value shared by lower- and middle-class persons, but the practical exigencies of lower-class life result in another force that creates a generalized tolerance and acceptance of public assistance despite its nonrespectable qualities.[17]

The Nonreciprocal Character of Welfare Status

While the nonrespectable quality of welfare income is only one force differentiating the status of the public assistance recipient from that of the breadwinner, there is a second general quality of welfare status that widens the gap between welfare and nonwelfare recipients.

This quality arises from the nonreciprocal character of the welfare status. There is no way in which the welfare client can act that gives his status a positive quality. E. Wight Bakke has described with great insight the impact of welfare status on the self-reliance of the client.

It is one of the tragic consequences of the lack of jobs in which the worker can prove he is capable of self-support that many must learn new ways of proving that they cannot support themselves. When a man's chief problem, which must be solved if he and his family are to survive, is to prove that he has no resources and has been unable to find ways of renewing them, the stimulus to self-reliance is severely curtailed. The basic cause of this curtailment, however, lies in the nature of the task he must perform and the factors that he must manipulate in the performance. Men become what they practice. What they practice must be adapted to the nature of the problems they face [1940, p. 282].

The only self-reliance that the client can display is to manipulate the system. The more self-reliant he is in terms of his welfare status, the more it appears that he is conning the system. This aspect of the welfare system feeds into a value element that is part of lower-class life. This dilemma operates with equal force

---

[16] As previously indicated in Chapter 13, this interpretation fits the argument presented by Hyman Rodman in his paper "The Lower-Class Value Stretch" (1965).

[17] In developing an Index of Status Characteristics (or ISC) for the class placement of individuals, W. Lloyd Warner and associates (1949) utilized "source of income" as one status indicator, and rated public welfare as the lowest point on the "source of income" scale.

for both the welfare client and the welfare worker. The very character of welfare status makes it difficult if not impossible to differentiate *in action* between those who are attempting to be self-reliant and those who are operating as con-men. The only acceptable solution to the status is to get out of it.

Welfare status unconnected to any form of work relief thus treats the self-reliance central to a breadwinner role and con-men attitudes inimical to this role, in an undifferentiated manner. An extended exposure to the welfare status has the aggregate effect of weakening the husband's capacity to fulfill the breadwinner role.[18]

Reduction in Income Level and Level of Living. Despite the effort to obtain as complete information as possible on the economic history of the 1200 families, there are a number of difficulties in using these data to describe shifts in the economic fortunes of these families from the predependency to welfare periods of their lives.[19]

The current annual income of the three groups classified by dependency status was: NOA, $3,682; STA, $3,190, and LTA, $3,068. From the data presented in Chapter 7, it seems probable that the annual median income of the STA and LTA families in prior years showed more variation than the NOA families. At the same time, it also seems clear that the protracted welfare status of the LTA families has reduced their income below what it was during the predependency period.

On all the indexes of economic security and level of living, the LTA cases ranked the lowest. There can be little question, then, that protracted welfare status has meant a lowering in the family level of living. This lowering of the family's level of living over a protracted period of time functions to accelerate the effects of the feedback cycle between environmental conditions and personal orientation. Its effect is to further lower the husband's flexibility of response and to accelerate a change in his self-definition as a breadwinner.

Increased Social Isolation. The data in Chapters 4 and 5 show clearly that the LTA families manifest the largest degree of social isolation. We have labeled this

---

[18] Amendments to the Social Security Act passed by the Congress in 1962 providing for a system of work relief and training for AFDC-U families have led to reciprocal legislation by many states, including a new California law passed in 1963. The programs of work relief and work training made possible under this law offer a possibility for welfare clients to act in ways that signify self-reliant behavior. Unfortunately, the implementation of programs called for by the new law has been very slow indeed, due in major degree to lack of public financial resources.

[19] It is quite difficult to know precisely how much the income of the LTA families has dropped by virtue of their protracted welfare experience without accurate data on their annual income in prior years. Nevertheless, the data on these workers' minimum and maximum monthly earnings for the jobs of longest duration provide a basis for estimates. These indexes, when combined with facts about seasonality of work and unemployment, lead to the conclusion that the STA and LTA families' annual income in prior years probably oscillated more than the NOA families, but was on the average at approximately the same level (Table 7-9).

pattern one of social withdrawal. This withdrawal constitutes an increase in social isolation from the family's social network during the predependency period.

Bakke, Cavan and Ranck, and Komarovsky all pointed to a characteristic pattern of withdrawal from kinship and other social relations on the part of the unemployed and welfare families that they studied. As some significant portion of the husbands in these families were not very low status workers, it can be argued that their social withdrawal during the welfare experience was a response to loss of status.

The 808 families in our sample with some welfare experience are not living in the middle of a nationwide depression, and have always occupied a very low socioeconomic status. It could be argued that these families have little to lose on entering a welfare status, and hence would manifest little or no social withdrawal.

The facts concerning their social life reveal that this argument is invalid. Our interpretation of the lowered social participation of the LTA families is that the threat to the husband's self-definition as a breadwinner becomes greater as the welfare dependency period lengthens. Social withdrawal from both kin and non-kin relationships is part of the husband's and the family's attempt to preserve self-respect and to resist participation in the subcultural pattern of the alienated nonworker.

Change in Self-Definition. The dependency feedback cycle just described is a prolongation of the predependency cycle, but includes additional elements that act powerfully to weaken the worker's self-definition as a breadwinner while simultaneously attacking his self-respect.

It is not clear at what point in the welfare experience a change in the worker's self-definition takes place. Despite considerable variations in the adjustments made by particular families to unemployment and welfare experience, Bakke, Cavan and Ranck, and Komarovsky each posited a general sequence of stages in the adaptation made by families to the husband's nonworker status. Following an initial effort to preserve a nonwelfare existence, families went through a period of disequilibrium. Some then established a new equilibrium, other families disintegrated, and in still others, the husband's adjustment took some form of psychological escape or changed self-definition.

Our case history data indicate that the LTA husbands have experienced some considerable loss of self-definition as breadwinners. Their verbal statements suggest they are attempting to sustain their self-definition as workers while realizing that they have largely become nonworkers. Their self-conception rests upon an effort to cope with irreconcilable elements arising from the feedback between their personal orientation and their environment.

Linkage of the Two Feedback Cycles. The mechanics of the process whereby a family's predependency experience links up with welfare dependency experience is not clear from the data collected in this study. It may be that those families entering a welfare status who manifest the widest range of economic, social and medical handicaps experience events that move them in a given direction. Out of a large number of families and a large number of random events, those families with the largest number of handicaps are most liable to move along a path weakening their capacity for participation in the breadwinner role. This movement takes place over time and produces the LTA family. Expressing the perspective of the public welfare worker, we would say that these families have been unable to cope successfully with the crises that have placed them on public welfare, and that during their protracted welfare experience, the husband has lost, in considerable measure, his capacity to fulfill a breadwinner role.

Lower-Class Life and Welfare Dependency. The foregoing interpretation suggests that the life of workers at the bottom of the American lower class is a product of contradictory forces. One set of forces creates a life style centering on family stability and continuity of work. The breadwinner role is at the very center of this life style. Participation in this role is vital in maintaining the self-respect of the very low status worker and in attaching him to the values of the larger society. For these persons, identification with the value of occupational achievement and a rising standard of living are manifested mainly in their aspirations for their children.

Another mode of life involves rejection of the family stability and job continuity incorporated in the breadwinner role. This life style involves alienation from these two master values of the larger society. Types of work and sources of income considered as nonrespectable by the larger society are incorporated into this life style. The mutual expectations of the participants constitute a subcultural system that provides support for the individual's life style.

The life the very low status male worker and his family consists of a continuous struggle between these two life styles. In dealing with adult male workers and thier families, we have outlined the combination of economic, social, and psychological forces that maintain the very low status male worker's self-definition as a breadwinner, and have described in detail, the feedback cycles that weaken and ultimately destroy this self-definition.

Welfare dependency appears to function as a halfway house between these two opposed life styles. While there are no adequate statistics to document the number of low-status workers who have had welfare experience during their working lives, the number of such experiences per worker, or their aggregate length, it seems plausible that welfare experience is much more common for these workers than is popularly supposed.

The halfway house of welfare dependency, while necessary for his survival, threatens the worker's self-respect and tends to produce a social isolation weakening his linkage to the very mode of life that he is struggling to maintain.

Implications for Policies and Programs

Any significant attempt to cope with the problem of male welfare dependency involves strengthening those forces in lower-class life that support workers in the breadwinner role in order to offset the effects of an opposed life style—that of the nonworker.[20]

Of those factors maintaining the worker in a breadwinner role, none seems more important than decreasing his economic insecurity by maintaining his continuity of employment and raising his income level. At the same time, the analysis of the feedback cycle that results in welfare dependency has pointed to social, psychological and health factors, as well as the economic determinants that affect the male worker's role performance.

Thus, the provision of increased employment opportunities for the very low status worker is a necessary but not sufficient condition to alter the feedback cycle that is the true cause of welfare dependency. Social, psychological, and health factors that narrow the worker's flexibility of response and lower his capacity to cope with crisis also need to be altered if any large-scale reduction in welfare dependency is to be expected.

More adequate health programs, adequate day care child centers, moving allowances, community development programs, adult education, job preparation and job training programs, and casework oriented to crisis therapy, are all significant weapons in breaking through the cycle that reduces the low-status worker's flexibility of response and his capacity for coping with crisis. For those persons already in a welfare status, work relief represents an attempt to maintain some elements of the breadwinner role for the welfare recipient.

These programs, taken in conjunction with policies tending toward full employment and toward the development of new opportunity structures for the low-status worker, would have two effects.[21] The first would be to increase the stability of the breadwinner role for many low-status workers, while increasing occupational mobility for this group. The second would be to increase the flexibility of response of these workers to the dynamics of a continuously changing labor market.

The combined result would be a significant change in the general quality of life for many low-status families and a reduction in the incidence of welfare dependency.

These same effects cannot be posited for the Long-Time Aid families. Due to the feedback cycle operating during their dependency experience, their response to changes in their environment is more limited and their social isolation is more marked. The provision of work relief, though limited in its significance, would be a first step in changing their condition. Demonstration programs of intensive casework with these "hopeless" families have produced surprising results and

---

[20]The study did not include families with a female head of household who represent a much larger proportion of the welfare caseload than do AFDC-U families. While our analysis is relevant only for policies and programs that relate to the AFDC-U family, we can suggest that the theoretical frame of reference would be valuable in analyzing the dilemmas and contradictions in the role played by the low-income female head of household.

[21]The analysis given in Pearl and Riessman's *New Careers for the Poor* (1965) points to the need for development of large-scale job opportunities for the low-status worker.

point the way toward further efforts at rehabilitation.[22] Community development programs may offer still another method of breaking through the social isolation and withdrawal that characterize these people's lives. Perhaps the greatest reduction in the numbers of Long-Time Aid families would come from a reduction in the number of short-time welfare cases.

Analysis of the life style of the 1200 families indicates that economic elements in their mode of living are primarily a product of their occupational roles and not of their ethnic status. While ethnic status molds family life and general outlook, as well as other aspects of life not investigated in this study, it does not dictate the husband's orientation toward work.

Because blacks and Spanish-speaking Americans are found in disproportionate numbers in very low status jobs, they are found on the unemployment and welfare rolls in disproportionate numbers. Thus, all the discriminatory factors that tend to hold members of these minority groups in a fixed and low occupational status also operate indirectly to maintain their disproportionately high representation in the welfare population.

---

[22] See, for example, Wiltse, Kermit T., "The 'Hopeless' Family," *Social Work*, October, 1958; also the programs initiated by Community Research Associates. The research and demonstration work of this group is summarized by Bernice Madison in "Analysis of Studies Conducted by or under the Supervision of Community Research Associates," San Francisco State College, 1964 (unpublished).

Bibliography

Angell, Robert C. *The Family Encounters the Depression.* New York: Charles Scribner's Sons, 1936.

Arnold, David, ed. *The Sociology of Sub-Cultures.* Berkeley, Calif.: The Glendessary Press, 1969.

Bakke, E. Wight. *Citizens Without Work.* New Haven: Yale University Press, 1940.

_____. *The Unemployed Worker.* New Haven: Yale University Press, 1940a.

Bernard, Sydney E. *The Economic and Social Adjustment of Low-Income Female-Headed Families.* The Florence Heller Graduate School for Advanced Studies in Social Welfare, Brandeis University, 1964.

Besner, Arthur. "Economic Deprivation and Family Life Styles," *Welfare in Review*, Vol. 3, No. 9 (Sept. 1965).

Billingsley, Andrew, and Amy Tate Billingsley. "Negro Family Life in America," *Social Service Review*, Vol. 39, No. 3 (Sept. 1965).

Blum, Alan F. "Social Structure, Social Class, and Participation in Primary Relationships" in *Blue-Collar World.* Edited by Arthur B. Shostak and William Gomberg. New Jersey: Prentice-Hall, Inc., 1964.

Bradley, Nelson. "The Work Addict," *Sales Management*, Vol. 87, No. 1 (July 7, 1961).

Caplowitz, David. *The Poor Pay More.* New York: The Free Press, 1963.

Cavan, Ruth S., and Katherine H. Ranck. *The Family and the Depression.* Chicago: University of Chicago Press, 1938.

Clark, Margaret. *Health in the Mexican-American Culture.* Berkeley: University of California Press, 1959.

Davis, Allison. "The Motivation of the Underprivileged Worker" in *Industry and Society*. Edited by William Foote Whyte. New York: McGraw Hill Book Co., 1946.

Dubin, Robert. "Industrial Workers' Worlds: A Study of the Central Life Interests of Industrial Workers' Worlds," *Social Problems*, Vol. 3, No. 3 (Jan. 1956).

Dyer, William G. "Work and the Family" in *Man, Work, and Society*, Chapter 3, Section 15. Edited by Sigmund Nosow and William H. Form. New York: Basic Books, Inc., 1962.

Ferman, Louis A., and Michael T. Aiken. "The Adjustment of Older Workers to Job Displacement" in *Blue-Collar World.* Edited by Arthur B. Shostak and William Gomberg. New Jersey: Prentice-Hall, Inc., 1964.

First Annual Report. State Social Welfare Board. Sacramento: State of California, Department of Social Welfare, (Jan. 1965).

Friedmann, E.A., and R.J. Havighurst. "Work and Retirement" in *Man, Work, and Society*, Chapter 5, Section 2. Edited by Sigmund Nosow and William H. Form. New York: Basic Books, Inc., 1962.

Gans, Herbert. *The Urban Villagers.* New York: The Free Press of Glencoe, 1962, Chapter 11.

_____. "Subcultures and Class" in *Poverty in America*. Edited by Louis A. Ferman, Joyce L. Kornbluh, and Alan Haber. Ann Arbor: University of Michigan Press, 1965.

Gardner, Burleigh. *Human Relations in Industry*. Chicago: Richard D. Irwin, Inc., 1945.

Gildea, Margaret C.L., John C. Glidewell, and Mildred B. Kantor. "Maternal Attitudes and General Adjustment in School Children" in *Parental Attitudes and Child Behavior*. Edited by John C. Glidewell. Springfield: Charles C. Thomas, 1961.

Goodman, Leonard. *Welfare Administration Cooperative Research Project No. 125*. Washington: U.S. Department of Health, Education and Welfare, 1965.

Gordon, Milton M. *Assimilation in American Life*. New York: Oxford University Press, 1964.

Gordon, Milton, and Charles Anderson. "The Blue-Collar Worker at Leisure" in *Blue-Collar World*. Edited by Arthur B. Shostak and William Gomberg. New Jersey: Prentice-Hall, Inc., 1964.

Gross, Edward. *Work and Society*. New York: Thomas Y. Crowell Co., 1958.

Himelson, Alfred, and Paul Takagi. *Research Report 7, Parole Panel Study, Report A*. Sacramento: Department of Welfare, 1963.

Hodges, Harold M. *Peninsula People: Social Stratification in a California Megapolis*. San Jose: Spartan Bookstore, San Jose State College, 1964.

Holmes, Emma G. "Expenditures of Low-Income Families," *Family Economics Review* (March, 1965).

Hughes, Everett C. 'Ethnic Relations in Industry and Society" in *Man, Work, and Society*. Edited by Sigmund Nosow and William H. Form. New York: Basic Books, Inc., 1962.

Hurvitz, Nathan. "Marital Strain in the Blue-Collar Family" in *Blue-Collar World*. Edited by Arthur B. Shostak and William Gomberg. New Jersey: Prentice-Hall, Inc., 1964.

Kalish, Carol B. "Portrait of the Unemployed," *Monthly Labor Review*, Vol. 89, No. 1 (Jan. 1966).

Kluckhohn, Clyde, *et al.* "Value and Value-Orientations in the Theory of Action" in *Toward a General Theory of Action*. Edited by Talcott Parsons and Edward Shils. New York: Harper and Row (Torchbook Edition), 1962.

Kluckhohn, Florence, and Fred Strodtback. *Variations in Value Orientations*. Evanston: Row, Peterson and Co., 1961.

Komarovsky, Mirra. *Blue-Collar Marriage*. New York: Random House, 1964.

_____. *The Unemployed Man and His Family*. New York: The Dryden Press, 1940.

Kornhauser, Arthur. *Mental Health of the Industrial Worker*. New York: John Wiley and Sons, Inc., 1965.

Lamphere, Arthur. "The Relationship between Dependency Factors and Goal-Setting Behavior in Duodenal Ulcer Patients." Unpublished doctoral dissertation, University of Washington, Seattle, Wash., 1953.

Lewis, Oscar. *La Vida*. New York: Vintage Books, Random House, 1965.

Litwak, Eugene. "Occupational Mobility and Family Cohesion," *American Sociological Review*, Vol. 25, No. 1 (Feb. 1960).

Loether, Herman J. "The Meaning of Work and Adjustment to Retirement" in *Blue-Collar World*. Edited by Arthur Shostak and William Gomberg. New Jersey: Prentice-Hall, Inc., 1964.

MacDonald, Robert Wesley. "Intergenerational Family Helping Patterns." Unpublished doctoral dissertation, University of Minnesota, June, 1964.

McConnell, John W. *The Evolution of Social Classes*. Washington, D.C.: American Council on Public Affairs, 1942.

McKinley, Donald Gilbert. *Social Class and Family Life*. New York: The Free Press of Glencoe, 1964.

Madison, Bernice. "Analysis of Studies Conducted by or under the Supervision of Community Research Associates," San Francisco State College, 1964 (unpublished).

Matza, David. "The Disreputable Poor" in *Social Structure and Mobility in Economic Development*. Edited by Neil Smelzer and Seymour Lipset. Chicago: Aldine Press, 1966.

Miller, Delbert C., and William H. Form. *Industrial Sociology*. New York: Harper and Row, 1962.

Miller, Henry. "Characteristics of AFDC Families," *Social Service Review*, Vol. 39, No. 4 (Dec. 1965).

Miller, S.M., and Frank Riessman. "The Working Class Subculture: A New View" in *Blue-Collar World*. Edited by Arthur B. Shostak and William Gomberg. New Jersey: Prentice-Hall, Inc., 1964.

———. "American Lower Classes: A Typological Approach" in *Blue-Collar World*. Edited by Arthur B. Shostak and William Gomberg. New Jersey: Prentice-Hall, Inc., 1964.

Miller, Walter B. "Focal Concerns of Lower-Class Culture" in *Poverty in America*. Edited by Louis A. Ferman, Joyce L. Kornbluh, and Alan Haber. Ann Arbor: University of Michigan Press, 1965.

Morse, Nancy C., and R.S. Weiss. "The Function and Meaning of Work and the Job" in *Man, Work, and Society*. Edited by Sigmund Nosow and William H. Form. New York: Basic Books, Inc., 1962.

Pearl, Arthur, and Frank Riessman. *New Careers for the Poor*. New York: The Free Press, 1965.

Rainwater, Lee, Richard P. Coleman, and Gerald Handel. *Workingman's Wife*. New York: Oceana Publications, 1959.

Reiss, P.J. "The Extended Kinship System: Correlates of and Attitudes on Frequency of Interaction," *Marriage and Family Living*, Vol. 24, No. 4 (Nov. 1962).

Rodman, Hyman. "The Lower-Class Value Stretch" in *Poverty in America* Edited by Louis A. Ferman, Joyce L. Kornbluh and Alan Haber. Ann Arbor: University of Michigan Press, 1965.

Schaefer, Earl S., and Richard Bell. "Development of a Parental Attitude Research Instrument," *Child Development*, Vol. 29, No. 3 (Sept. 1958).

Schlamp, Fredric T. "Social Characteristics Associated with Long-Term Social Aid." Department of Social Welfare, Sacramento, Calif., 1962 (duplicated).

Shannon, Lyle W., and Elaine M. Krass. "The Economic Absorption of In-Migrant Laborers in a Northern Industrial Community," *The American Journal of Economics and Sociology,* Vol. 23, No. 1 (Jan. 1964).

Shostak, Arthur B., and William Gomberg. *Blue-Collar World.* New Jersey: Prentice-Hall, Inc., 1964.

Simmel, Georg. "The Poor," *Social Problems* (trans. by Jacobson and Clair), Vol. 13, No. 2 (Fall, 1965).

Smith, M.G. *West Indian Family Structures.* Seattle: University of Washington Press, 1962.

Srole, Leo. ' Social Integration and Certain Corollaries: An Exploratory Study" in *American Sociological Review,* Vol. 21, No. 21 (Dec. 1956).

"Survey of Financial Characteristics of Consumers," *Federal Reserve Bulletin,* (March 1964).

Valentine, Charles. *Culture and Poverty.* Chicago: The University of Chicago Press, 1968.

Warner, W. Lloyd, Marchia Meeker, and Kenneth Eells. *Social Class in America.* New York: Stratford Press, Inc., 1949.

Warner, W. Lloyd, and Paul S. Lunt. *The Social Life of a Modern Community.* Yankee City Series, Vol. 1. New Haven: Yale University Press, 1941.

Wellisch, William. "The 'Culture of Poverty': Analysis of the Concept as an Analytical Device in Stratification Studies and as an Instrument for Social Action." Unpublished master's thesis, University of Missouri, 1968.

Wiltse, Kermit. "The 'Hopeless' Family," *Social Work,* Vol. 3, No. 4 (Oct. 1958).

Appendixes

Appendix A: Issues of Reliability and Sampling

After potential respondents had been identified by name and address, the first step was to send them a letter indicating that an interviewer would call on them requesting an interview. Black interviewers were to be used for black respondents, and Spanish-speaking interviewers for Spanish-speaking respondents. It was also planned that husbands would be interviewed by themselves, and in those cases where wives were to be interviewed, the husband should not be present. At the end of the interview, a certificate was presented to the respondent with his name on it. The certificate expressed the appreciation of San Francisco State College for the respondent's participation in the study.[1] One important variation from this initial plan occurred when black interviewers were used to interview whites and vice versa. There were also a good many cases where the wife was present while the husband was being interviewed.

Interviewers were trained in a three-hour session where the interview schedule was studied question by question. After the first interview was completed, the interviewer was called in and a supervisor edited the completed questionnaire. As additional questionnaires were turned in by a given interviewer, they were edited in the field office and corrections were made either by telephone or when the interviewer returned to the field office.

Despite these control devices over the interviewing procedures, there were a number of questions that gave the interviewers a great deal of difficulty, particularly the sections on the husbands' work history and welfare experience. The completed questionnaires were less accurate than desired at a number of points. In a study involving 1200 interviews, it could be expected that some few interviewers might engage in dishonest practices and fill out questionnaires without actually taking an interview. Some spot checking of the interviews was done, and one case was discovered where an interview had been taken on the telephone. This case was reinterviewed. Without extensive random checking on the completed interviews, it is not possible to know with real precision, the error created by cases of interviewer dishonesty. At the same time, our knowledge of the interviewers and the high motivation and loyalty expressed by the vast majority of them, leads us to believe that falsified questionnaires were probably less than 1% of the total of 1200.

After the interviews were completed, the data were transcribed onto code sheets. These sheets were processed by IBM machines that automatically translated the data onto punched cards. Processing of these cards by the IBM 1620 Computer produced the tables that are contained in the report.

The sources of error or bias generic to this type of study may be listed as follows: (1) biases created by the questions themselves; (2) incorrect presenta-

---

[1] The use of a certificate of appreciation was copied from the procedure employed by Lyle Shannon in his study of Racine, Wisconsin.

tion of the questions by the interviewer, or incorrect recording of the answer given by the respondents; (3) failure by the interviewer to complete a given question; (4) falsification of answers by the interviewer or the respondent; (5) failure of a coder to score a given answer properly; (6) failure of the IBM machine in translating code scores onto a punched card; (7) incorrect programming of the computer; and, (8) failure of the computer to read the punched cards accurately and to print correct results. Of these error sources, the major ones in this study seemed to be failure of the interviewer to complete a given question and failure of the IBM machine to translate coded scores onto a punch card.

A random sample of one percent of the questionnaires was checked for accuracy in coding. Certain questions were found where the coder error was as high as 10%, and these questions were recoded for the entire 1200 interviews. Coder error seemed to group by questions rather than being randomly distributed. Some of the coder error was reduced by checking each of the punches on the 8600 IBM cards that represented an unallowable answer. The completed questionnaire itself was scrutinized, and the unallowable answer corrected. It was found that many of these errors had been created by the IBM scanning machine itself.

In any large-scale study, the use of standardized procedures always creates undetermined error and bias, and the investigator is haunted by the possibility that his results may be simply a function of uncontrolled errors. In attempting to cope with this possibility, we did not make inferences about similarities or differences between subgroups of the sample unless several indexes showed the same pattern. Furthermore, for each such pattern, we attempted to determine if the results were internally consistent. In most cases, such consistency was found. A case in point where this was not so occurred in the answers concerning coverage under Social Security. On most of the indexes, the sample families in the San Joaquin Valley showed high economic handicaps. For example, less than 50% had ever belonged to a union. Nevertheless, the Valley cases showed a higher percentage of cases having Social Security coverage than any of the other three geographic areas. This finding is internally inconsistent and thus is untrustworthy unless some other facts can be adduced that would explain the inconsistency.

*Selection of AFDC-U Cases in the
San Joaquin Valley*

As explained in Chapter 3, in the two Valley counties, it was impossible to fill the sample quota of 150 families who were current AFDC-U cases. The number of current AFDC-U families declined almost to zero during the months of June, July, and August. Consequently, we were forced to substitute families who had been welfare cases during the spring of 1964. Table A-1 gives a frequency distribution of families by distance in months from a public assistance status.

When families are classified as current welfare or nonwelfare families the Merced and Stanislaus county sample is badly distorted. However, when the cases are reclassified in terms of the dependency index described in Chapter 3, the same problem does not obtain. The determination of how a family will be classified as to dependency status no longer rests on the single *criterion* of current welfare status.

There is a possibility, however, that the selection procedure that was used in these two counties might reduce the number of persons in the sample who have never had welfare experience. The 392 families falling in this NOA category are distributed geographically as follows: San Francisco, 27.3%; San Jose, 18.9%; Valley, 24%; and Los Angeles, 29.8%. These figures show that the Valley sample is not disproportionately low in the number of families falling in the NOA group.

Table A-1
Distribution of AFDC-U Sample Families in Stanislaus and Merced Counties by Distance, in Months, from Public Assistance Status

Months	Number of Families	Percent of Families
0	67	44.7
1	19	12.7
2	36	24.0
3	22	14.7
4	3	2.0
5	3	2.0
6		
7		
	150	100.0

Table A-2
Distribution of Cases by Ethnic Status in the Group Designated "Other"

Ethnic Status	Number
American Indian	12
Filipino	10
Portuguese	9
Puerto Rican	4
Chinese	2
Syrian	1
Polynesian	1
Japanese	1
Persian	1
Spanish	1
	44

Appendix B: Measuring Dependency

Psychological Dependency. Table B-1 shows the questionnaire item number and the source from which the question was drawn for each scale reported in Chapter 8.

Table B-2 gives the weighted mean score for each item in the attitude section of the questionnaire. There are some questions reported on in this table that were not utilized in the scales described in Chapter 8.

Psychological Dependency. These items in the attitude section were all drawn from an unpublished doctoral dissertation by Lamphere (1953). In an attempt to measure dependency-related factors in duodenal ulcer patients, Lamphere constructed a scale of dependency. A number of dependency-related items were rated by professional clinical psychologists. These clinicians judged if the items were *good* descriptions of dependent behavior, or good descriptions of the dependent feelings typical of the psychologically dependent person. All of these dependency-oriented statements were later rated in terms of social-acceptability by another panel of judges.

Table B-1
Items Comprising Each Attitude Scale, Identified by Source and Question Number

Attitude Scale	Questionnaire Item Number	Source
Dependency feeling scale	88, 89, 94, 95, 99, 100	Lamphere
Dependency acceptable feeling scale	88, 94, 99	Lamphere
Dependency unacceptable feeling scale	89, 95, 100	Lamphere
Dependency behavior scale	86, 87, 92, 93, 98, 102	Lamphere
Dependency acceptable behavior scale	86, 92, 93	Lamphere
Dependency unacceptable behavior scale	87, 98, 102	Lamphere
Total acceptable dependency scale	86, 88, 92, 93, 94, 99	Lamphere
Total unacceptable dependency scale	87, 89, 95, 98, 100, 102	Lamphere
Child responsibility	15a, 15b, 15c	Shannon
Dependency on family of orientation-P.A.R.I. scale	104, 106, 108	P.A.R.I.
Fostering child dependency-P.A.R.I. scale	90, 96, 101	P.A.R.I.
Autonomy of child-P.A.R.I. scale	91, 97, 103	P.A.R.I.
Anomie scale	72, 73	Himelson and Takagi
	70, 75, 83	Original
	78, 82	Shannon
Gildea responsibility scale	105, 107, 109	Gildea

Table B-2
Weighted Mean Scores for Items Used in the Attitude Scales[1]

Questionnaire Number	Cases Classified by Dependency				Cases Classified by Area					Cases Classified by Ethnicity				
	NOA	STA	LTA	Total	S.F.	S.J.	VAL.	L.A.	Total	Black	Span.	White	Other	Total
15a	.77	1.00	.91	.91	.98	.86	.94	.83	.91	1.04	.83	.88	.88	.91
15b	.90	1.06	.98	.99	1.11	.89	.99	.97	.99	1.18	.96	.89	.86	.99
15c	.82	.98	.92	.92	.82	.85	1.02	.96	.92	.97	.85	.95	.81	.92
70	−.17	.13	.27	.06	−.05	.17	.19	−.09	.06	−.04	.24	−.06	.02	.06
71	1.25	1.28	1.24	1.26	1.38	1.16	1.29	1.22	1.26	1.46	1.09	1.31	1.14	1.26
72	.15	.31	.48	.29	.24	.37	.22	.35	.29	.10	.63	.09	.16	.29
73	.07	−.03	.24	.06	.01	.09	−.12	.25	.06	−.09	.60	−.36	−.44	.06
74	.95	1.17	1.09	1.08	1.01	1.04	1.17	1.11	1.08	1.30	1.12	.96	.32	1.08
75	.18	.33	.45	.30	.48	.16	.23	.35	.30	.70	.39	.00	−.61	.30
76	1.18	1.19	1.19	1.19	1.17	1.14	1.09	1.34	1.19	1.36	1.15	1.10	1.02	1.19
77	1.00	1.29	1.20	1.18	1.13	1.33	1.22	1.03	1.18	.95	1.36	1.17	1.05	1.18
78	.34	.62	.66	.53	.49	.64	.74	.28	.53	.46	.83	.28	.36	.53
79	1.77	1.79	1.71	1.76	1.70	1.79	1.79	1.78	1.76	1.77	1.83	1.69	1.74	1.76
80	.71	.97	.91	.87	.97	.46	1.26	.80	.87	1.05	.47	1.14	1.21	.87
81	1.28	1.45	1.39	1.38	1.28	1.48	1.37	1.39	1.38	1.33	1.41	1.43	.98	1.38
82	−.36	−.32	−.07	−.29	−.23	−.21	−.44	−.27	−.29	−.22	.01	−.62	−.59	−.29
83	−.95	−.97	−.78	−.92	−.68	−1.15	−.89	−.98	−.92	−.81	−1.00	−.97	−.73	−.92
84	−.68	−.54	−.36	−.55	−.50	−.20	−.86	−.64	−.55	−.53	−.39	−.76	−.39	−.55
85	−.43	−.50	−.46	−.47	−.51	−.41	−.40	−.55	−.47	−.69	−.24	−.58	−.14	−.47
86	1.16	1.10	1.20	1.14	1.09	1.16	1.18	1.12	1.14	1.22	1.18	1.04	1.07	1.14
87	−.66	−.61	−.46	−.60	−.74	−.40	−.63	−.62	−.60	−.78	−.44	−.62	−.64	−.60

88	.07	.21	.10	.14	.18	.19	.24	-.03	.14	.16	.08	.20	.11	.14
89	-.72	-.70	-.47	-.66	-.69	-.48	-.67	-.82	-.66	-1.04	-.27	-.79	-.77	-.66
90	.64	.83	1.01	.80	.96	.63	1.01	.79	.80	.91	1.05	.44	.74	.80
91	.41	.58	.69	.54	.72	.47	.44	.55	.54	.85	.18	.67	.91	.54
92	1.20	1.13	1.20	1.17	1.05	1.07	1.41	1.14	1.17	1.14	1.23	1.12	1.12	1.17
93	1.54	1.58	1.50	1.55	1.44	1.53	1.63	1.61	1.55	1.53	1.54	1.57	1.66	1.55
94	1.59	1.63	1.67	1.62	1.62	1.58	1.63	1.66	1.62	1.71	1.66	1.52	1.61	1.62
95	-.46	-.62	-.44	-.53	-.52	-.41	-.69	-.49	-.53	-.40	-.29	-.87	-.71	-.53
96	1.22	1.36	1.47	1.34	1.37	1.30	1.34	1.34	1.34	1.58	1.48	1.02	1.00	1.34
97	.05	-.01	.24	.06	.21	.00	-.13	.14	.06	.43	-.07	-.09	-.07	.06
98	-.08	.05	.14	.02	.10	-.02	.15	-.15	.02	.18	.16	-.23	-.21	.02
99	1.04	1.05	1.15	1.06	1.00	1.07	1.03	1.16	1.06	1.23	1.04	.95	1.18	1.06
100	-.51	-.42	-.34	-.43	-.60	-.07	-.45	-.59	-.43	-.66	-.09	-.64	-.27	-.43
101	1.01	1.08	1.00	1.04	.77	1.03	1.39	.97	1.04	.97	1.30	.82	.86	1.04
102	-.65	-.60	-.36	-.57	-.79	-.32	-.56	-.60	-.57	-.78	-.16	-.84	-.66	-.57
103	.13	.33	.49	.30	.39	.21	.06	.52	.30	.54	.07	.33	.43	.50
104	.04	-.07	.28	.03	.09	-.07	.00	.12	.03	.09	.23	-.23	.02	.03
105	.82	.88	.95	.87	.90	.84	.89	.86	.87	1.05	.90	.73	.55	.87
106	.18	.31	.33	.27	.18	.31	.57	.04	.27	.12	.46	.23	-.12	.27
107	.28	.20	.26	.24	.06	.32	.29	.28	.24	.03	.61	-.01	.38	.24
108	.63	.60	.85	.66	.71	.83	.45	.65	.66	.79	.88	.34	.37	.66
109	.85	.92	.76	.87	.66	1.02	1.02	.77	.87	.65	.98	.89	1.14	.87

[1]Scoring formula:

Where a = scoring weights 2, 1, 0, −1, −2
n = number of persons per group
i = ith score per item

Twelve of the 96 items of the Lamphere scale were selected for inclusion in the current interview schedule. It was felt that these items most closely measured aspects of what, in this report, has been called psychological dependency. The sophisticated nature of the scale derivation; the presence of a social desirability factor; and the results of a factor analysis all conspired to make this a useful instrument for investigating dependency factors. Since the entire Lamphere Dependency Scale was not administered, some of the factors resulting from the factor analysis are represented on the interview schedule by only two or three items. The subgroups showing highest and lowest scores for the factors identified by Lamphere are reported in Table B-3.

The P.A.R.I. Scales. The Parental Attitude Research Instrument (P.A.R.I.) was constructed by Schaefer and Bell (1958). To develop a set of rating scales for maternal behavior, they tentatively defined each fundamental concept. Attitudes of the respondents were item analyzed and weighted to present the most clear-cut measure of the particular scale, which they then named from the content of the scale. Eventually, they formed 23 scales that were consistent enough to encourage further use. In the present study, the father's form of the

Table B-3
Groups Showing Highest and Lowest Scores on the Lamphere Dependency Scale's Factored Scores

Factor[1]	Cases Classified by Dependency		Cases Classified by Ethnicity		Cases Classified by Area	
	High	Low	High	Low	High	Low
A	LTA	NOA	Spanish	White	S.J.	S.F.
B	LTA	NOA	Spanish	Black	S.J.	S.F.
D[2]	STA	NOA	Spanish	White	S.J.	S.F.
E	LTA	NOA	Spanish	Black White	S.J.	S.F.
F	LTA	NOA	Spanish	Black White	S.J.	S.F. L.A.
G	LTA	NOA	Spanish	White	S.F. S.J.	L.A.

[1] Factors listed here are represented by questionnaire items as follows:

A = 88, 89, 92, 93, 94, 102
B = 92, 97
D = 87, 99, 100, 102
E = 89, 95, 102
F = 88, 102
G = 95, 98

[2] There was no Factor "C" included in our sample of questions.

P.A.R.I. was the source of items for the questionnaire (and the respondent's form). Three scales were selected as being most appropriate for use in the present study. These were (1) Autonomy of the Child; (2) Dependency on Family of Orientation; and (3) Fostering Dependency. For each of these scales, three items were chosen that correlated most highly with the total scale. These items were included in our questionnaire.

Responsibility and Child Rearing. Gildea *et al.* (1961) constructed a scale for responsibility, comparing responses given by parents whose children were doing well in school with those whose children were not as successful. A resulting scale labeled responsibility differentiated these two groups. The responsible mothers seemed to have a feeling that they could take charge of their own lives, that they were responsible for their children's behavior, and that personal action was required in order to help their children. This obviously measures an aspect of family role behavior. Items 105, 107 and 109, heavily weighted on this responsibility factor, were used in the interview schedule.

Scoring. All of the items mentioned in this section were scored in the same way. Each of the questions is in the form of a statement to which the subject may indicate his agreement. Categories of agreement are: strongly agree; mildly agree; neither agree nor disagree; mildly disagree; or strongly disagree. The assumption is made that each statement is a continuum, and that a person could not check in two places on the question. Therefore, one's check on such a scale is a measure of the degree to which he accepts the statement. Strongly agree was given a score of two, mildly agree was given a score of one, neither disagree nor agree zero, mildly disagree a minus one and strongly disagree a minus two score.

An equal interval was thus assumed, and although this may not be entirely defensible, some method was needed to make the items comparable. As a result of the item scaling, each group of respondents has a distinctive score for each item based upon the sum of the scores of the people within that particular group. The group scales were scored by combining the appropriate item scores.

By scoring items in this way, one could have two groups with the same score, although they had a different percent response in each of the categories. For example, if half of one group checked strongly disagree and the other half checked strongly agree, the total score would be zero. Exactly the same score would be obtained if half had checked mildly agree and half mildly disagree, or if all of the group had checked neither agree nor disagree. In all of these cases, the total feeling of the group would be the same, using the group as a hypothetical construct. The scoring system, while allowing easy and ready comparison between group feelings, may indeed mask certain differences based upon the scatter within the group.

Significance of the Difference between Items and Scales. The significance of the difference between two attitude items on any major variable depends upon three things:

1. the size of the sample;
2. the dispersion of the answers; and
3. the size of the mean score differences.

The Size of the Sample. The number of persons answering the item helps determine the size of the difference between groups needed to reach statistical significance. The larger the group, the smaller the difference between two items will have to be in order to be significantly different. The number of people answering is essentially the same for all of the items. Approximately 1,200 persons answered each item. For comparison between different sized groups, however, smaller numbers of persons would be involved. For example, comparing the black group with the white group would involve only 716 persons, if everyone answered the question.

The Dispersion of the Answers. The dispersion of the answers determines the significance of a difference between two groups. Here, if there is a tight dispersion, or variance, it means that a much smaller difference between the means can be accepted as significant. A general idea of the range encountered is illustrated by Items 97 and 98. In Item 98, which is an ' acceptable-behavioral dependency" statement, "I do a great many things just to avoid criticism," the answers are almost all on the left-hand side, or agree portion. The standard deviation of this question is .8. Item 97 states: "Parents should keep out of children's activities as much as possible so the children can learn to do the things on their own.' This item has a wide range of answers. The standard deviation for this question is 1.6, or approximately twice as large as the variance for Item 98.

The Difference between the Means. The size of the mean difference is crucial to determining the significance of the difference between means. The means are somewhat correlated with the standard deviation. As the means approach either end of the distribution of possible scores, the variance decreases. This is not marked enough to affect the rough test of significance that we apply, however. Using a varying total N for comparison (i.e., black versus white group equal 716) and the number of items in the scale (i.e., from 3 to 7), the differences required to produce a significant difference between means at the 5% level of confidence have been computed. In a sense, this establishes fiducial limits for differences significant at the 5% level. Tables B-5 and B-4 give the differences required to reach significance for items with a broad dispersion and for items with a tight dispersion. The largest difference required in order that the means be significantly different is a comparison of only 400 cases on one item of broad dispersion. In this case, a difference of .23 is significant, using Table B-5. In Table B-4, for comparisons of over 1,000 and with over 3 items in the scale, a difference of .01 or less becomes significant. For our purposes, the significance of the difference between means was judged by the conservative estimates provided by Table B-5.

Table B-4
The Differences in Mean Values of Attitude Scales[1] Required for a 5% Level of Significance (2 sigma) for a Tight Dispersion Made up of "N" Items

Total N for each comparison (i.e., black vs. white 316 + 440 = 756)	Items in Scale						
	1	2	3	4	5	6	12
400	.036	.018	.012	.009	.007	.006	.003
500	.032	.016	.011	.008	.006	.005	.003
600	.029	.015	.010	.007	.006	.005	.002
700	.027	.014	.009	.007	.005	.005	.002
800	.025	.013	.008	.006	.005	.004	.002
900	.024	.012	.008	.006	.005	.004	.002
1000	.023	.012	.008	.006	.005	.004	.002

[1] Attitude scale scoring formula:
$$\frac{\sum_j^n \sum_i^m a_i X_{ij}}{nm}$$
Where: a = scoring weights 2, 1, 0, −1, −2
n = number of persons per group
m = number of items per scale
j = j^{th} item in scale
i = i^{th} score per item

Table B-5
The Differences in Mean Values of Attitude Scales[1] Required for a 5% Level of Significance (2 sigma) for a Broad Dispersion Made up of "N" Items

Total N for each comparison (i.e., black vs. white 316 + 440 = 756)	Items in Scale						
	1	2	3	4	5	6	12
400	.226	.113	.075	.057	.045	.038	.019
500	.202	.101	.067	.051	.040	.034	.017
600	.185	.093	.062	.046	.037	.031	.015
700	.171	.086	.057	.043	.034	.029	.014
800	.160	.080	.053	.040	.032	.027	.013
900	.151	.076	.050	.038	.030	.025	.013
1000	.143	.072	.048	.036	.029	.024	.012

[1] Attitude Scale scoring formula:

Where: a = scoring weights 2, 1, 0, −1, −2
n = number of persons per group
m = number of items per scale
j = j^{th} item in scale
i = i^{th} score per item

Meaning of Differences in Scale Scores. At this point, it seems appropriate to point out the various ways in which differences in percent of agreement can come about between two groups. It is conceivable that a large number of people mark answers which are only slightly divergent. In this case, we might have some reason for believing that small but general overall differences were important. On the other hand, a small number of persons might quite well be extremely divergent and cause sizeable group differences. In the latter case, we may quite well have a series of types of individuals or types of adjustments to an environment. This may produce a series of divergent answers which are indeed greater than we might expect by chance alone but, nonetheless, not necessarily consistent with one another. In our own data, we do not know what proportion of these patterns exist. A correlational analysis will eventually answer this question.

In the situation in which a great number of people, or the majority of people, checked slightly divergent answers, we would have an argument for large, sweeping pressures or life-shaping forces. In the case of a small number of people checking widely divergent answers, we would have a situation arguing for psychological types, individual family circumstances of limited situational variables. It seems obvious from our analysis that both of these situations exist in differing degrees with differing portions of the sample studied.

Table B-6
Attitude Items

Questions	Source of Question
70. In general, lots of things are going downhill. Lots of people have less today and less chance than was true in the past.	Original
71. Since 1900, people's ideas of things have changed a lot, but there are still some absolute guides to conduct.	Himelson and Takagi
72. Nobody cares whether you attend church or not, except the clergy (ministers).	Himelson and Takagi
73. Cheating on income tax is nobody's business but the government's.	Himelson and Takagi
74. Most people do not trust one another anymore.	Original
75. People who go out of their way to help a personal friend are usually disappointed.	Original
76. The best job you can have is one where you are part of the group, all working together, even if you don't get much individual credit.	Shannon
77. The real way of happiness is not expecting too much, but being content with what comes your way.	Shannon
78. Planning only makes a person unhappy, since your plans hardly ever work out anyway.	Shannon
79. It is always a good idea to put away some of your money for a rainy day.	Shannon
80. Not many things in life are worth the sacrifice of being away from your family.	Shannon
81. When a man is born, the success he is going to have is *not* already in the cards; each makes his own fate.	Shannon
82. Nowadays, with world conditions the way they are, the wise person lives for today and lets tomorrow take care of itself.	Shannon
83. One man said that if he won a lot of money next week, say $1,000, he would certainly buy a lot of things that he'd been wanting, but felt he couldn't afford, you know, items like dressy clothes, color television, and eating out in restaurants. How do you feel about his outlook?	Original
84. Another man got some extra money, but he felt that in the long run it made more problems than it helped. How do you feel about this outlook?	Original
85. Not many things in life are worth the sacrifice of moving away from old friends.	Shannon
86. When planning something, I try to get suggestions from other people whose opinions I respect.	Lamphere
87. I feel afraid of being alone, or of not being wanted.	Lamphere
88. I am very much concerned about what others think of my actions.	Lamphere

Table B-6 (cont.)

89.	I secretly wish that I were a child again.	Lamphere
90.	Parents should know better than to allow their children to be exposed to difficult situations.	P.A.R.I.
91.	If children plan their own work and do it without the direction of parents they are more willing to help, and they do more.	P.A.R.I.
92.	I accept the leadership of people I admire.	Lamphere
93.	I usually follow instructions and do what is expected of me.	Lamphere
94.	I feel that people should help each other more than they do.	Lamphere
95.	I feel a person must "play politics" to get promotions or increases in pay and jobs.	Lamphere
96.	A father should do his best to avoid any disappointment for his child.	P.A.R.I.
97.	Parents should keep out of children's activities as much as possible so that children can learn to do things on their own.	P.A.R.I.
98.	I do a great many things just to avoid criticism.	Lamphere
99.	I enjoy cooperating with others more than working by myself.	Lamphere
100.	I feel out of sorts if I have to be myself for any length of time.	Lamphere
101.	A child should be protected from jobs which might be too tiring or hard on him.	P.A.R.I.
102.	Because I want to be liked, I tend to be apologetic and don't stand up for what I know are my real feelings.	Lamphere
103.	Managing their own affairs without interference develops responsible children.	P.A.R.I.
104.	The responsibilities of taking care of his wife and children should not keep a husband from spending plenty of time with his own parents.	P.A.R.I.
105.	No matter what the parents try to do, there are children who don't change at all in the way they behave.	Gildea
106.	There is no excusing a wife who tries to come between a man and his parents.	P.A.R.I.
107.	When neighbors or teachers complain about the behavior of a child this shows that the parents haven't done a good job.	Gildea

Appendix C: Outlines of Family Historys

Case History I

I. Demographic Information
   A. Ethnic group: White
   B. Class group: Welfare
   C. Religion: Lutheran
   D. Family composition: Husband, age 32
      Wife, age 32
      Son
      Daughter, age 7
      Son, in Cupertino cared for by paternal aunt

   E. Neighborhood: North Beach, high percentage of black population but significant percentage of non-black
   F. Residence:
      External: Public housing project, Francisco St. Project, two-story cement building
      Internal: 4-room apartment, generally disorderly
   G. Occupation:
      Past: Husband in military, wife was waitress for one month
      Present: Husband, part-time, some work for coal and wood wholesale-retail store, trying to join carpenter's union
   J. Length of time on welfare: at least six months

II. Attitudes
   A. Welfare: Welfare has become part of the "given" in their lives, especially for wife whose planning appears to be in relation to the welfare check. Welfare is considered an interim solution until the husband can achieve a position (information here from wife).
   B. Employment: There is no apparent desire for a job. This rests mainly on the fact that no attempts were being made to train for a position or to become acceptable to the union. The husband particularly did not want the wife to work. Wife wants to be a housewife. Husband seems to be interested in outside (of home) friendships and associations.
   C. Education: The parents had some occupational goals for their children. However, the children are retarded. There is no attempt to help children with their schoolwork or encourage education.

III. Value Orientations
   A. Human Nature: Neutral.
   B. Man-Nature: Harmony: (this category rests on the relationship of mother

to children and the problem of children's retardation and the acceptance of this, no real striving to overcome it).
  C. Time: Present (Things just happened; not planned. Husband's presences and absences from home are irregular and taken as a matter of course.)
  D. Activity: Being (Things are done to fill up time.)
  E. Relational: Lineal for wife (Concern with children, also relationship with grandmother and aunt who cares for child). Individual for husband (no close relationship with relatives or children, mainly his own friendships outside of home).

IV. Family Themes
  A. Conform strongly to traditional American ideal values, except for leaning toward acceptance and passivity and some fatalism.
  B. The family feels that a gap exists between themselves and the surrounding community. The family feels itself different from the rest of the people in the public housing project. They feel themselves happier. The interviewer did not perceive them as being very happy.

Case History 2

I. Demographic Information
  A. Ethnic group: White
  B. Class group: Matching
  C. Religion: Weak; husband—Episcopalian; wife—Catholic
  D. Family composition: Husband, age 33
     Wife, age 27
     Daughter, age 5
     Daughter, age 19 months
     Mother-in-law, age 67
     Wife's brother, age 22

  E. Neighborhood: Racially mixed—Italian, Anglo, Mexican, black
  F. Residence:
     External: Forty-year-old house (top apartment), outside in "terrible" rundown condition
     Internal: Cheap, contemporary style of furniture, crowded together. Generally dirty and cluttered.
  G. Occupation: Delivery boy on motorcycle, two jobs at this
  H. Number of months employed per year: full time
  I. Income: first job: $100 per week
             second job: $ 70 per week

II. Attitudes
  A. Welfare: Wife states she didn't like idea of being on welfare and would

baby-sit before going on it. At another time, she stated that city residents had the right to accept welfare. The grandmother is on welfare since her income is depleted.
   B. Employment: Husband has two jobs and wishes he had more education and training so he could get a better job.
   C. Education: Wife feels education is important economic necessity and that each child should make a choice as to the type of education. She said she would like to take some business training if possible.

III. Value Orientations
   A. Man-Nature: Subjugated (in their educational and work history)
      Mastery (in the fact that husband has two jobs, use of hospitals in illness, birth control)
   B. Time: Present for wife (in terms of household management and lack of planning)
      Slight future for husband
   C. Activity: Being (no activities planned, no ambition for self-improvement)
   D. Relational: Lineal (in that mother-in-law and brother live with them and there is little contact with other relatives)

IV. Family Themes
   The interviewer traced family occupations and socioeconomic class five generations on one side and four on the other. He submits that the present family is a regression from an upper-middle-class position several generations back, due to a breakdown in educational and vocational background and ability to maintain the position in the social order. The interviewer maintains that the family probably doesn't realize that they no longer belong to the social class of their great-grandparents. By and large they hold to middle-class values.

Case History 3

I. Demographic Information
   A. Ethnic group: Husband, Mexican-American (born in San Francisco)
      Wife, Mexican
   B. Class group: Matching
   C. Religion: Catholic
   D. Family composition: Husband, wife, three children
   E. Neighborhood: South of Market, fringe of skid row between Folsom and Howard and 6th and 7th Streets. Street is slumlike alley with broken glass, litter, garbage
   F. Residence: Middle flat of three-story tenement-type house. Rundown and dirty.
   G. Occupation: Apprentice for electrical contractor

    H. Number of months employed: Seasonal work (but never applied for welfare).

II. Attitudes
    A. Welfare: Although husband (or family) has never received aid, he thinks there is nothing wrong with getting government assistance and it is an available income if he were to need it. He criticized those who supplement their welfare or lied to get it. He believes an adequate amount of welfare should be available. If the reason is unemployment, people should be offered jobs.
    B. Employment: He blames lack of jobs on racial prejudice and the unwillingness and mistrust from the white world (concept of the gringo).
    C. Education: He feels sorry to have dropped out of school and hopes his children would finish. He does not seem to link the lack of education with low economic status, rather it is the white world's reaction to them which prevents them from making money and getting ahead.

III. Value Orientations
    A. Outlook: Optimistic: ("things will get better" "devil may care")
    B. Man-Nature: Harmony (if you follow prescribed courses things will be okay). Subjugation (in terms of the dominant society but tries to seek identity and prestige within the Mexican-Indian community).
    C. Time: Present-Future. (Lives in present but leans to future. Some family planning and credit buying.)
    D. Activity: Being in Becoming (e.g., he is serving an apprenticeship and learning a trade. There is also a routine of recreational behavior, e.g., Friday night out with the boys, fishing).
    E. Relational: Collateral (Strong extended family orientations. Strong compadre relationship with friends.)

IV. Family Values
    A. Concept of the gringo is the term the investigator uses. This essentially means that they believe that the whites (dominant society) try to exploit them (the Spanish-speaking) and consider them untrustworthy and lazy, etc. The Spanish-speaking get back at them in little ways, e.g., slacking off from the job and being clannish and forming "in groups."
    B. Compadres, the male peer group, is important for associations, recreation and mutual aid.
    C. Husband is dominant in family.

Case History 4

I. Demographic Information
    A. Ethnic group: Puerto Rican

B. Class group: Welfare
C. Religion: Catholic
D. Family composition: Husband, Wife, five children
E. Neighborhood: Potrero Hill Project, racially mainly Puerto Rican
F. Residence: House was dirty, drab; yard is grassless, strewn with litter and garbage
H. Occupation:
   Previous: Worked in furniture factory as upholsterer
   Present: Something part time
J. Length of time on welfare: two years

II. Attitudes
   A. Welfare: This is what is keeping the family going, but husband thinks the amount received is inadequate for a decent standard of living. He feels security in getting welfare rather than in holding a job in which he could be easily laid off.
   B. Employment: Blames racial prejudice and white dominant society for holding down employment possibilities. When working, however, he tries to create impression of hard work and get as much as possible with the minimum of effort (to get back at the gringo world). Recently took the civil service exam for the Post Office but failed.

III. Value Orientations
   A. General view: Pessimistic, welfare check represents security.
   B. Man-Nature: Harmony (If you follow prescribed course, e.g., illness, everything is okay.) Subjugation in terms of receiving welfare and the gringo concept, but mastery in terms of making it on the side.
   C. Time: Present (few future plans, live in present)
   D. Activity: Being (Little concern with self-improvement. He aspires to civil service job, but has not made effort to be in better position to pass test. Complains about lack of education. Wife enrolled in IBM and typing class at Mission Adult School. Husband against it.)
   E. Relational: Individual (emphasis on nuclear family).

IV. Family Themes
   A. Gringo concept (c.f. Case History).
   B. Husband economically subordinate to wife (e.g., asks for cigarettes and money, etc.).

Case History 5

I. Demographic Information
   A. Ethnic group: Black
   B. Class group: Matching

C. Religion: Baptist
  D. Family composition: Husband, age 57
     Wife, age 47
     Eight children

  E. Neighborhood. Hunter's Point Housing project
  F. Residence
     Exterior: Bungalow, apartment building
     Interior: Furnishing worn but in good serviceable repair, clean, neat.
  G. Occupation: General construction work. Sand mixer and jackhammer operator.
  I. Annual income: $4720 per year

II. Attitudes
  A. Welfare: He works hard and has never been on welfare and doesn't ever intend to be.
  B. Employment: Be a hard worker
  C. Education: The family realizes that education allows one to control world better. Therefore, they stress education for their children even though they never finished high school. The family places high value on getting a high school education.

III. Value Orientations
  A. Human Nature: Neutral, (mixture of good and evil), the wife feels that human nature is all a matter of learning and training; the husband, that it is shaped by God. Also, that man's nature is subject to corruption.
  B. Man-Nature: Subjugation (accepts what comes along and are pragmatic about life). Realize that education is key to overcome subjugation. Mastery in medical attention.
  C. Time: Present (look to future somewhat insofar as children's education). Husband rejects past.
  D. Activity: Being in Becoming and Doing (concerned with getting details of everyday life done, e.g., wife keeps children disciplined, fed and clothed to best of her ability, house clean; husband concerned with making best living possible).
  E. Relational: Individualistic (nuclear family) minding their own business and making their own way in the world.

IV. Family Themes
  A. Industriousness and hard work
  B. Tendency to be very individualistic, almost loners.

Case History 6

I. Demographic Information
  A. Ethnic group: Black

B. Class group: Matching
C. Religion: Pentecostal Holiness
D. Family composition: Husband, age 29
   Wife, age 20
   Son, age 2½
   Daughter, age 17 months
   Daughter, age 7 months
E. Neighborhood: Haight-Ashbury District, paved, steep street, with papers and wood laying about. Predominantly black, but some white and Chinese families.
F. Residence: Exterior of building fairly well kept—paint in good condition, but somewhat dirty. The interior of the residence is very clean and tidy, and is a contrast to the other units in the building. It is located on the second of three floors.
G. Occupation:
   Husband—dishwasher at present, supervises other kitchen employees in South San Francisco restaurant.
   Wife—former telephone operator, and later printing apprentice, now tries to sell line of clothes and shoes to friends and neighbors.

II. Attitudes
   A. Welfare: Family on welfare in 1962, but did not like having to accept such help. Wife feels strongly that people can do for themselves with the help of friends and relatives if things get too bad. Husband generally disagrees with idea of welfare for his family, but this seems to be due to the disapproval of the wife in accepting such aid.
   B. Employment: Husband works to provide for family, and also feels that a person should work. Wife helps out so that her children will be better off.
   C. Education: Wife wants children to finish high school and possibly go on to college. Husband says high school is enough. Wife says more training would have given her better employment today. None of the children are of school age at present.

III. Value Orientations
   A. Human Nature: Neutral to good on part of wife. She feels that people are basically good, and if they sometimes misbehave, they are not necessarily basically bad; behavior can be changed by proper influences. Husband is neutral, but feels he is in control of his behavior.
   B. Man-Nature: Both husband and wife feel that they are responsible for what they are, although wife is devoutly religious and feels that God must make the final decisions. Wife feels that she can master fate, while husband feels more in harmony with nature.
   C. Time: Present-to-Future orientation. Husband buying life insurance, but at same time works to provide for immediate needs of his family. Wife is somewhat more future-oriented, concerned with what her children will do and be when they grow up.

D. Activity: Doing orientation on part of wife—she solicits for her clothing business, active in church, and pushes husband in his work. Husband is more being-oriented, willing to go along as he is now.
  E. Relational: Individualistic. Husband spends some time with wife's cousin, but family group remains isolated from relatives for most part. Wife states that it is important to have friends, but she seems to maintain individualism within social sphere.

IV. Family Themes
  A. Wife feels that she is for most part responsible for the maintenance of the family group, aside from earning money. She does keep husband motivated in job area, and pushes him to take on more responsibility to better himself and children.
  B. Wife is greatly concerned with education for children when they grow up, and tries to educate herself more by reading and talking to people.
  C. Strict child training which stems from wife's religious beliefs.

Case History 7

I. Demographic Information
  A. Ethnic group: Black
  B. Class group: Welfare
  C. Religion: Methodist (A.M.E.)
  D. Family composition: Husband, age 54
                          Wife, age 47
                          Son, age 15
                          Son, age 10
                          Daughter, age 7

  E. Neighborhood: Bayview District, unpaved street littered with garbage and glass. Mostly black, although some whites and Mexicans.
  F. Residence:
      Exterior: Upper flat, building rundown
      Interior: Generally disarrayed
  G. Occupation:
      Husband: Past—painter, burner; present—part-time junk dealer, odd jobs
      Wife: Past—registered nurse
  J. Length of time on welfare: Since February 1962

II. Attitudes
  A. Welfare: Wife feels that welfare necessary to maintain life especially for children's sake. Family circumstances (wife's blindness and husband's injury while on the job) was cause of welfare status. Husband once said he didn't like being on welfare and planned to repay it.

B. Employment: Husband works to get money, wouldn't work if he didn't have to. Wife worked as a nurse.
C. Education: Very strong belief in necessity of education for better jobs and for mobility. Very strong emphasis on children's education, wife helps them with homework.

III. Value Orientations
A. Human Nature: Neutral-Good (mutable) (people have choice to control their own destiny and to bring out their innate good qualities. Often corrupted by the world around).
B. Man-Nature: Subjugation (to circumstances in life especially at present, some mastery in that husband has concept of making it and not letting the world trample on him). Also very concerned with using medical facilities, although mainly in curing, not preventive medicine.
C. Time: Present (live in the present, no planning, buying at moment of need)
D. Activity: Being (at present time, the wife probably had a doing orientation as indicated by her becoming a nurse, but has no present plans for self-improvement).
E. Relational: Individualistic (no kin relationships maintained, but very interested in children).

IV. Family Themes
A. Family feels themselves different (and better) or perhaps, atypical of neighborhood. Mother and children religious; keep out of trouble with law, don't have drinking problem.
B. Concern with education
C. Leniency in child training

Case History 8

I. Demographic Information
A. Ethnic group: Black
B. Class group: Welfare
C. Religion: Baptist
D. Family composition: Husband, wife, ten children
E. Neighborhood: Hunter's Point
F. Residence: Interior was newly painted, neat and clean
G. Occupation:
Husband: Past: used to be in construction work, also janitor for S.W. Airlines. Present: some part-time work.
Wife: Present: domestic, one or two days per week.
J. Length of time on welfare: At least since 1959

II. Attitudes
A. Welfare: Husband used to take welfare check and spend (squander) it. Five months previous to interviewing, wife had it made out to her.

B. Employment: Husband can't get back into union since he was kicked out and doesn't have dues money. Feels that he can't do anything besides construction work because he lacks training and education. Gaining employment is viewed as a matter of luck and God. He doesn't seriously look for a job. Wife feels life would improve if he got a job but he doesn't want to.
C. Education: Feels that lack of education inhibits getting job. Some concern with children's education but more in behavior concerns at school.

III. Value Orientation
A. Human Nature: Good-Mutable (Human nature is getting better).
B. Man-Nature: Wife: Subjugation (some mastery in terms of her own industriousness). Husband: Subjugation (dependent upon luck and God).
C. Time: Present: Wife: (some future as far as children are concerned). Husband: (time spent in pleasure living in present).
D. Activity: Being-Doing (doing because of wife's industriousness). Husband: Being (little ambition to improve).
E. Relational: Lineal for wife (concern with children)
    Individualistic (minimal concern with relatives)
    Collateral (for husband a wide circle of friends outside the home)
    (children tend to stick together).

IV. Family Themes
Probably a good example of matricentered family. Very bad husband–wife relationship. She kicks him out of house for drinking, carousing with other women, beating her. She calls welfare agency and police at such times.

Appendix D: Open-Ended Questions from the Women's Questionnaires

27. Now, we want something about the history of your family. That is, something about your life since you've been married. People usually remember things easiest when they think of the best things that have happened to them, and also of the worst or most difficult things. I've listed down a number of topics to ask you about, but we don't have to follow them in any order.
    Looking back over the time that you've been married, what would you say were the best and worst things that have happened in that time.
28. What about best and worst things with reference to children? (Child care problems for example?)
29. Good and bad things about marriage itself?
30. Health or sickness?
31. Jobs and work of either yourself or your husband?
32. Money matters?
33. Relatives, in-laws, parents?
34. What about planning family size (birth control) and things like that?
35. Chances for improving yourself and your family in different ways?
36. Moving from place to place—good or bad things?
37. Things having to do with the police, with courts, or with other things like that?
38. a. Let's take a look at your family the way it is now, can you tell me about all the people that are part of your family, or live with you? Tell me if there have been any changes in the last couple of years.
    b. What age are you now? _____
39. How about before this? What was your family like in 1960?—that's four years ago. Can you tell me who you were living with, or was living with you? Were there any changes during this time?
40. Now can you remember as far back as ten years ago? Say 1955? Can you tell me about your family then? Who were you living with, or was living with you? Can you tell me any changes that took place, marriage or births, or people living with you, or people leaving? Tell me if they left for any amount of time, even if it was just a short time.
41. Now, how about before that. Let's go back to 1945, you must have been only _____ then. From 1945 to 1955, what happened during this time? Who were you living with, and just like the other things in the answers you have given me above.
42. I'd like to know about all that happened like you have been talking about, but any of these things that may have happened 20 years ago. That was 1945 and before. Tell me about your family then, and who you lived with.

Index

Activity, self-help, 60, 166–167, 171 176, 200
AFDC program, 1
AFDC-U program, 1, 234
  policies of, 24, 27
Age: classification by husband's, 40
  See also Old age
Aid: from relatives, 53, 59, 90
  to relatives, 59
  sources of, 206
    See also Mutual aid; Public assistance
Alcohol, use of, 177
Anomie, 199
  attributes of, 140
  defined, 133–134
  interclass comparison, 216
  scales for measurement of, 140
Aspirations, 246
  interclass comparison, 228
Attitudes and outlooks of dependents, 198–199
  test for, 134
Automobiles, ownership of, 88, 196, 212

Bakke, E. Wight, 63, 64, 83, 93, 148, 225, 240, 242, 243, 245
Beliefs and behavior, themes of, 160–161, 173, 200
Bell, Richard, 135, 262
Bernard, Sidney, 230, 242
Breadwinner, role of, 6, 150, 227, 230
Burial insurance, 93

Caplowitz, David, 103
Case histories, 177–185, 269–278
Cavan, Ruth, 148–149, 240, 245
Checking accounts, 93
Child, desire for autonomy of, 138
Child-rearing, responsibility for, 139–142
Classification (of sample cases): by dependency, 29–33, 34
  by ethnicity, 34–35

by geography, 34, 36
by income, 36–37
Controls (study), 3
Credit unions, membership in, 93
Culture of poverty, 203, 218, 222–223
  the alienated nonworker, 231–232

Davis, Allison, 228, 231
Debts, family, 97, 197
Dependency: causes of, 63, 247
  correlates with, 201
  defined, 133
  effects of, 63, 195, 196, 199–200, 201–202, 241, 244–245
  kinship bonds and, 50, 52, 53, 63–64
  meaning of, 241–242, 243–244
  prevention of, 33, 247
  stages in adjustment to, 148
    See also Psychological dependency
Dependency feedback cycle, 239–241, 245–246
Dependency index, 4, 29–33, 36, 38, 40, 239
Dependency rate, 32–33
Design, of study, 2–5, 45
  problems in, 34, 36, 37–38
Discrimination, 118, 145
Dubin, Robert, 228

Economic characteristics of dependents, 196–197
Economic security, 83–103, 197, 210
Education: classification by, 40
  interclass differences, 204
  levels of, 14–15, 18, 175
Employability, influences on, 230, 232
Employment: barriers to, 117–122, 128, 129, 198
  continuity of, 107–111, 113, 198, 214
  job-finding, 122–123, 213
  by relatives, 59
  seasonal, 24
Error sources of study, 255–256

Ethnic groups, differences among, 14–15, 88
Ethnicity: correlation of, with personal orientation, 135, 138, 139, 140, 142
  earning power and, 113
  economic security and, 102–103
  husband-wife roles and, 157–158
  influences of, 198, 199, 200, 201, 202
  kinship patterns and, 63
  level of living and, 102–103
  neighborhood stability and, 66
  occupation, income, and level of living and, 116–117
  sampling problems, 34, 36
  savings and, 93
  self-responsibility and, 139
  significance of, 140, 144–146
  social interaction and, 74

Family: characteristic LTA, 234
  matricentered, 176
  self-evaluation by, 122
  size, 204
Family organization, 161, 169–170, 171, 176–177, 200
  effect of unemployment on, 148–150
Foresight practices, 88–93, 113, 197
Friendships: number of, 68
  sources of, 6, 76, 79, 123, 196, 207–208, 229

Gans, Herbert, 226, 228, 230, 231
Geographic differences, 63, 66
Gildea, Margaret C. L., 139, 263

Health, 118, 230
  interclass comparison of, 210
Himelson, Alfred, 140
Hirabayashi, James, 5, 159, 173, 200
Holmes, Emma G., 97
Household size, 40
Housing: cost of, 97
  ownership of, 97, 210
Hurvitz, Nathan, 228
Husband-wife roles: differences in, 155–157
  interclass comparison, 215–216
  shifts in, 147–148, 157, 199, 200
  similarities in, 150–154

Income, 111, 129, 244
  case matching for, 35–37
  determinants of, 116
  education and, 18
  function of, 102–103
  interclass differences, 204
  level of living and, 85, 197
  median, 85
  retirement, 102
  of sample family, 12, 14–15
Insurance, 93, 197, 210
Interviews, 4–5
  methods and problems of, 255–256

Job-finding, 122–123
  help from relatives, 59
  interclass comparison, 213
Job history, 107–111

Kinship: function of, 49, 53, 59, 76, 79
  as a social system, 49, 63, 195
Kinship bonds, 161, 168–169, 171, 176, 200
  interclass differences, 206
Kluckhohn, Clyde, 160
Kluckhohn, Florence, 160
Komarovsky, Mirra, 74, 76, 148, 149, 228, 233, 240, 245

Lamphere, Arthur, 134, 259
Level of living, 83–103, 197
  determinants of, 116
  effect of dependency on, 244
Life insurance, 93, 210
Life style, 171
  dependency and, 246
  factors affecting, 63, 201
  level of living in, 83
LTA (long-time-aid) families: case history, 177–185
  characteristics of, 171, 240
  characteristic worker in, 234–235
  defined, 4, 33 *n.*
  handicapping factors, 201

McConnell, John, 83, 93, 97
Marriage, stability of, 40
Matching sample cases, 13–14, 33–40
Matza, David, 231
Microculture of work, 6
Miller, Dr. Henry, 2
Miller, S.M., 107, 230, 231
Miller, Walter B., 230
Mobility, 40
   occupational, 107–111, 197, 227–228
   residential, 204
      See also Stability
Money, husband/wife control of, 152, 155
Morse, Nancy C., 228
Motivation, influences on, 230
Mutual aid: kin, 53, 59
   nonkin, 66–74
   sources of, 74–76, 79

Neighborhood utilization index, 66
NOA (never-on-aid) families, 4, 33, 171
   case history, 185–191
   characteristic worker in, 232–233
   characteristics of, 231–232

Occupation: advancement in, 227
   grouping by, 16–17, 21, 105–107
   level of, 113, 197
   self-definition of, 105
   status from, 227
Old age, economic security for, 88–90, 100, 210
Old Age and Survivors Insurance program, 90
Open-ended questions, 279
   results of, 171
   use and analysis of, 159–163, 200
Organizations, association with, 68, 207
Orientation of dependent families, 142, 198–201

Parental Attitude Research Instrument, 135, 138, 362
Pensions, 90, 210
Poor, the: compared with the affluent, 203–223
   ethnic composition of, 204–205
   and nonpoor, similarities between, 218
Population, characteristics of, in sample area, 22–25
Pensions, 100, 196
Possessions: interclass comparison of, 212
   survey of, 85–88
Poverty, culture of, 174, 203, 218, 222–223, 231–232
Poverty line, 18, 100, 203
Predependency feedback cycle, 235–239, 245–246
Psychological dependency, 133–146, 199, 237
   interclass comparison, 216
   measurement of, 134–135, 259–268
   significance of, 142–144
Public assistance: arguments for and against, 1–2
   attitudes toward, 2, 241–243
   effects of, 142–144
   risk population for, 32

Questionnaires, number, of, 5

Rainwater, Lee, 228
Ranck, Katherine, 148–149, 240, 245
Reading, 88, 116, 196, 212
Relatives: availability of, 50, 63, 64
   interaction with, 50–59, 63, 176, 195
   use of, 53, 63, 123, 206
Responsibility, feelings of, 139, 199
   scale for, 263
Riessman, Frank, 230
Rodman, Hyman, 223
Rosal, Gerardo, 159
Rotman, Arthur, 173

Sampling: criteria for, 4, 12
   methods of, 3–4, 11–13
   problems of, 256–257
   reliability of, 263–266
   representativeness of, 12–18, 20–27
Savings, 93, 102, 197, 210
Schaefer, Earl S., 135, 262

Scoring, method of, 263
Segregation, 21, 145
Self-definition, 5-7, 105, 222, 227, 231, 241
   changes in, 245
Shannon, Lyle W., 139, 140
Simmel, Arthur B., 241
Situational control attitudes, 160, 163-165, 171, 175-176, 200
Social characteristics of dependents, 195-196
Social network: husband and wife, 74, 79
   lower- vs. middle-class, 208-209
   work in, 79-80, 196, 215
Social relationships, 65-80, 176, 196
   effects of dependency on, 74, 80, 196, 245
   husband and wife differences in, 74-79
   interclass differences, 206-208
   significance of work to, 79, 218, 229
Social Security, 90, 100, 210
Social world, local: importance of, 79, 196, 208
Socioeconomic status: interclass differences, 204
   measures of, 45
Spring, Anita, 159, 173
Srole, Leo, 140
STA (short-time-aid) families: characteristic worker in, 233
   defined, 4, 33 n.
Stability: employment, 113
   family, 230
   marital, 40
   residence, 65-66, 206
State Employment Service, 122, 123
State Social Welfare Board, 27
Strodtbeck, Fred, 160
Subjugation, attitudes of, 164-165, 171, 174, 175-176, 200

Takagi, Paul, 140
Themes of beliefs and behavior, 160-161, 173, 200
Time, attitudes toward, 160, 165-166, 171, 176, 200

Unemployability, index of, 231
Unemployment, 113, 198
   effects of, 7, 63
   interclass comparison, 210
   stages of adjustment to, 148-150
Unemployment compensation, 90
Unemployment rates, 17-18
Union experience, 90-93, 123
Urban-rural differences, 14, 35, 38, 113, 118, 130, 140, 197, 198

Value orientations defined, 160
Values, 229, 230
   interclass comparison, 223

Wage histories, 111
Warner, W.L., 97
Weiss, R.S., 228
Welfare: attitudes about, 174
   defined, 3 n.
   See also Public assistance
Welfare experience, 29, 32
Welfare status: nonreciprocal nature of, 241, 243
   See also Dependency
Wellisch, William, 203
Withdrawal, social, pattern of, 74, 81, 196
Wives, working, 154, 157
Work: attitudes toward, 5, 123, 128, 175, 198, 213-214
   factors involved in, 5-6
   identification with the world of, 228, 229-231
   significance of, 225-229
   social relationships and, 79, 218, 229
Work addict, the, 5, 7
Work histories, 111, 113, 129
Workers, characteristic low-status, 232-235